EFFANBEE

A Collector's Encyclopedia

1949 - Present
by John Axe

*Happy Birthday
Patsy Joan*

Published by Hobby House Press, Inc.
Grantsville, Maryland 21536

ACKNOWLEDGMENTS

There are many reasons why Effanbee dolls are worthy of being collected. The company has been manufacturing dolls in America for more than 70 years; some of the designs that Effanbee has produced are considered "classics"; Effanbee dolls have always been a high-quality product. More than anything else, Effanbee dolls are fun to collect.

It has been possible to gather information about Effanbee dolls because of the generosity of many people who gave their time to share memories, experiences, research materials and their doll collections. I am particularly grateful to the following:

From the Effanbee Doll Corporation -

Eugenia Dukas, Effanbee's chief designer; Al Kirchof, an Effanbee doll salesman for more than 50 years; Leroy Fadem, (former) Chairman of the Board; Arthur Keller, (former) Vice President and (former) Sales Manager; Roy R. Raizen, (former) President; Robyn Richards, (former) National Sales Manager; and Erica Seiz, (former) Assistant to Eugenia Dukas.

From the new Effanbee Doll Corporation -

Stanley Wahlberg, President; and Irene Wahlberg, Vice President of Merchandising.

Collectors whose dolls are shown in this book -

Sherry Baloun of Gigi's Dolls and Shirley's Teddy Bears, Inc.

Shirley Bertrand of Shirley's Dollhouse

Shirley Buchholz, Patricia Gardner, Rosemary Hanline, Emily and Ruth Jones, Pam Petcoff, Agnes Smith, Marjorie Smith, Sararose Smith and Virginia Tomlinson.

For the loan of dolls for photographs -

Suzanne Chordar of The Doll's Nest.

For help with research material and photographs -

Dorothy S. Coleman, The Library of Congress, *Playthings* (magazine), Marge Meisinger, Bea Skydell of Bea Skydell's Dolls & Friends, John Stafford, Joyce Stafford and Alma Wolfe.

For their help with research and photography -

John Schoonmaker and Patricia N. Schoonmaker.

For her support and her friendship -

Editor Donna H. Felger.

For helping to sort information and compile listings on Effanbee dolls -

My sister, Patricia E. Axe.

Front Cover: Effanbee offered an exact reproduction of the original 1946 *Patsy Joan* doll in 1995. The 17in (43cm) beauty is molded from the original 1946 Patsy, authentic in every detail from her puppy sleep eyes and rosebud lips, to her striped cotton dress with matching bonnet and gold, heart-shaped Effanbee wrist tag. This doll even bears the exact markings of the original "EFFANDBEE" on the torso, the only doll to ever be marked in this way. Made of specially formulated, collectible vinyl, *Patsy Joan* feels like the original composition doll. *Patsy Joan* was offered with the **Patsy Doll Family Encyclopedia**, by Patricia N. Schoonmaker (Hobby House Press, Inc., 1992).

Title Page: Happy Birthday Patsy Joan. 17in (43cm). Limited to 1996. This *Patsy Joan* is part of the Patsy Family Collection. For further information and photographs of other Patsy members, see pages iv, v, vii, ix, 2-3 and the 1995 and 1996 Catalog listings found on pages 287-290.

Back Cover: At the left is Joyce Stafford's *Orange Blossom* for Effanbee; at the right is her porcelain original *Poppy*. *Poppy* is from the *Shirley Bucholz Collection*. For a full length photograph, see page 10.

Additional copies of this book may be purchased at $24.95 (plus postage and handling) from

Hobby House Press, Inc.

1 Corporate Drive
Grantsville, Maryland 21536
1-800-554-1447
or from your favorite bookstore or dealer.

Printed in the United States of America

ISBN: 0-87588-470-9

TABLE OF CONTENTS

Effanbee.
Dolls that touch your heart.

This 1996 13in (33cm) *Skippy®* is molded from the original doll.

This 1996 13in (33cm) *Patsy®* is molded from the original 1928 doll.

INTRODUCTION

In 1910 two businessmen who had become acquainted by operating adjoining shops on the Boardwalk in Atlantic City, New Jersey, formed a partnership to sell toys and dolls. In 1913 they decided to manufacture dolls. The trade name for the company was based on the initials of the last names of the two friends. The company became Fleischaker and Baum — EffanBee. The owners were Bernard E. Fleischaker and Hugo Baum. The successor doll company still exists today as the Effanbee Doll Company.

The company name is pronounced EFFanBEE to accent the initials of Fleischaker and Baum. Effanbee has produced many successful commercial dolls which today are very desirable collectibles. The company's best selling dolls helped to make it one of the most important American doll companies. The greatest successes in the past were *Bubbles* in the 1920s, *Patsy* and *DyDee Baby* in the 1930s. Growth of the Effanbee firm was aided by the arrival of Walter Fleischaker, Bernard's brother, who was Effanbee's top salesman until his retirement in 1945. In 1923 Morris Lutz joined the company.

Hugo Baum died in 1940 and Bernard Fleischaker moved to California and began a new business, Fleischaker Novelties, which also made dolls. Effanbee in New York was operated by Hugo Baum's son, Bernard, and his brother, Walter. In 1946 the company was sold to Noma Electric, a manufacturer of Christmas tree decorations. Noma Electric did not continue a strong interest in the doll business, and the once important Effanbee Doll Company began to slide into a second-rate position. In 1953 a new partnership was formed by Bernard Baum, Perry Epstein, and Morris Lutz who repurchased the Effanbee part of the business from Noma and began to restore it to its former leadership in the industry.

Walter Fleischaker died in 1965 and Bernard Baum died in 1966. Perry Epstein retired from the company in 1969 and Morris Lutz left in 1972, after "officially retiring" in 1971, having spent more than 50 years with Effanbee dolls.

Stanley Wahlbeg, President and Irene Wahlberg, Vice President of Merchandising of the Effanbee Doll Coporation.

Margiann Flanagan, Vice President of Design of the Effanbee Doll Corporation.

OPPOSITE PAGE: *Patsy* — the doll with *"IT"* is a classic design that spans the ages. Effanbee introduced a Patsy Family Collection modeled after the ever-popular 1930s Patsy Dolls, starting in 1995. Each Patsy, exact in every detail, has been molded from an original doll and has been crafted of specially formulated vinyl that looks and feels like the original composition material. For additional photographs and information about the Patsy Doll Family, see pages vii, ix, 2-3, and the 1995 and 1996 Catalog Listings found on pages 287-290.

Illustration 1. Patsy is one of the most important dolls upon which Effanbee based its reputation and its success. *Patsy* is all-composition and fully-jointed with painted hair and is 13-1/2in (34cm). *From left to right:* From 1928 with brown painted hair and brown painted eyes; back marked: 'EFFanBEE // PATSY // PAT. PEND. // DOLL;" old, but replaced clothing. From 1933 with green sleep eyes and red hair; wears original yellow silk dress; head marked; 'EFFanBEE // PATSY;" back marked: 'EFFanBEE //PATSY //DOLL." From 1933 with brown painted eyes and red painted hair without the molded headband; marked like the sleep-eye *Patsy* in the center.

Illustration 2. Eugenia Dukas, Effanbee's costume designer from 1947 to approximately 1988 with *Suzie Sunshine,* her favorite Effanbee doll.

An important force with Effanbee dolls was always Al Kirchof, who was an Effanbee doll salesman from 1930 until his retirement from the company in 1980. Al Kirchof was with Effanbee during the Depression of the 1930s, when he felt fortunate if he could interest a retail store in a few *Kali-Ko-Kate* cloth dolls, showing buyers the one sample that he carried with him around his territory (the north central part of the United States). He was still with Effanbee 50 years later when buyers would accept his advice on which dolls they should stock, hardly glancing at the color catalogs that he showed them.

In 1971 the Effanbee Doll Corporation was purchased by Leroy Fadem and Roy R. Raizen. Fadem served as Chairman of the Board and Raizen as President of the corporation. Under the guidance of these gentlemen (1971-1986), Effanbee prospered and expanded to become a national play and collectible doll company.

The collectibility of Effanbee dolls is based on the classic dolls from the company's past history. Raizen and Fadem returned to this well formed foundation while also introducing new artists and dolls into the doll line. They created a *Craftsmen's Corner Collection* in 1979 including such doll artists as Faith Wick, Astry Campbell, Joyce Stafford, and Jan Hagara. This new sculpted artist look diversified the line and increased the collectible factor.

In 1974 Roy Raizen introduced the concept of the Effanbee Limited Edition Doll Club. This became quite a popular club with dolls produced in limited quantities from 1974-1988.

The Effanbee dolls on which this book concentrates are all noted for their well-designed and attractive costumes. This can be credited to the various doll designers who have worked with the company. One of the biggest contributions was made by Eugenia Dukas, who designed the costumes for Effanbee dolls from 1947 to approximately 1988.

Eugenia Dukas grew up in Newburg, New York. As a young girl she was inspired by her aunt, also called Eugenia, who worked with fine fabrics in clothing design. Eugenia wanted to design clothes for the theater but unable to find such work, she began working for Effanbee in 1947. She quickly became interested in all aspects of doll production and began designing the dolls themselves, working with sculptors who executed the dolls based on her plans. Her favorite of all doll designs is *Suzie Sunshine* (1961) "because she is a typical little girl". Eugenia was still designing dolls in the prosperous years of the Raizen and Fadem ownership.

In 1987 the Effanbee company was sold to Russ Berrie and much like the Noma Electric ownership in 1946, Effanbee declined in position from 1988 to 1991.

In 1992 Effanbee changed hands once again. The company was purchased by the Alexander Doll Company, and was operated independently. It was during that period that Effanbee started their climb back as a play and collector doll favorite. Leading the company was the husband-wife team of Stanley and Irene Wahlberg. With this new enthusiasm for Effanbee's playability and rich heritage, the line once again turned to its strong foundation of recreating the lovable dolls of history.

In June of 1995, the Wahlbergs, together with Margiann Flanagan purchased Effanbee from the Alexander Doll Company. Today, the company is headed by Stanley Wahlberg, President, Irene Wahlberg, Vice President of Merchandising and Margiann Flanagan, Vice President of Design.

"Effanbee has such a rich and beautiful history of creating the greatest American doll creations. We want to capture that magic again. Our goal is to recreate the Effanbee favorites that the baby boomers grew up with, in an affordable price range so that past doll favorites can be recaptured and shared with future generations. The classic dolls are the ones Irene grew up with and we are focusing on bringing that classical look back into the Effanbee line," says Stanley Wahlberg, President of Effanbee Doll Company.

The Effanbee of the future is the rebirth of the Effanbee company of the past. The Company is re-introducing collections that were long ago retired. In 1994 they brought the *Age of Elegance Collection* back to life under the *Ladies of Elegance* category. Within a few years they hope to revitalize the Effanbee Limited Edition Collector's Club. Recently Effanbee brought back the Legends series with George Burns, an outstanding success. Working with a new type of vinyl that duplicates the look of the composition dolls of the 1920s, '30s, and '40s, Effanbee is also bringing back new versions of the best loved dolls of this era.

Effanbee dolls are not only works of art for collectors to put away and admire but are also play toys for children. The only mission of the Effanbee company until the 1970s was to produce America's playthings. The dolls in the 1990s are being made in both vinyl and porcelain to appeal to both children and collectors.

Illustration 3. 10in (25.4cm) *Babykin*, circa 1949. All-composition and fully-jointed with reddish painted hair. The doll on the left is all-original and has blue sleep eyes with lahes. The doll on the right has blue painted eyes. These dolls are the same mold as *Patsy Baby* from the 1930s, but the paint finishing is less shiny and more muted in tone. The heads are marked: "EFFANBEE // PATSY BABY." The backs are marked: 'EFFANBEE // 'PATSY BABY'."

Illustration 4. John Wayne. The very popular *Legend Series* featured *John Wayne* in 1981.

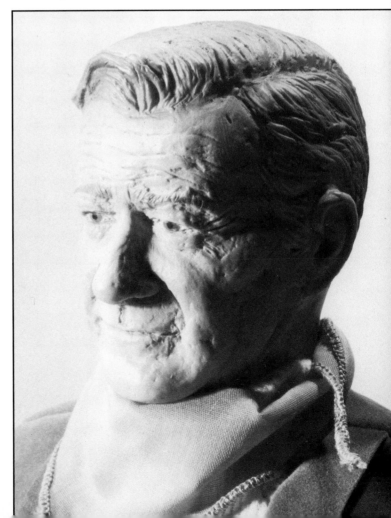

RIGHT: (Clockwise) *Mella*, SP107, 18in (46cm), 2-piece shoulder-plate head; *Merrie*, MP127, "First Annual Christmas Doll," 15in (38cm) musical that plays Silent Night, production limited to 5000; *Melanie*, MP126, "First Annual Doll," 18in (46cm), 2-piece shoulder-plate head and production limited to 1994; *Rebecca*, MP110, 18in (46cm), includes basket of flowers, 2-piece shoulder-plate head; *Shelby*, MP116, 20in (51cm).

OPPOSITE PAGE: The *Patsy Trunk Set* includes a 13in (33cm) *Patsy*, two additional costumes, and a trunk that is made in the style of a 1930s suitcase. *Patsy* is molded from the original 1928 composition doll. For further Patsy dolls, see pages i, iv, 2, 3 the 1995 and 1996 Catalog Listings found on pages 287-290, and the front cover.

RIGHT: (Clockwise) *Elizabeth*, MP111, 18in (46cm), 2-piece shoulder-plate head; *Kimberly*, MP128, 15in (38cm), limited to 2500; *Kristen*, MP130, 16in (41cm), includes plush teddy bear, limited to 2500; *Allison*, SP106, 16in (41cm), limited to 2500; *Alice*, MP129, 16in (41cm), limited to 2500; *Ashley*, MP105, 16in (41cm), 2-piece shoulder-plate head.

OPPOSITE PAGE: 15in (38.1cm) *Dy-Dee Jane*, 1955.

ABOVE: 20in (50.8cm) *Honey Walker as Junior Miss, A Doll with Glamour,* 1956.

ABOVE RIGHT: 15in (38.1cm) *Honey as a majorette*, 1952.

BELOW: 15½in (39.4cm) *Honey as a bridesmaid and as a bride, 1952. Honey* bride from *Patricia Gardner Collection*.

BELOW RIGHT: 13½in (34.3cm) *Honey, circa 1949, and 18½in (47cm) Honey Walker*, 1954.

Illustration 5a. 15in (38cm) reproduction of famous *Patsy* doll. The head is molded from an original Effanbee *Patsy* and the costume is a reproduction of the 1930s doll. A gold plated reproduction of the original Effanbee heart tag comes with each doll. Limited to 5000 pieces.

Illustration 5b. 9in (23cm) *Babyette*, circa 1949. All-composition and fully-jointed with brown painted hair and blue sleep eyes with lashes. These dolls are the same mold as *Patsy Babyette f*rom the 1930s. The heads are marked: "EFFANBEE." The backs are marked: "EFFANBEE/ /PATSY BABYETTE." These dolls also came with dark brown lamb's wool wigs. *Photograph courtesy of Al Kirchof.*

Illustration 6. 19in (48.3cm) and 23in (58.4cm) *Howdy Doody*, circa 1949. Composition heads and hands, cloth bodies. Brown sleep eyes without lashes; open/closed mouths with painted and molded teeth. The dolls are not marked. (*Howdy Doody* was made with hard plastic components by Ideal in 1954.) *Photograph courtesy of Al Kirchof.*

I. EFFANBEE DOLLS—1949-1983

1949 was the first year that Effanbee dolls were made with plastic components. Modern thermoplastics were developed during the 1940s, and their use was mainly restricted to governmental work during World War II. Plastics are chemical by-products of petroleum, and there are many different formulas for making the materials known as "hard plastics," "soft vinyls" and "rigid vinyls." The early dolls made of plastic materials were of "synthetic rubber," a wartime development. This material darkened and became "sticky," unlike modern vinyls. The first dolls made of this substance, usually referred to as "magic skin," were produced in the 1940s.

In general hard plastic is a synthetic, rigid material that is relatively unbreakable and it is firm and solid. Its advantage over composition as a material for the manufacture of play dolls was that it was more durable and the medium allowed for more detailing in the modeling. *Honey* was the first Effanbee doll in hard plastic in 1949.

By 1954 Effanbee was advertising *Baby Cuddle-Up* as made of "all washable vinyl plastic" and citing the fact that "her Saran hair is individually rooted." Soft vinyl is a plastic material that is soft to the touch and it is much more resilient and pliable than hard plastic. Vinyl is completely unbreakable and it became a perfect medium for play dolls. Vinyl does not deteriorate with age, although it is receptive to accepting ink and other coloring agents by absorbtion and it can discolor in time.

By the 1960s Effanbee dolls were made of a combination of soft and rigid vinyl. Soft vinyl can also be rigid, if the component part of a doll is made with a thick layer of vinyl. Rigid vinyl seems like hard plastic but it is much thinner in volume, and it usually shows seam markings. A common example of rigid vinyl is the material used for the bottles in which liquid bleaching compounds are sold.

1949-1958

There were not always catalogs for Effanbee dolls every year. According to Effanbee salesman Al Kirchof, some years dolls were introduced to retailers by having the salesman exhibit samples of completed dolls or by showing buyers company photographs of the dolls. The doll catalogs were produced for the benefit of salesmen and buyers in stores. Later the catalogs were mailed to stores, or were presented by salesmen, so the buyers could study the models pictured to determine which dolls they should purchase for their stores. It is because of the demand of collectors that catalogs have been more available in recent years.

From 1946 to 1953 the Effanbee Doll Company was owned by Noma Electric. There was a scarcity of new models in those years, as there was no personal driving force behind doll production. One real advantage to the company was the employment of Eugenia Dukas in 1947.

In 1949 Effanbee was still producing dolls with composition parts. *Dy-Dee* was still sold with a composition head that had rubber ears. *Howdy Doody* came in sizes of 19in (48.3cm) and 23in (61cm) with composition head and hands and a cloth body.

The most important dolls from 1949 to 1958 were *Honey* in hard plastic, *Dy-Dee* with a plastic head and a vinyl body, and *Mickey, the All-American Boy*, in all-vinyl.

The listings for dolls show the models that were advertised and sold during each year. When available, stock numbers are given.

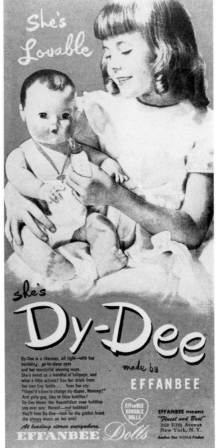

Illustration 7. Advertisement for *Dy-Dee Baby* from *Children's Activities*, December 1949.

TOP LEFT: In 1995 Effanbee produced the *Pink Patsy Ornament* and *Blue Patsy Ornament.* The 3in (8cm) ornaments were made of hand cast porcelain and were the first Christmas Ornaments that Effanbee had ever produced. *Top RIGHT:* The *Wee Patsy Travel Set* includes: a paper doll book, ***Effanbee's Wee Patsy™ Paper Dolls & Playhouse*** by John Axe (Hobby House Press, Inc., 1996); a doll house travel case with artwork by John Axe; 5-1/4in (13.65cm) Wee Patsy girl and boy dolls which look like the original composition versions; and five accessories including a rocking chair, clothes tree, jack-in-the-box, train, and black cat. All costumes are created from ***Effanbee's Wee Patsy™ Paper Dolls & Playhouse.*** *BOTTOM LEFT: Patsy Joan with Wig* and *Black Patsy Joan.* Each 17in (43cm) doll has been molded from the original 1946 doll. *Bottom Right: Porcelain Patsy.* This 14in (36cm) Patsy is all porcelain and is holding an all vinyl Wee Patsy. Limited Edition of 7,500.

2

ABOVE: Two notable members of the 1995 Porcelain Collection were *Patsy* dolls (*TOP RIGHT*), in limited editions of 5,000 each. Also pictured: (*TOP LEFT*) *Girl With A Hoop*; (*BOTTOM: LEFT to RIGHT*) *Girl With Watering Can; Waltz of Flowers; Clara;* and *Sugar Plum Fairy.*
RIGHT: 17in (43cm) *Christmas Patsy Joan* comes with her own *Wee Patsy* attired in appropriate Christmas dress.
BOTTOM: The 13in (33cm) *Candy Kid* comes with an additional coat, bonnet and muff set. Molded from the original 1946 doll.

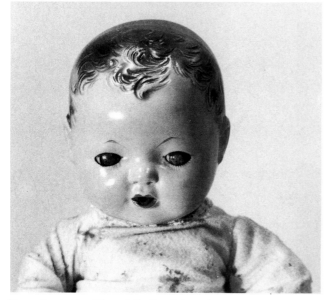

Illustration 8. 15in (38.1cm) *Dy-Dee Baby* with a composition head and a rubber body. Brown painted hair; brown sleep eyes with lashes; open mouth. Back marked: "EFF-AN-BEE // DY-DEE BABY // three lines of indiscernible US patent numbers, one line of a patent number for England, two lines of patent numbers for France, one line of patent numbers for Germany // OTHER PATENTS PENDING." This is the version of *Dy-Dee* made from the 1930s through the 1940s.

Illustration 9. Dy-Dee Baby. Note the unfortunate condition of the fully-jointed rubber body. The natural rubber has shrunken, cracked, hardened and is flaking away.

Illustration 10. Beautee Skin Baby, circa 1949. Composition head with painted hair and sleep eyes with lashes. The body is made of latex. This is an original Effanbee promotional photograph. The body of this doll would now be "sticky" and darkened with age, as latex dolls do not maintain their original condition. *Photograph courtesy of Al Kirchof.*

4

Illustration 11. Beautee Skin Baby, circa 1949. Photograph courtesy of Al Kirchof.

1949

Dolls that were still being produced:

Little Lady	All-composition and fully-jointed.	15in (38.1cm)
		18in (45.7cm)
		21in (53.3cm)
	(27in [68.6cm] size also called *Formal Honey*.)	27in (68.6cm)
Portrait Dolls	All-composition and fully-jointed (unmarked).	11in (27.9cm)
Three lady dolls *Majorette* *Bride* and *Groom*		
*Babyette**	All-composition and fully-jointed. (This is the same doll that was sold as *Patsy Babyette* during the 1930s.)	9in (22.9cm)
*Babykin**	All-composition and fully-jointed. (This is the same doll that was sold as *Patsy Baby* during the 1930s.)	10in (25.4cm)
Howdy Doody	Composition head and hands; cloth body.	19in (48.3cm)
		23in (58.4cm)
Dy-Dee Baby	Composition head; rubber body; applied rubber ears.	11in (27.9cm)
		15in (38.1cm)
		20in (50.8cm)
Beautee Skin Baby	Composition head with sleep eyes; latex body.	14in (35.6cm)
		17in (43.2cm)
		19in (48.3cm)
L'il Darlin'	All-latex or with cloth body; painted eyes.	20in (50.8cm)

New dolls for 1949:

Honey (also called *Honey Girl)*	All-hard plastic and fully-jointed.	13½in (34.3cm)
		16in (40.6cm)
		18in (45.7cm)
Mommy's Baby	Hard plastic head; stuffed latex body.	17in (43.2cm)
		21in (53.3cm)
		28in (71.1cm)

*There is no evidence to support the belief that these dolls were ever produced in hard plastic.

Effanbee revived its *Legend Series* in 1996 with the introduction of an authentic *George Burns* doll. Molded of special collector quality vinyl, the 17in (43cm) doll is meticulously crafted and hand-painted to be exact in every detail from George Burn's trademark cigar, to his tuxedo, and endearing smile. He even has actual folding glasses. This doll is personally authorized by George Burns himself.

A special 1995 angels category featured (*TOP: LEFT TO RIGHT*): a 6in (15cm) all porcelain *Littlest Angel* and *Grandma's Little Angel* with an available monogramed pillow; (*BOTTOM: LEFT TO RIGHT*): a 12in (31cm) porcelain with stuffed body *Pink Angel* and a 9in (23cm) vinyl *Guardian Angel*.

OPPOSITE PAGE: *Huckleberry Finn* and *Mark Twain*, 1983. Photographed at the Effanbee factory.

Eugenia Dukas' *Crowning Glory*, the Effanbee Limited Edition Doll Club doll of 1978. *Marjorie Smith Collection.*

Patsy '76 and *Skippy* of the Effanbee Limited Edition Doll Club dolls.

Susan B. Anthony, the 1980 Effanbee Limited Edition Doll Club selection. *Marjorie Smith Collection.*

Illustration 12. L'il Darlin', circa 1949. Latex head and body. Some of these dolls had a cloth body with latex limbs; others were all-latex. These dolls have not darkened with age as much as they have become very "sticky" to the touch. *Photograph courtesy of Al Kirchof.*

Illustration 14. Mommy's Baby, circa 1949. Hard plastic head with painted hair and sleep eyes with lashes. The latex body is stuffed with cotton batting. *Photograph courtesy of Al Kirchof.*

Illustration 13. L'il Darlin', circa 1949. Made with latex components. Latex is a synthetic rubber, first produced during World War II when Japan had cut off the American source of raw rubber from southeast Asia. *Photograph courtesy of Al Kirchof.*

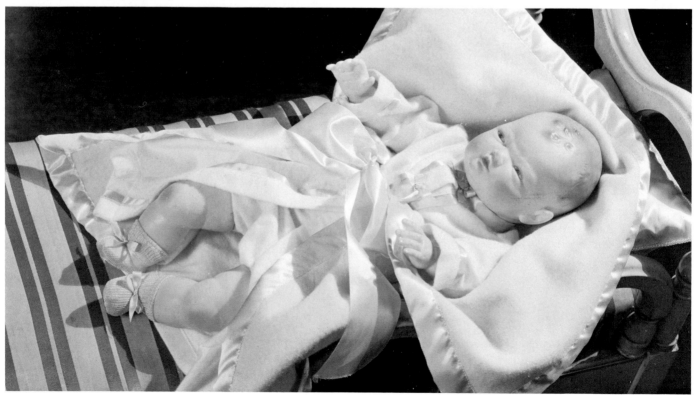

Illustration 16. 13½in (34.3cm) *Honey*, circa 1949. All-hard plastic and fully-jointed. Blue sleep eyes with lashes; blonde synthetic wig. All-original in pale pink organdy dress. Marked on the head and back: "EFFANBEE."

Illustration 15. *Honey*, 1949. All-hard plastic and fully-jointed. Blue sleep eyes with lashes; synthetic wig. *Photograph courtesy of Al Kirchof.*

9

TOP RIGHT: The *Sammie Trunk Set* includes a 9in (23cm) vinyl *Sammie* doll in a party dress, together with a fabric covered trunk that includes a clothes rack, hangers, and accessory drawers. Additional outfits — pajamas, bathrobe, slippers, play outfit, sneakers, slippers, pillow and teddy bear complete the ensemble. *Sammie* is available in a blonde and brown hair version and has additional outfits which are sold separately. See pages 288 and 290 for a complete listing of her current outfits.

BOTTOM LEFT: The 1996 Porcelain Collection features wonderful artist creations such as: Peggy Dey's *Mardi Gras* (top left), *Fairy Princess* (top left), and *Juliette* (bottom right); and Linda Steele's *Guinevere* (bottom left).

Illustrations 17, 18 and 19. *Honey* from about 1949 in original publicity stills. All the *Honey* dolls were fully-jointed hard plastic. *Photographs courtesy of Al Kirchof.*

12

1950

New Dolls:

Noma, the Electronic Doll	Hard plastic head; cloth body; vinyl limbs. Battery-operated "talking doll."	28in (71.1cm)
Dy-Dee Baby	Hard plastic head; rubber body. Molded hair or wigs of lamb's wool.	11in (27.9cm) 15in (38.1cm) 20in (50.8cm)

Dating Dy-Dee Baby

1933-1946	Composition head; fully-jointed rubber body.
1947-1949	Composition head; fully-jointed rubber body. Applied rubber ears.
1950-1954	Hard plastic head; fully-jointed rubber body. Applied rubber ears.
1955-1958	Hard plastic head; fully-jointed vinyl body. Applied rubber or vinyl ears.

Note: There can be some overlaps in the time periods during a change in design.

Illustration 20. Advertisement for *Noma, the Electronic Doll, Children's Activities,* December 1950.

Illustrations 21 and 22. *Dy-Dee Jane,* 1950. Hard plastic head with sleep eyes and applied rubber ears; fully-jointed rubber body; open mouth that leads to a rubber hose that drains from a valve in the torso so that *Dy-Dee* can "drink" from her bottle. *Photographs courtesy of Al Kirchof.*

13

Illustrations 23 and 24. Dy-Dee Baby in different sizes from about 1950. This is the doll with the hard plastic head and rubber ears on a rubber body. Photographs courtesy of Al Kirchof.

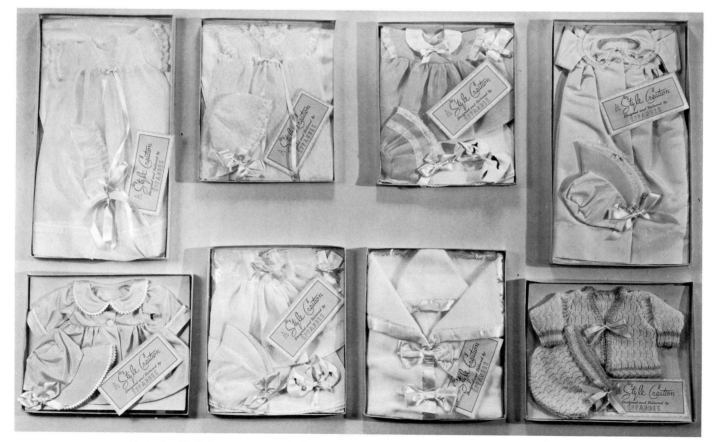

Illustration 25. Extra costumes for Dy-Dee Baby from about 1950. Photograph courtesy of Al Kirchof.

14

Illustration 27. Effanbee "Baby Doll" or "Mama Doll" with an open mouth and upper teeth from about 1950. *Photograph courtesy of Al Kirchof.*

Illustration 26. Effanbee "Baby Doll" or "Mama Doll" with a closed mouth from about 1950. *Photograph courtesy of Al Kirchof.*

1951

New dolls:

Tintair	All-hard plastic.	14in (35.6cm)
	Honey doll with white hair	16in (40.6cm)
	that could also be tinted	18in (45.7cm)
	"glossy chestnut" or	
	"carrot top."	
Schiaparelli Dressed Dolls	All-hard plastic.	18in (45.7cm)
	Honey with dresses by "world	
	famous French Coutuiére Madame	
	Elsa Schiaparelli." These dolls	
	were to "be limited to America's	
	finest stores on a franchise basis."	

Illustration 28. Advertisement for the *Tintair Doll* from the Sunday comic section of a newspaper dated November 25, 1951.

Illustration 29. 16in (40.6cm) *Tintair*, 1951. All-hard plastic and fully-jointed. Blonde Dynel wig that still has traces of "redhead" coloring in it. Head and back marked: "EFFANBEE."

FAR RIGHT: *Illustration 30.* Advertisement from *Better Homes and Gardens*, December 1951. This ad cites the advantages of *Honey's* Saran hair and points out how Saran is used in the manufacture of many products. This was not an advertisement for Effanbee, but for The Saran Yarns Company. *Courtesy of Patricia N. Schoonmaker.*

RIGHT: *Illustration 30-A.* 18in (45.7cm) *Honey Walker* in all-hard plastic and fully-jointed. This is one of the Schiaparelli designed costumes. The doll sold for $19.95 at John Wanamaker in New York, New York. Advertisement from *Today's Woman*, December 1951.

1952

New Dolls:

Honey Walker	All-hard plastic. *Honey* with a walking mechanism.	18in (45.7cm)
Sweetie Pie	Hard plastic head; cloth body; vinyl limbs. Same doll as *Noma* of 1950 without voice mechanism. With painted hair or synthetic wigs.	27in (68.6cm)
Miss Lollipop	Toddler version of the above doll.	27in (68.6cm)
TV Puppets: *Jambo* *Kilroy* *Toonga* *Pimbo*	Puppets on strings packaged with a record.	

Dating Honey

1949-1957	All-hard plastic; five-piece body.
1952-1957	All-hard plastic; five-piece body with walking mechanism.
1956-1957	All-hard plastic and fully-jointed with extra joints at ankles and knees.
1957	Hard plastic head, torso and legs; jointed also at ankles and knees. Vinyl arms, jointed or unjointed at the elbows.

Illustration 31. Honey was a widely imitated doll. She was produced from 1949 to about 1957 in many different versions and costumes and was the mainstay of Effanbee during the years that the company was owned by Noma Electric. This doll is 14in (35.6cm) and is a fully-jointed hard plastic walker. She has a dark blonde synthetic wig; blue sleep eyes with molded plastic lashes. The maker is unknown. The head is marked: "14." The back is marked: "MADE IN U.S.A." in an embossed circle. Note the poor quality finishing of the seams at the arms and legs.

Illustration 32. Honey as a brides-maid and a bride. Both dolls are 15½in (39.4cm) tall. (The advertisements for dolls of this size would call the measurement 16in [40.6cm].) All-hard plastic and fully-jointed. The bridesmaid has red hair; the bride has blonde hair. The former has the usual synthetic hair found on *Honey* dolls; the bride has a floss-type wig. Both dolls are marked on the head and back: "EFFANBEE." The bride is from the *Patricia Gardner Collection.*

Illustration 34. Honey as a bridesmaid from *Illustration 32.*

Illustration 33. Honey as a bride from *Illustration 32. Patricia Gardner Collection.*

Illustration 35. 15in (38.1cm) *Honey* as a majorette in all-hard plastic. Dark brown wig; blue sleep eyes with lashes. The original box refers to this doll as style number 7524. Head and back marked: "EFFANBEE."

Illustrations 36 through 40. *Honey* in various costumes from glossy photographs that were used by Effanbee salesmen. *Photographs courtesy of Al Kirchof.*

20

Illustration 41. Five versions of *Honey* from 1952. Left to right, the stock numbers of the dolls are: 7623, 7621, 7642, 7641 and 7622. *Photograph courtesy of Al Kirchof.*

Illustration 42. Four versions of *Honey* from 1952. These dolls were also called *Honey Girl.* The stock numbers of the dolls are, from left to right: 7625, 7626, 7644 and 7624. *Photograph courtesy of Al Kirchof.*

Illustration 43. Three of the more elaborately attired *Honey* dolls from 1952. Left to right, the stock numbers are: 8964, 8963 and 8965. *Photograph courtesy of Al Kirchof.*

Illustration 44. Three elegant versions of *Honey* from 1952. Left to right, the stock numbers are: 8621, 8661 and 8642. *Photograph courtesy of Al Kirchof.*

Illustration 45. *Honey* as *Cinderella* and *Prince Charming*, 1952, stock numbers 8523 and 8524. Note the "glass slipper" in the prince's right hand. *Photograph courtesy of Al Kirchof.*

Illustration 46. *Honey* as *Cinderella*, No. 8523, 1952. *Photograph courtesy of Al Kirchof.*

Illustration 47. The various boxes from original *Honey* dolls. The black markings on the boxes (i.e., "Hard Body") were added by a seller on the secondary market.

Illustration 48. 27in (68.6cm) *Sweetie Pie* from 1952. Hard plastic heads with sleep eyes and an open mouth with upper teeth; cloth bodies; vinyl arms and legs. The wigs are lamb's wool, mistakenly called "caracul" by collectors. Left to right, the stock numbers are: 2771, 2774T, 2776T and 2777T. *Photograph courtesy of Al Kirchof.*

Illustration 49. 27in (68.6cm) *Sweetie Pie* from 1952, numbers 2774T and 2771. Hard plastic heads, cloth bodies, vinyl arms and legs. Of special note are the well-designed shoes worn by these dolls. *Photograph courtesy of Al Kirchof.*

24

New Dolls:

Baby Cuddle-Up	Vinyl head, arms and legs; vinyl-coated cloth body; molded or rooted hair.	20in (50.8cm) 23in (58.4cm) 27in (68.6cm)

Was $9.95
NOW
$8.89
27-inch

Illustration 50. 27in (68.6cm) *Sweetie Pie*, 1952. Hard plastic head, cloth body, vinyl arms and legs. Saran glued-on wig. This costume is the same one that *Noma, the Electronic Doll* wore. It is pink rayon taffeta with black and white check trim. *Sears Christmas Book 1953.*

Illustration 51. The ever-popular *Dy-Dee Baby*, 1952. The open lid of the box calls this doll "the new Effanbee Dy-Dee Baby." This refers to the fact that the doll was made at this time with a hard plastic head. The doll is not to be confused with the one later described as *New Dy-Dee Baby*, called *Dy-Dee Darlin'* in 1968 and *Dy-Dee Baby* in 1969, both of which were in all-vinyl. *Photograph courtesy of Al Kirchof.*

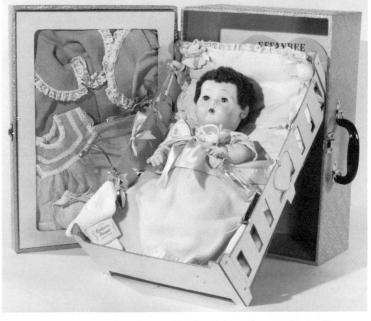

Illustrations 52 and 53. In 1953 *Dy-Dee Baby* still came with a rubber body. This can be noted by the curved fingers and the seams in the arms. The vinyl-body *Dy-Dee Baby* has fingers that are straighter in molding. The tear ducts in *Dy-Dee's* eyes appeared before the doll had a vinyl body. *Photographs courtesy of Al Kirchof.*

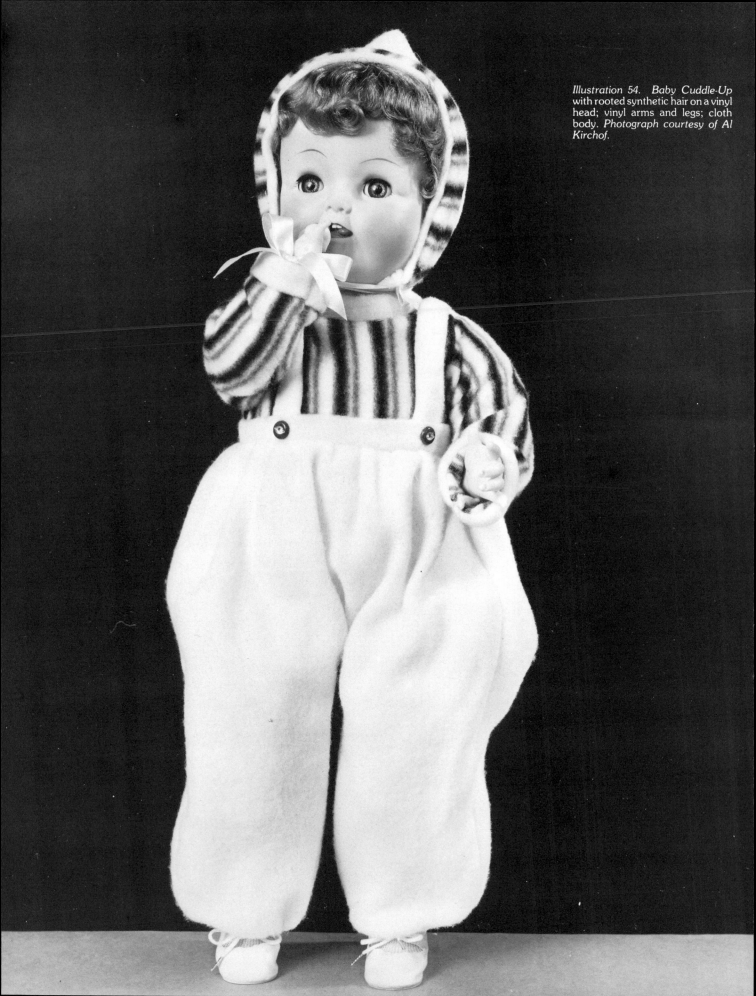

Illustration 54. Baby Cuddle-Up with rooted synthetic hair on a vinyl head; vinyl arms and legs; cloth body. *Photograph courtesy of Al Kirchof.*

1954 Catalog

Baby Cuddle-Up　　　　　　　Vinyl head, arms and legs;
　　　　　　　　　　　　　　　vinyl-coated cloth body.
　　　　　　　　　　　　　　　Molded hair or rooted hair.

9553	Molded hair	Dressed in bunting suit.	20in (50.8cm)
9753	Molded hair	Dressed in bunting suit.	23in (58.4cm)
9953	Molded hair	Dressed in bunting suit.	27in (68.6cm)
9583	Rooted hair	Dressed in bunting suit.	20in (50.8cm)
9783	Rooted hair	Dressed in bunting suit.	23in (58.4cm)
9983	Rooted hair	Dressed in bunting suit.	27in (68.6cm)
9554	Molded hair	Dressed in a "chinchilla" cloth snowsuit.	20in (50.8cm)
9754	Molded hair	Dressed in a "chinchilla" cloth snowsuit.	23in (58.4cm)
9954	Molded hair	Dressed in a "chinchilla" cloth snowsuit.	27in (68.6cm)
9584	Rooted hair	Dressed in a "chinchilla" cloth snowsuit.	20in (50.8cm)
9784	Rooted hair	Dressed in a "chinchilla" cloth snowsuit.	23in (58.4cm)
9984	Rooted hair	Dressed in a "chinchilla" cloth snowsuit.	27in (68.6cm)
9551	Molded hair	Dressed in a taffeta dress with a matching bonnet.	20in (50.8cm)
9751	Molded hair	Dressed in a taffeta dress with a matching bonnet.	23in (58.4cm)
9951	Molded hair	Dressed in a taffeta dress with a matching bonnet.	27in (68.6cm)
9581	Rooted hair	Dressed in a taffeta dress with a matching bonnet.	20in (50.8cm)
9781	Rooted hair	Dressed in a taffeta dress with a matching bonnet.	23in (58.4cm)
9981	Rooted hair	Dressed in a taffeta dress with a matching bonnet.	27in (68.6cm)
9552	Molded hair	Dressed in cotton overalls with a matching hat.	20in (50.8cm)
9752	Molded hair	Dressed in cotton overalls with a matching hat.	23in (58.4cm)
9952	Molded hair	Dressed in cotton overalls with a matching hat.	27in (68.6cm)
9582	Rooted hair	Dressed in cotton overalls with a matching hat.	20in (50.8cm)
9782	Rooted hair	Dressed in cotton overalls with a matching hat.	23in (58.4cm)
9982	Rooted hair	Dressed in cotton overalls with a matching hat.	27in (68.6cm)
9555	Molded hair	Dressed in a print nylon party dress.	20in (50.8cm)
9755	Molded hair	Dressed in a print nylon party dress.	23in (58.4cm)
9955	Molded hair	Dressed in a print nylon party dress.	27in (68.6cm)

Baby Cuddle-Up continued from page 27.

9585	Rooted hair	Dressed in a print nylon party dress.	20in (50.8cm)
9785	Rooted hair	Dressed in a print nylon party dress.	23in (58.4cm)
9985	Rooted hair	Dressed in a print nylon party dress.	27in (68.6cm)
9587	Rooted hair	Dressed in a nylon coat over a taffeta dress.	20in (50.8cm)
9787	Rooted hair	Dressed in a nylon coat over a taffeta dress.	23in (58.4cm)
9987	Rooted hair	Dressed in a nylon coat over a taffeta dress.	27in (68.6cm)

Illustration 56. Baby Cuddle-Up. Vinyl head with rooted hair, vinyl arms and legs, cloth body. Dressed in a printed nylon party dress with a matching bonnet. Packaged with a small teddy bear. *1954 Effanbee catalog illustration.*

Illustration 55. Baby Cuddle-Up. Vinyl head with rooted hair, vinyl arms and legs, cloth body. Dressed in corded checked overalls with matching hat. The plush teddy bear wears matching overalls. *1954 Effanbee catalog illustration.*

| 9541 | Molded hair | Dressed in a christening dress. | 20in (50.8cm) |

Candy-Ann   Vinyl head, arms, legs; cloth body.

2582	Rooted hair	Dressed in an organdy pinafore.	20in (50.8cm)
2782	Rooted hair	Dressed in an organdy pinafore.	24in (61cm)
2982	Rooted hair	Dressed in an organdy pinafore.	29in (73.7cm)
2583	Rooted hair	Dressed in a taffeta nylon coat, straw bonnet and nylon dress. Came with a stuffed dog, also wearing a straw bonnet.	20in (50.8cm)
2783	Rooted hair	Dressed in a taffeta nylon coat, straw bonnet and nylon dress. Came with a stuffed dog, also wearing a straw bonnet.	24in (61cm)
2983	Rooted hair	Dressed in a taffeta nylon coat, straw bonnet and nylon dress. Came with a stuffed dog, also wearing a straw bonnet.	29in (50.8cm)

Illustration 57. Candy-Ann. Vinyl head, arms and legs; cloth body. Rooted synthetic wig; sleep eyes with lashes. Dressed in a nylon coat over a print nylon dress. The plush dog wears a flower-trimmed straw bonnet, as does the doll. 1954 Effanbee catalog illustration.

Honey Walker		All-hard plastic and fully-jointed.	
7442	Synthetic wig	Dressed in striped taffeta dress.	15in (38.1cm)
7642	Synthetic wig	Dressed in striped taffeta dress.	19in (48.3cm)
7742	Synthetic wig	Dressed in striped taffeta dress.	21in (53.3cm)
7942	Synthetic wig	Dressed in striped taffeta dress.	25in (61cm)
7443	Wig in pigtails	Gingham dress; white organdy blouse.	15in (38.1cm)
7643	Wig in pigtails	Gingham dress; white organdy blouse.	19in (48.3cm)
7743	Wig in pigtails	Gingham dress; white organdy blouse.	21in (53.3cm)
7943	Wig in pigtails	Gingham dress; white organdy blouse.	25in (61cm)
7444	Synthetic wig	Printed chintz dress.	15in (38.1cm)
7644	Synthetic wig	Printed chintz dress.	19in (48.3cm)
7744	Synthetic wig	Printed chintz dress.	21in (53.3cm)
7944	Synthetic wig	Printed chintz dress.	25in (61cm)
7446	Synthetic wig	Raincoat and hat over print dress. Plush puppy dressed in raincoat.	15in (38.1cm)
7646	Synthetic wig	Raincoat and hat over print dress. Plush puppy dressed in raincoat.	19in (48.3cm)
8412	Synthetic wig	Bridesmaid in nylon gown.	15in (38.1cm)
8612	Synthetic wig	Bridesmaid in nylon gown.	19in (48.3cm)
8712	Synthetic wig	Bridesmaid in nylon gown.	21in (53.3cm)
8912	Synthetic wig	Bridesmaid in nylon gown.	25in (61cm)
8413	Synthetic wig	Bride dressed in satin gown.	15in (38.1cm)
8613	Synthetic wig	Bride dressed in satin gown.	19in (48.3cm)
8713	Synthetic wig	Bride dressed in satin gown.	21in (53.3cm)
8913	Synthetic wig	Bride dressed in satin gown.	25in (61cm)

Illustration 58. 18½in (47cm) *Honey Walker*, No. 7642. All-hard plastic and fully-jointed. Blonde wig; green sleep eyes with lashes. She wears a striped taffeta dress and a pink straw hat. Head and back marked: "EFFANBEE." (The catalog calls this size 19in [48.3cm].)

Illustration 59.   Close-up of *Honey Walker* from 1954. The head sits rather high on the neck and it turns from side-to-side as the doll "walks," which is accomplished by taking her hand and gliding her.

Illustration 60.   *Honey Walker* in all-hard plastic. Dressed in a checked gingham guimpe dress and white organdy blouse. On her head she has a straw beanie hat. *1954 Effanbee catalog illustration.*

Illustration 61.   *Honey Walker* in all-hard plastic. She is dressed in printed chintz with braid and button trim and a straw hat. *1954 Effanbee catalog illustration.*

Illustration 62.   All-hard plastic *Honey Walker* with puppy. She wears a plastic rain slicker and rain hat with matching rain boots. Under the coat is a print dress; under the boots are shoes. The plush dog on a chain leash wears a matching raincoat. *1954 Effanbee catalog illustration.*

Patricia Walker	Vinyl head with rooted hair; hard plastic body that is fully-jointed.	
7681	Dressed in organdy party dress.	19in (48.3cm)
7781	Dressed in organdy party dress.	21in (53.3cm)
7981	Dressed in organdy party dress.	25in (61cm)
7683	Dressed in velvet coat with matching leggings and hat.	19in (48.3cm)
7783	Dressed in velvet coat with matching leggings and hat.	21in (53.3cm)
7983	Dressed in velvet coat with matching leggings and hat.	25in (61cm)
8481	Dressed in formal metallic striped nylon gown.	15in (38.1cm)
8681	Dressed in formal metallic striped nylon gown.	19in (48.3cm)
8781	Dressed in formal metallic striped nylon gown.	21in (53.3cm)
8981	Dressed in formal metallic striped nylon gown.	25in (61cm)
7407 *Little Lady* gift set with "Little lady Toiletries" designed by Helène Pessl, Inc.	All-vinyl and fully-jointed with rooted hair.	15in (38.1cm)
7401 *Honey Walker* in carrying case with extra clothing and accessories.	All-hard plastic and fully-jointed.	15in (38.1cm)
7403 *Honey Walker* in steamer trunk with extra clothing and accessories.	All-hard plastic and fully-jointed.	15in (38.1cm)

Illustration 63. Patricia Walker. Vinyl head with rooted hair; fully-jointed hard plastic body. She is wearing an organdy party dress and a straw hat. *1954 Effanbee catalog illustration.*

Illustration 64. *Patricia Walker* with a vinyl head and a hard plastic body. She is dressed in a velvet coat with matching leggings and bonnet. Under this are slacks and a blouse. In her hand she has a white plush muff. *1954 Effanbee catalog illustration.*

Illustration 65. *Patricia Walker.* Vinyl head with rooted hair; hard plastic body. She is costumed in a formal metallic striped nylon gown with a silver metallic cloth bodice. The dolls of 15in (38.1cm), 19in (48.3cm) and 21in (53.3cm) carried a little fan. The 25in (63.5cm) size carried a ruffle trimmed striped nylon parasol to match her gown. *1954 Effanbee catalog illustration.* In 1954 the 25in (63.5cm) doll retailed for $37.95, which was quite expensive at the time.

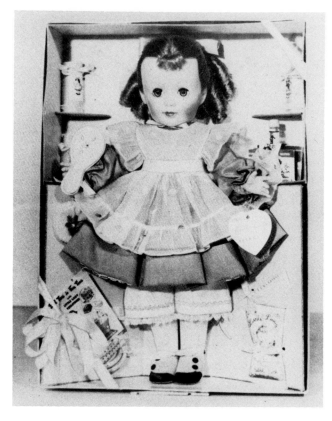

Illustration 66. 15in (38.1cm) *Little Lady*, No. 7407. All-vinyl and fully-jointed. Rooted hair set in an "old-fashioned" style with long curls; sleep eyes with lashes. Costumed in a long-sleeved dress and an organdy pinafore. The package included "Little Lady Toiletries"—cologne, perfume, shampoo, soap, talcum powder, bubble bath, powder puff, comb, mirror and curlers. The toiletries were designed by Helène Pessl, Inc., a maker of children's toiletries. *1954 Effanbee catalog illustration.*

Illustration 67. 15in (38.1cm) *Honey Walker* in all-hard plastic with a Saran wig. She was packaged in a carrying case with a metal catch and handle that included extra costumes and accessories, such as hangers, a comb, brush and mirror set, bobby pins, barrettes, necklace, a bouquet of flowers, bonnet, sunglasses, a pocket book and curlers. *1954 Effanbee catalog illustration.*

Illustration 68. 15in (38.1cm) *Honey Walker*, No. 7403. All-hard plastic and fully-jointed; Saran wig; blue sleep eyes with lashes. The wood and metal steamer trunk included extra clothing, hats, shoes and hair accessories. This ensemble retailed for $19.95. *1954 Effanbee catalog illustration.*

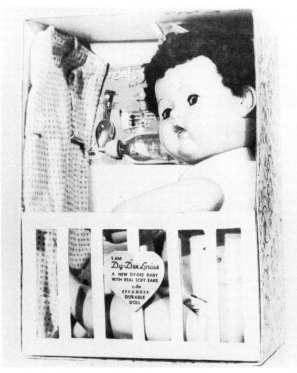

Illustration 69. Electric display unit for retailers to use in connection with the promotion of *Dy-Dee Baby*. The plastic drinking cup would light up, causing the plastic drinking straw to heat and bubble, simulating drinking. Promotional literature stated that "All *Dy-Dee Dolls* are made of finest quality, long-lasting, natural rubber. All joints are air and water tight. *Dy-Dee* has durable plastic head with eyes that can stay open even when the doll lays down or close while doll is upright. *Dy-Dee* drinks from bottle, spoon or straw — while sitting, laying down, or standing up. ONLY EFFANBEE MANUFACTURES *DY-DEE*—no other doll has so much play-value!" *1954 Effanbee catalog illustration.*

Illustration 70. "Fully-tubbable" *Dy-Dee Louise.* She was dressed in a shirt and diaper and her "clearvue playpen box" also included flannel pajamas and a bottle, bubble pipe, pacifier, feeding spoon, sipping straw and Q-Tips. *1954 Effanbee catalog illustration.*

Hard plastic head; fully-jointed rubber
body; painted hair or "washable
tousle wigs" (fur wigs).

Dressed in a shirt and diaper and packaged
in a "playpen box," that includes pajamas
and accessories.

5121	Painted hair	11in (27.9cm)
5322	Painted hair	15in (38.1cm)
5722	Painted hair	20in (50.8cm)
5191	Tousle wig	11in (27.9cm)
5392	Tousle wig	15in (38.1cm)
5792	Tousle wig	20in (50.8cm)

Dressed in a shirt and diaper and packaged
in a hinged carrying case that includes
a layette and accessories.

5123	Painted hair	11in (27.9cm)
5323	Painted hair	15in (38.1cm)
5723	Painted hair	20in (50.8cm)
5193	Tousle wig	11in (27.9cm)
5393	Tousle wig	15in (38.1cm)
5793	Tousle wig	20in (50.8cm)

Dressed in a shirt and diaper and packaged
in a wood-frame carrying case; layette
and accessories included.

5124	Painted hair	11in (27.9cm)
5324	Painted hair	15in (38.1cm)
5724	Painted hair	20in (50.8cm)
5194	Tousle wig	11in (27.9cm)
5394	Tousle wig	15in (38.1cm)
5794	Tousle wig	20in (50.8cm)

Dressed in a shirt and diaper and packaged
in a wood-frame convertible suitcase;
layette and accessories included.

5395	Tousle wig	15in (38.1cm)
5795	Tousle wig	20in (50.8cm)

ROOTIE KAZOOTIE AND POLKA DOTTIE
lovable television characters

Favorites of the kiddie television audience of the American Broadcasting Company, appearing on national hook-ups. Cute and lovable, they appeal even where the program does not appear.

711—21"—5.95 Rootie Vinyl Head— Vinyl Fabric Body
712—21"—5.95 Polka Dottie—Vinyl Fabric Body, Vinyl Head
700—4.95 Gala-Poochie Pup
723—5.95 Fully jointed plastic Rootie Walkers—Vinyl Head
724—5.95 Fully joined plastic Polka Dottie Walkers—Vinyl Head

Not pictured
701—11"—3.95 Rootie Vinyl Head Latex Body-Washable
702—11"—3.95 Dottie Latex Body-Washable
722—7.95 Twins of above

Effanbee means finest 🖤 and best

Illustration 71. Rootie Kazootie and *Polka Dottie* from the 1954 Effanbee catalog. Rootie Kazootie and Polka Dottie were puppet characters from the ABC-TV children's show "Rootie Kazootie," which was a 30 minute entry from January 3, 1952, to February 5, 1954. Other characters on the program were Rootie's wide-eyed dog, Gala Poochie Pup; El Squeako, the mouse; Nipper Catador and Poison Sumac.

Dy-Dee Layettes

51/10	11in (27.9cm)	Diapers (packaged 1 dozen).
53/10	15in (38.1cm)	Diapers (packaged 1 dozen).
57/10	20in (50.8cm)	Diapers (packaged 1 dozen).
51/11	11in (27.9cm)	Shirts (packaged 1/2 dozen).
53/11	15in (38.1cm)	Shirts (packaged 1/2 dozen).
57/11	20in (50.8cm)	Shirts (packaged 1/2 dozen).
51/12	11in (27.9cm)	Flannel pajamas.
53/12	15in (38.1cm)	Flannel pajamas.
57/12	20in (50.8cm)	Flannel pajamas.
51/13	11in (27.9cm)	Short dress, cap, slip.
53/13	15in (38.1cm)	Short dress, cap, slip.
57/13	20in (50.8cm)	Short dress, cap, slip.
51/14	11in (27.9cm)	Long dress, cap, slip.
53/14	15in (38.1cm)	Long dress, cap, slip.
57/14	20in (50.8cm)	Long dress, cap, slip.
51/15	11in (27.9cm)	Short silk coat and hat.
53/15	15in (38.1cm)	Short silk coat and hat.
57/15	20in (50.8cm)	Short silk coat and hat.
51/16	11in (27.9cm)	Long silk coat and hat.
53/16	15in (38.1cm)	Long silk coat and hat.
57/16	20in (50.8cm)	Long silk coat and hat.
51/17	11in (27.9cm)	Nightie, cap and booties.
53/17	15in (38.1cm)	Nightie, cap and booties.
57/17	20in (50.8cm)	Nightie, cap and booties.
51/18	11in (27.9cm)	Pinafore, slacks and hat.
53/18	15in (38.1cm)	Pinafore, slacks and hat.
57/18	20in (50.8cm)	Pinafore, slacks and hat.
51/19	11in (27.9cm)	Coat, hat and leggings.
53/19	15in (38.1cm)	Coat, hat and leggings.
57/19	20in (50.8cm)	Coat, hat and leggings.
5/102		Accessory card (packaged 1 dozen).
5/103		Pacifiers (packaged 1 dozen).
5/104		Bottles (packaged 1 dozen).
5/106		Utility kits (packaged 1 dozen).

Illustration 72. 12in (30.5cm) *Candy Kid Twins*, No. 341. All-vinyl and fully-jointed with molded and painted hair. The twins were dressed in red and white checked gingham. He carried a yo-yo; she had a plush monkey. *1954 Effanbee catalog illustration.* (These are the same dolls as *Katy.*)

141	*Katy*	Vinyl head with stationary glassine eyes; fully-jointed hard plastic body.	12in (30.5cm)
241	*Candy Walker*	Vinyl head, arms and legs; vinyl-coated fabric body.	13in (33cm)
	Rootie Kazootie		
711		Vinyl head; vinyl fabric body.	21in (53.3cm)
723		Vinyl head; fully-jointed hard plastic body.	21in (53.3cm)
701		Vinyl head; latex body.	11in (27.9cm)
	Polka Dottie		
712		Vinyl head; vinyl fabric body.	21in (53.3cm)
724		Vinyl head; fully-jointed hard plastic body.	21in (53.3cm)
702		Vinyl head; latex body.	11in (27.9cm)
722	*Rootie Kazootie* and *Polka Dottie* twins.	Vinyl heads; latex bodies.	11in (27.9cm)
700	*Gala-Poochie Pup*	Stuffed plush.	about 21in (53.3cm)
341	*Candy Kid Twins*	All-vinyl and fully-jointed; molded, painted hair. Dressed in red and white gingham outfits. The boy carries a yo-yo; the girl has a small plush monkey.	12in (30.5cm)

1955

New Dolls:
Rusty and *Sherry* from "Make Room for Daddy"

Rusty	All-vinyl and fully-jointed with painted and molded hair; blue sleep eyes with lashes. Dressed in bibbed overalls.	20in (50.8cm)
Sherry	Vinyl head with rooted hair in braids; hard plastic, fully-jointed body with walker mechanism. Dressed in schoolgirl dress.	19in (48.3cm)
Dy-Dee Baby	Hard plastic head; fully-jointed vinyl body. Tear ducts in eyes.	
Dy-Dee Wee		9in (22.9cm)
Dy-Dee Ellen		11in (27.9cm)
Dy-Dee Jane		15in (38.1cm)
Dy-Dee Louise (also called *Dy-Dee Lou*)		20in (50.8cm)
Tiny Tubber	All-vinyl and fully-jointed with painted hair. Sleep eyes with molded lashes.	8in (20.3cm)

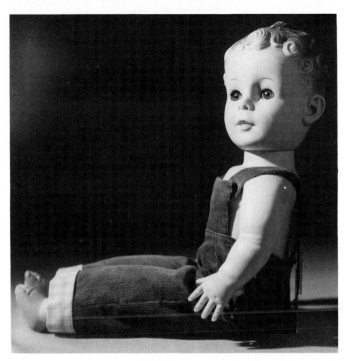

Illustrations 73 and 74. 20in (50.8cm) *Rusty*. All-vinyl and fully-jointed. Molded curly hair; blue sleep eyes with lashes. The bibbed overalls are replaced, but this is the type of costume the doll originally wore. Head marked: "EFFANBEE // RUSTY // ©." *Pam Petcoff Collection. Photograph by John Schoonmaker.*

Rusty is from the ABC-TV show "Make Room for Daddy," which ran from September 1953 to September 1964. Rusty Williams was played by Rusty Hamer (born February 15, 1947), and he was the son of Danny Williams, played by Danny Thomas. There was a doll called *Sherry*, also from about 1955, that capitalized on the same television program. This is Sherry Jackson, who played Terry Williams (Sherry Jackson was born Sharon Diane Jackson, *also* on February 15, 1947).

Illustration 75. 15in (38.1cm) *Dy-Dee Jane*. Hard plastic head with brown painted hair and blue sleep eyes with lashes. There are tear ducts at the corners of the eyes so that she can "weep real tears." The ears that are attached to the head are rubber. The body is fully-jointed vinyl. The doll is marked on the back:

EFFANBEE
DY-DEE BABY
U.S. PAT. 1859485
U.S. PAT. 1859485
ENGLAND D 380060
FRANCE 723980
GERMANY 585647
U.S. 2007784
OTHER PAT. PENDING
OTHER PAT. PENDING

Note the identification bracelet on *Dy-Dee*'s right wrist.

Illustration 76. The original box for *Dy-Dee* in *Illustration 75*. She is style number 5562V.

Illustrations 78 and *79. Tiny Tubber. Photographs courtesy of Al Kirchof.*

Illustration 77. 8in (20.3cm) *Tiny Tubber.* All-vinyl and fully-jointed. Painted hair; sleep eyes with molded plastic lashes; open mouth nurser. The doll was sold dressed like this and cost $3.00. She is No. 2111. *Photograph courtesy of Al Kirchof.*

Illustration 80. Tiny Tubber modeling some of her fashions. Left to right: No. 161 broadcloth dress and cap, No. 131 sunsuit and bonnet, and No. 331 short dress, cap, shoes and socks. *Photograph courtesy of Al Kirchof.*

Illustration 81. Tiny Tubber wearing a christening dress. *Photograph courtesy of Al Kirchof.*

1956

New Dolls:

Mickey, the All-American Boy	All-vinyl and fully-jointed with molded hats. Painted eyes. *Baseball Player.* *Football Player.* *Fireman.* *Soldier.* *Sailor.* *Policeman.*	10in (25.4cm)
Honey	All-hard plastic. A walker with extra joints at ankles and knees. Wore high heel shoes. *Junior Miss* is an example of this doll.	20in (50.8cm)
Melodie	Vinyl head with rooted hair; hard plastic body. A fully-jointed walker with bending knees. A battery-operated record player in the torso allowed her to talk and sing.	27in (68.6cm)

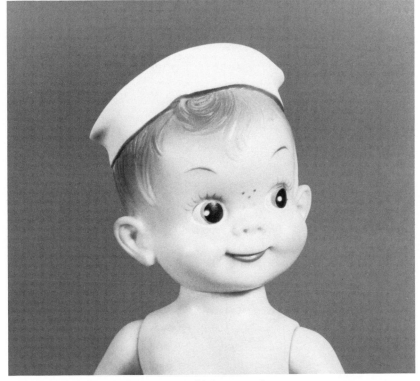

Illustration 83. Mickey as a sailor.

Illustration 82. 11in (27.9cm) (including molded hat) *Mickey, the All-American Boy* as a sailor. All-vinyl and fully-jointed. Molded hair and hat; blue painted eyes. The top of the suit is missing. Head marked: "MICKEY // EFFANBEE." Back marked: "10 // EFFANBEE // 8."

Illustrations 84 through 88. Honey Walker. All-hard plastic and fully-jointed, including jointed knees. These were Effanbee salesmen's sample pictures. *Photographs courtesy of Al Kirchof.*

Illustrations 89 through 93. Honey Walker from Effanbee salesmen's sample pictures. All-hard plastic and fully-jointed with extra joints at the ankles and knees. The joints at the ankles permitted the doll's feet to wear flat shoes or high heel shoes and to assume the positions of a dancing ballerina. *Photographs courtesy of Al Kirchof.*

Illustration 92.

Illustration 93.

Illustration 94. 20in (50.8cm) *Honey Walker,* called *Junior Miss, A Doll with Glamour.* This is the same doll as in *Illustration 93.* All-hard plastic and fully-jointed, with extra joints at the ankles and knees. Dark brown wig; blue sleep eyes with lashes. The original box calls her *Honey Walker,* style 8641; the gold heart tag tied to her wrist cites her other name. Head and back marked: "EFFANBEE."

Illustration 95. 20in (50.8cm) *Honey Walker/Junior Miss.*

Illustrations 96 and 97. 20in (50.8cm) *Honey Ballerina* in all-hard plastic. Extra joints at the feet and knees. The doll is also a "walker." *Patricia N. Schoonmaker Collection. Photographs by John Schoonmaker.*

Illustration 98. 27in (68.6cm) *Melodie,* 1956. Vinyl head with blonde rooted hair; blue sleep eyes with lashes. Hard plastic body with extra joints at the knees so that *Melodie* could "pray." The record player inside the torso operated by having the child "push the magic button." The original dress is flowered viole; the shoes and socks are replacements. Marked on head: "EFFANBEE // MELODIE // 2." *Virginia Tomlinson Collection. Photograph by John Schoonmaker.*

Illustration 99. Back view of *Melodie's* torso. Small records fit into the record player. *Melodie* would recite "One, Two, Buckle My Shoe," "Simple Simon" and "Now I Lay Me Down to Sleep." She sang "Eensie Weensie Spider," "Sing a Song of Sixpence," "Twinkle, Twinkle Little Star" and "Rock-a-Bye Baby." *Virginia Tomlinson Collection. Photograph by John Schoonmaker.* Note: In 1956 *Melodie* retailed for "only" $29.95.

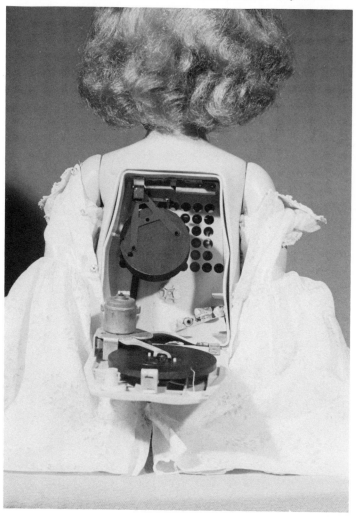

New Dolls:

Fluffy	All-vinyl and fully-jointed. Rooted hair.	8in (20.3cm) 10in (25.4cm)
Lawrence Welk's Champagne Lady	Vinyl head with rooted hair; blue sleep eyes with lashes. Vinyl arms; the remainder of the fully-jointed body is hard plastic.	21in (53.3cm) 25in (63.5cm)
Honey Ballerina	Hard plastic with vinyl arms	18in (45.7cm)

FLUFFY'S FASHIONS

No. 101	Two-piece pajama set	$1.00	No. 255	Ice skating ensemble with ice skates	$2.50
No. 102	Long robe	$1.00	No. 257	Dungarees, shoes, yo-yo	$2.50
No. 103	Percale dress	$1.00	No. 258	Fleece snowsuit	$2.50
No. 104	Dress trimmed with "rickrack"	$1.00	No. 301	Gingham dress	$3.00
No. 105	Cotton dress	$1.00	No. 302	Organdy party dress	$3.00
No. 106	Sunsuit and hat	$1.00	No. 303	Organdy party dress and hat	$3.00
No. 152	Two-piece shorty pajamas	$1.50	No. 304	Permanent pleated ensemble	$3.00
No. 203	Percale dress and hat	$2.00	No. 306	Velvet party dress	$3.00
No. 204	Taffeta dress and straw hat	$2.00	No. 307	Tulle formal and slippers	$3.00
No. 205	Cotton dress and pinafore	$2.00	No. 308	Majorette with baton	$3.00
No. 206	Slack suit and hat	$2.00	No. 309	Borgana coat and hat	$3.00
No. 207	Sailor boy suit	$2.00	No. 310	Rodeo girl with gun	$3.00
No. 208	Sailor girl suit	$2.00	No. 311	Ski outfit with skis	$3.00
No. 209	Nurse ensemble	$2.00	No. 312	Roller skating outfit	$3.00
No. 210	Rain cape and boots	$2.00	No. 314	Nylon formal and slippers	$3.00
No. 251	Hat and coat	$2.50	No. 316	Southern Belle	$3.00
No. 252	Plaid dress and beret	$2.50	No. 401	Bride ensemble	$4.00
No. 253	Ballerina and slippers	$2.50			

FASHIONS for TINY TUBBER
Fluffy's Little Sister

No. 81	Flannel robe	$ .80
No. 82	Flannel pajamas	$ .80
No. 131	Sunsuit and bonnet	$1.00
No. 132	Play dress and bonnet	$1.00
No. 161	Broadcloth dress and cap	$1.50
No. 231	Bunting -- flannel sacque with hood	$2.00
No. 261	Coat and hat	$2.50
No. 262	Snowsuit and hat	$2.50
No. 331	Short dress, cap, shoes and socks	$3.00
No. 332	Long dress and cap	$3.00

Presenting **FLUFFY** *and her fashions*

EFFANBEE DOLL CORPORATION
200 FIFTH AVENUE • NEW YORK 10, N.Y.

Illustration 100.

Illustration 101. 10in (25.4cm) *Fluffy.* All-vinyl and fully-jointed. Rooted hair; sleep eyes with plastic lashes. This is stock number 1121 and she retailed for $3.00. *Photograph courtesy of Al Kirchof.*

Illustration 102. 10in (25.4cm) *Fluffy*, wearing No. 253 ballerina with dancing slippers, No. 205 dotted cotton dress with organdy pinafore, and No. 206 slack suit and hat. *Photograph courtesy of Al Kirchof.*

Illustration 103. Fluffy wearing No. 101 two-piece pajama set and No. 102 long robe that is lace-trimmed. *Photograph courtesy of Al Kirchof.*

Illustration 104. *Fluffy* dressed in No. 316 southern belle, No. 401 bride ensemble, and No. 310 rodeo girl with gun and holster and shoes. *Photograph courtesy of Al Kirchof.*

Illustration 105. *Fluffy* in little girl dresses. They are No. 104 printed percale with rickrack, No. 103 printed percale, and No. 105 embossed cotton. *Photograph courtesy of Al Kirchof.*

Illustration 106. *Fluffy* modeling her fashions, No. 204 striped taffeta with straw sailor hat and No. 106 sunsuit and hat. *Photograph courtesy of Al Kirchof.*

Illustration 107. Three different *Fluffy* dolls posing in outfits No. 203 printed percale with matching hat, No. 208 sailor girl with whistle and No. 207 sailor boy with whistle. *Photograph courtesy of Al Kirchof.*

Illustration 108. Fluffy modeling her "better clothes." They are No. 301 gingham dress, No. 309 Borgana coat and hat and No. 304 permanent pleated ensemble with hat, shoes and socks. *Photograph courtesy of Al Kirchof.*

Illustration 109. Fluffy sporting No. 252 plaid taffeta dress with matching beret, No. 210 rain cape and boots, and No. 306 velvet party dress and hat. *Photograph courtesy of Al Kirchof.*

Illustration 110. 10½in (26.3cm) *Fluffy* with stationary eyes.

Illustration 111. Fluffy is ready for play in fashions No. 257 dungaree outfit with shoes and yo-yo, an unnumbered two-piece swimsuit, and No. 258 fleece snowsuit. *Photograph courtesy of Al Kirchof.*

Illustration 112. Other doll companies, such as Molly-'es, had unmarked dolls that looked like Effanbee's *Fluffy.* At the left is an 11¾in (29.9cm) lass with bright orange hair and bright green sleep eyes. She is all-vinyl and fully-jointed. At the right the 10½in (26.7cm) nude doll has blonde hair and blue sleep eyes with molded lashes. The head and arms are soft vinyl; the torso and legs are rigid vinyl. Head marked: "4092 // K 32."

Illustration 113. Two different versions of Effanbee's *Fluffy.* Both measure 10½in (26.3cm) and are all-vinyl and fully-jointed. The doll at the left has dark brown rooted hair and blue sleep eyes with lashes. Her head is marked: "FLUFFY." The doll on the right has red rooted hair and blue stationary eyes. Her head is marked: "EFFANBEE // LITTLE LADY // © FLUFFY."

1958 Catalog

My Fair Baby

All-vinyl and fully-jointed with sleep eyes.
Wears flannel robe and diaper and is in zippered quilted bunting.

4695	Rooted hair		18in (45.7cm)
4895	Rooted hair		22in (55.9cm)
4625	Molded hair		18in (45.7cm)
4825	Molded hair		22in (55.9cm)
4421	Molded hair		14in (35.6cm)

Toddle Tot

All-vinyl and fully-jointed.

6392	Rooted hair	Dressed in pique playsuit.	13in (33cm)
6592	Rooted hair	Dressed in pique playsuit.	19in (48.3cm)
6792	Rooted hair	Dressed in pique playsuit.	22in (55.9cm)
6342	Molded hair	Dressed in pique playsuit.	13in (33cm)
6542	Molded hair	Dressed in pique playsuit.	19in (48.3cm)
6742	Molded hair	Dressed in pique playsuit.	22in (55.9cm)
6796	Rooted hair	Dressed in sleeper with covered feet. Carries plush teddy bear.	22in (55.9cm)
		Same as above without teddy bear.	22in (55.9cm)

Illustration 114. 23in (58.4cm) *Bubbles* with rooted hair. Vinyl head and limbs; cloth body stuffed with kapok. *Photograph courtesy of Al Kirchof.*

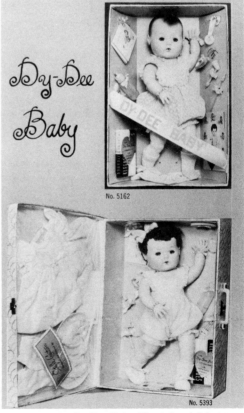

Illustration 115. Dy-Dee Baby. Plastic head; fully-jointed vinyl body. *1958 Effanbee catalog illustration.*

Dy-Dee Baby		Plastic head; fully-jointed vinyl body.	
5162	Molded hair	Dressed in cotton playsuit.	12in (30.5cm)
5362	Molded hair	Dressed in cotton playsuit.	17in (43.2cm)
5762	Molded hair	Dressed in cotton playsuit.	21in (53.3cm)
5192	Lamb's wool wig	Dressed in cotton playsuit.	12in (30.5cm)
5392	Lamb's wool wig	Dressed in cotton playsuit.	17in (43.2cm)
5792	Lamb's wool wig	Dressed in cotton playsuit.	21in (53.3cm)
5193	Lamb's wool wig	Packaged in deluxe carrying case. Wears playsuit and has layette and accessories.	12in (30.5cm)
5393	Lamb's wool wig	Packaged in deluxe carrying case. Wears playsuit and has layette and accessories.	17in (43.2cm)
5793	Lamb's wool wig	Packaged in deluxe carrying case. Wears playsuit and has layette and accessories.	21in (53.3cm)
5163	Molded hair	Packaged in deluxe carrying case. Wears playsuit and has layette and accessories.	12in (30.5cm)
5363	Molded hair	Packaged in deluxe carrying case. Wears playsuit and has layette and accessories.	17in (43.2cm)
5763	Molded hair	Packaged in deluxe carrying case. Wears playsuit and has layette and accessories.	21in (53.3cm)
7563	*Little Lady*	All-vinyl and fully-jointed. Rooted Saran hair, braided in pigtails. Dressed in checked gingham dress.	19in (48.3cm)
8651	*Jr. Miss*	Rigidsol vinyl plastic and fully-jointed. Rooted Saran hair. High heel feet. Dressed in flowered nylon formal.	21in (53.3cm)
Alice		All-vinyl and fully-jointed with rooted Saran hair. Dressed in organdy pinafore and organdy dress, as *Alice-in-Wonderland*.	
7364			15in (38.1cm)
7564			19in (48.3cm)
Jr. Miss Ballerina Walking Doll		Plastic body and legs; vinyl arms and head. Rooted Saran hair. Wears ballerina costume and nylon stockings.	
7431		Has jointed ankles.	15in (38.1cm)
7631		Has jointed ankles and knees.	21in (53.3cm)
8653	*Bride*	Rigidsol vinyl-plastic and fully-jointed. Rooted Saran hair. High heel feet.	21in (53.3cm)
My Precious Baby		All-vinyl and fully-jointed with extra joints at knees and elbows.	
6898P	Rooted hair		20in (50.8cm)
6858P	Molded hair		20in (50.8cm)

Bubbles		Vinyl head and limbs; cloth body stuffed with kapok.	
9851	Molded hair	Organdy dress.	23in (58.4cm)
9891	Rooted hair	Organdy dress.	23in (58.4cm)

My Fair Baby		All-vinyl and fully-jointed.	
4422	Molded hair	Dressed in organdy christening dress.	14in (35.6cm)
4622	Molded hair	Dressed in organdy christening dress.	18in (45.7cm)
4423	Molded hair	Dressed in christening dress with matching coat and pillow.	14in (35.6cm)
4623	Molded hair	Dressed in christening dress with matching coat and pillow.	18in (45.7cm)
4426	Molded hair	Wears organdy dress and bonnet.	14in (35.6cm)
4626	Molded hair	Wears organdy dress and bonnet.	18in (45.7cm)
4826	Molded hair	Wears organdy dress and bonnet.	22in (55.9cm)
4496	Rooted hair	Wears organdy dress and bonnet.	14in (35.6cm)
4696	Rooted hair	Wears organdy dress and bonnet.	18in (45.7cm)
4896	Rooted hair	Wears organdy dress and bonnet.	22in (55.9cm)

Illustration 116. Girl dolls from the 1958 Effanbee catalog. Top row: Little Lady, Alice and Jr. Miss Ballerina Walking Doll. Bottom row: Jr. Miss Doll and Bride Doll. See catalog listings for descriptions of these dolls. 1958 Effanbee catalog illustration.

Illustration 117. 19½in (49.6cm) Bride, No. 8653 (listed as 21in [53.3cm] in the 1958 catalog). Soft vinyl head with blonde rooted hair; blue sleep eyes with lashes; pierced ears for earrings. Rigid vinyl body with jointed arms, legs and waist, and an "adult" bosom. The white satin gown has a three-tiered overskirt. The original price in 1958 was $15.00, which was much lower than a comparable hard plastic Honey had been in the early 1950s. Head marked: "EFFANBEE // 19©66."

7474	Most Happy Family		
	Mother	Rigidsol vinyl and fully-jointed. Rooted Saran hair. High heel feet.	19in (48.3cm)
	Baby	All-vinyl and fully-jointed with molded hair. (*Tiny Tubber.*)	8in (20.3cm)
	Brother	All-vinyl and fully-jointed with molded hair and painted eyes. (*Mickey.*)	8in (20.3cm)
	Sister	All-vinyl and fully-jointed with rooted Saran hair and sleep eyes. (*Fluffy.*)	8in (20.3cm)
7676	Most Happy Family		
	Mother	Ridigsol vinyl and fully-jointed. Rooted Saran hair. High heel feet.	21in (53.3cm)
	Baby	All-vinyl and fully-jointed with molded hair. (*Tiny Tubber.*)	8in (20.3cm)
	Brother	All-vinyl and fully-jointed with molded hair and painted eyes. (*Mickey.*)	10in (25.4cm)
	Sister	All-vinyl and fully-jointed with rooted Saran hair and sleep eyes. (*Fluffy.*)	10in (25.4cm)

*Illustration 118. Most Happy Family,*No. 7474. 19in (48.3cm) *Mother* is all-vinyl and fully-jointed with rooted hair. She is dressed in an embossed taffeta dress, a straw pillbox hat, high heels, stockings, wedding and engagement rings and earrings. *Brother* is 8in (20.3cm) tall and is all-vinyl and fully-jointed with painted hair and eyes. *Sister* is 8in (20.3cm) and is all-vinyl and fully-jointed with rooted hair and sleep eyes with molded lashes. The *Baby* is 8in (20.3cm) and is all-vinyl and fully-jointed with an open mouth for "drinking and wetting." The original price was $18.00 for the set. *1958 Effanbee catalog illustration.*

Illustration 119. Most Happy Family, No. 7676. *Mother* is 21in (53.3cm) and is fully-jointed vinyl with rooted hair. She is dressed in a linen-look cotton skirt and bolero, a lace-trimmed blouse-slip combination, straw pillbox hat, high heels, wedding and engagement rings and earrings. The *Baby* is 8in (20.3cm) and is all-vinyl and fully-jointed with an open mouth. The *Brother* and *Sister* are 10in (25.4cm) and are fully-jointed vinyl. *Sister* has rooted hair; *Brother* has molded hair. (*Sister* is the *Fluffy* doll; *Brother* is *Mickey*; *Baby* is *Tiny Tubber.*) The original retail price for the set was $22.00. *1958 Effanbee catalog illustration.*

Illustrations 120 and 121. This Effanbee girl doll is an example of a "transitional doll." She dates from the late 1950s when doll manufacturers were changing hard plastic components over to vinyl and glued-on wigs to rooted wigs. She is 19in (48.3cm) and has a vinyl head stuffed with cotton batting and a jointed hard plastic body. The dark blonde hair is not rooted as evenly as hair was by the 1960s. The sleep eyes are blue; she has an open/closed mouth. The head and back are marked: "EFFANBEE." The original dress is royal blue velveteen and it is trimmed with white. The head looks like that of *Alyssa* of 1960; the body is the one used for *Honey* in the 1950s.

1959-1963

For the years 1959 through 1963 there are only three known Effanbee doll catalogs. Unfortunately, these catalogs have no dates on them. What seems to be accurate dates can be established by cross referencing Effanbee dolls with advertisements from trade magazines, such as *Playthings*, and with retail mail order catalogs from such companies as Sears and Wards.

No Effanbee dolls from these years are omitted here. To attempt to maintain accuracy the available catalogs are designated as I, II and III. From studying the available information, it seems most likely that I is 1960, II is 1961 and III is 1962.

New for 1959:

Mary Jane and Baby Sister in Bassinette

Mary Jane		Vinyl head with rooted Saran hair; walking mechanism.	32in (81.3cm)
Lil Darlin		All-vinyl drinking and wetting baby with rooted Saran hair.	16in (40.6cm)

CATALOG I

My Fair Baby		All-vinyl and fully-jointed with sleep eyes. Has identification bracelet and plastic nursing bottle.	
4431	Molded hair	Dressed in playsuit and bonnet with extra skirt.	14in (35.6cm)
4441	Molded hair	Dressed in fleecy bunting and hood.	14in (35.6cm)
4685	Rooted hair	Dressed in dimity dress with lace; matching bonnet.	18in (45.7cm)
4485	Rooted hair	Dressed in dimity dress with lace; matching bonnet.	14in (35.6cm)
4686	Rooted hair	Dressed in lace-trimmed fleece coat.	18in (45.7cm)
4646	Molded hair	Dressed in lace-trimmed fleece coat.	18in (45.7cm)
4648	Molded hair	Dressed in zippered quilted bunting.	18in (45.7cm)
4688	Rooted hair	Dressed in zippered quilted bunting.	18in (45.7cm)
4689	Rooted hair	Dressed in nylon dress.	18in (45.7cm)
4684	Rooted hair	Dressed in fleece coat and leggings.	18in (45.7cm)
4443	Molded hair	Dressed in fleece coat and leggings.	14in (35.6cm)
4643	Molded hair	Dressed in fleece coat and leggings.	18in (45.7cm)
4683	Rooted hair	Wears organdy dress and cap.	18in (45.7cm)
4642	Molded hair	Dressed in organdy dress and bonnet.	18in (45.7cm)
Twinkie		All-vinyl and fully-jointed with sleep eyes and molded hair. A drink and wet baby.	16in (40.6cm)
2532		Dressed in organdy dress with lace trim; lies on organdy covered pillow.	
0536		Dressed in lace-trimmed sacque with matching diaper. Packaged with a layette.	

Illustration 122. 14in (35.6cm) *My Fair Baby*, No. 4431, circa 1960. All-vinyl and fully-jointed. Molded hair; blue sleep eyes with lashes; open mouth nurser. She also has an identification bracelet and a plastic nursing bottle. She is dressed in a playsuit with a matching bonnet and has an extra skirt. *Photograph courtesy of Al Kirchof.*

Illustration 123. 16in (40.6cm) *Twinkie*, No. 2532, circa 1960. All-vinyl and fully-jointed. Molded hair; sleep eyes with lashes; open mouth nurser. She is wearing her identification bracelet and she has a nursing bottle. Her dress is organdy trimmed with lace and it has a matching jacket and bonnet. The pillow is covered with organdy. *Photograph courtesy of Al Kirchof.*

L'il Darlin'		All-vinyl and fully-jointed with sleep eyes and molded hair; has plastic nursing bottle.	
3311		Dressed in zippered bunting and ruffled hood.	13in (33cm)
3511		Dressed in zippered bunting and ruffled hood.	16in (40.6cm)
3312		Dressed in organdy christening dress with matching bonnet; tied in ruffled blanket.	13in (33cm)
3512		Dressed in organdy christening dress with matching bonnet; tied in ruffled blanket.	16in (40.6cm)
Fluffy		All-vinyl and fully-jointed with rooted hair and sleep eyes.	
1121			11in (27.9cm)
Candy Kids		All-vinyl and fully-jointed with rooted Saran hair and sleep eyes. Drink and wet toddlers.	16in (40.6cm)
2681		Dressed in two-piece butcher boy outfit with breton hat.	
2682		Dressed in percale dress with matching hat.	
2683		Dressed in lace-trimmed organdy dress.	
Sweetie Pie		All-vinyl and fully-jointed drink and wet baby with sleep eyes and mama voice.	22in (55.9cm)
4888V	Rooted hair	Dressed in zippered quilted crepe bunting.	
4848V	Molded hair	Dressed in zippered quilted crepe bunting.	
4884V	Rooted hair	Dressed in fleece coat and leggings.	
4889V	Rooted hair	Dressed in nylon waffle cloth frock.	
4843V	Molded hair	Wears organdy dress and cap.	
4883V	Rooted hair	Wears organdy dress and cap.	
Toddle Tot		All-vinyl and fully-jointed toddler with rooted Saran hair. Drinks and wets.	
6741		Dressed in "walk-a-blanket" and carries a teddy bear.	22in (55.9cm)
Patsyette Triplets		All-vinyl and fully-jointed with molded hair and sleep eyes. Drink and wet dolls.	8in (20.3cm)
2113		Dressed in organdy christening dresses.	
Tiny Tubber		All-vinyl and fully-jointed with molded hair and sleep eyes. Drink and wet babies.	10½in (26.7cm)
2312		Dressed in diaper and booties.	
2321		In zippered hat box with layette.	
2313		Dressed in print dress with bonnet.	
2322	*Twins*	Dressed in jersey knit pajamas and wrapped in a blanket.	

Illustration 125. 18in (45.7cm) *My Fair Baby,* No. 4683, circa 1960. All-vinyl and fully-jointed. Rooted Saran hair; sleep eyes with lashes; open mouth nurser. She is dressed in organdy and she wears her identification bracelet. *Photograph courtesy of Al Kirchof.*

Illustration 124. 16in (40.6cm) *Candy Kid* toddler, No. 2683, circa 1960. All-vinyl and fully-jointed. Rooted Saran hair; sleep eyes with lashes; open mouth. She is dressed in a lace-trimmed organdy dress with matching bonnet, taffeta slip and panties. *Photograph courtesy of Al Kirchof.*

Illustration 126. From the Effanbee Doll Corporation catalog, circa 1960. In the top row is *Tiny Tubber.* In the bottom row, from left to right: *Toddle Tot, Patsyette Triplets* and *Bubbles. Courtesy of Al Kirchof.*

TINY TUBBER

10½" All vinyl baby doll with moving arms, legs and head and moving eyes. Molded hair, drinks and wets.

No. 2321

No. 2312

No. 2322

No. 6741

No. 2113

Style No. 2312
Dressed in diaper and booties; wrapped in blanket with plastic bottle and hospital identification bracelet. 10½".
Retails at $2.98

Style No. 2321
In zippered hat box type carrying case with handle. Hat box has attached mirror.
Dressed in a two piece jersey knit denton type pajama.
Layette consists of dress, slip, diaper with pins, bottle, shoes and socks; birth announcement cards. 10½".
Retails at $7.98

Style No. 2313
Dressed in print dress and bonnet, and panties. Has nursing bottle. 10½".
Retails at $3.98

Style No. 2322
TINY TUBBER TWINS
Twins, each dressed in jersey knit pajamas. Wrapped in ruffle trimmed blanket. Each with her own nursing bottle. In attractive gift box. 10½".
Retails at $9.98

BUBBLES

HER FEATHER-LIGHTNESS MAKES "BUBBLES" THE PERFECT BIG DOLL FOR ALL AGES!

23" Feather light baby doll. Body is vinyl coated strong nylon fabric that can be washed with a damp cloth. Stuffed with soft kapok. Has moving eyes, vinyl arms, legs and head and mamma voice.

No. 9881

No. 9831

Style No. 9881
Dressed in crisp permanent finish organdy dress with matching bonnet trimmed with net ruching. Rayon taffeta slip and panties, shoes and socks. With rooted hair. 23".
Retails at $13.98

Style No. 9831—Molded hair — 23".
Retails at $11.98

TODDLE TOT
Style No. 6741
All vinyl standing toddler with soft flexible tiltable vinyl head with rooted saran hair that can be washed combed and set. Drinks and wets, and has nursing bottle. Dressed in authentic "walk-a-blanket". Has I.D. bracelet on wrist and carries soft teddy bear on arm. Shirt and diaper, under walk-a-blanket. 22".
Retails at $15.98

PATSYETTE TRIPLETS
Style No. 2113
8" soft flexible vinyl drinking and wetting dolls. Fully jointed with moving eyes and molded hair. Triplets, each dressed in lace trimmed long organdy christening dress with matching bonnet. All have taffeta slip, flannel diapers, socks and are wrapped in lace trimmed flannel blankets. Each baby has her own plastic bottle. Packed in gift box with combination of two pink blankets and one blue. 8".
Retails at $9.98

7

Bubbles	Vinyl head, arms and legs; kapok stuffed body that is a vinyl coated nylon fabric.	23in (58.4cm)
9881 Rooted hair	Dressed in organdy dress and hat.	
9831 Molded hair	Dressed in organdy dress and hat.	
Patsy Ann	All-vinyl and fully-jointed; rooted Saran hair; sleep eyes; freckles across nose.	15in (38.1cm)
621	Dressed in calico print dress.	
623	Dressed in polished cotton dress.	
624	Dressed in checked gingham dress.	
625	Dressed in nylon ballerina tutu.	
626	Dressed in velveteen skating outfit.	
627	Dressed in drum majorette costume.	
628	Dressed as a *Brownie Scout*.	
629	Dressed as a *Girl Scout of America*.	
0636	Dressed in organdy dress; packed in gift box with extra clothes.	

Illustration 127. Patsy Ann in vinyl from the Effanbee Doll Corporation catalog, circa 1960. *Courtesy of Al Kirchof.*

Illustration 127-A. 15in (38.1cm) *Official Girl Scout (Patsy Ann),* No. 629, 1960. All-vinyl and fully-jointed. Rooted Saran hair; sleep eyes with lashes; freckles across nose. *Patsy Ann* is dressed as an "official girl scout" with a uniform and panties made of the "authentic material used by the Girl Scouts of America." Her beret, dress, socks and belt are green. The tie is yellow and the shoes are brown. Head marked: "EFFANBEE // PATSY ANN // © 1959." Back marked: E F F A N B E E." *Patricia N. Schoonmaker Collection. Photograph by John Schoonmaker.*

Illustration 128. 15in (38.1cm) *Patsy Ann,* No. 621, circa 1960. All-vinyl and fully-jointed. Blonde rooted hair; blue sleep eyes with lashes; freckles across the nose. Head marked: "EFFANBEE // PATSY ANN // © 1959." Back marked: "E F F A N B E E." The calico print dress has a white apron. *Rosemary Hanline Collection.*

Illustration 129. 15in (38.1cm) *Patsy Ann.* This is the same doll as *Illustration 128.* Her bridal gown seems to be original, but there is no catalog listing for this costume.

ALYSSA —
ANOTHER EFFANBEE ORIGINAL WITH THE CONTINENTAL FLAIR!

No. 7732

No. 7731   No. 7711

No. 8721

BUD "THE BOY FRIEND"
Style No. 7711
24" rigisol vinyl, fully jointed boy doll,
also jointed at elbows. Has molded hair
and moving eyes.
Dressed in checked gingham shirt, cordu-
roy trousers, shoes and socks.
Retails at $9.98

No. 8722

LITTLE LADY
Style No. 8633
20" rigisol vinyl girl doll with flexible
vinyl head and rooted saran hair that
can be combed, washed and set.
Dressed in beautiful long embroidered
nylon bridal gown with long sleeves and
tight bodice. Has lace trimmed taffeta
slip and panty, long nylon hose and high
heeled shoes, and blue garter. Carries
bridal bouquet and has pearl earrings.
Wears engagement ring. Has pillbox
bridal hat with long net veil.
Retails at $14.98

No. 8633

THE PROFIT-PROTECTED LINE!

Illustration 131. 23in (58.4cm) *Alyssa,* No. 7732, circa 1960. All-vinyl and fully-jointed with extra joints at the elbows. Blonde rooted Saran hair; sleep eyes with lashes. She is wearing a broadcloth dress with a matching hat. The long stockings are nylon. *Photograph courtesy of Al Kirchof.*

Illustration 130. From the Effanbee Doll Corporation catalog, circa 1960. *Alyssa* and *Bud "The Boy Friend."* At the bottom left is *Little Lady.* Courtesy of Al Kirchof.

Bud, "The Boy Friend"	All-vinyl and fully-jointed, including elbows; molded hair and sleep eyes.	24in (61cm)
7711	Dressed in checked gingham shirt, corduroy trousers.	
Little Lady	All-vinyl and fully-jointed with rooted Saran hair; sleep eyes.	20in (50.8cm)
8633	Dressed as a bride in a nylon gown.	
Alyssa	All-vinyl and fully-jointed, including elbows; rooted Saran hair; sleep eyes.	23in (58.4cm)
8723	Dressed as a bride.	
8721	Bridesmaid in nylon tulle over taffeta.	
7731	Wears checked gingham dress.	
7732	Wears broadcloth dress and hat.	
8722	Dressed in organza party dress.	
Mickey, the All-American Boy	All-vinyl and fully-jointed; painted eyes; molded hair; molded hats.	10½in (26.7cm)
701	*Baseball Player.*	
702	*Football Player.*	
703	*Policeman.*	
704	*Soldier.*	
705	*Sailor.*	
706	*Fireman.*	
707	*Boy Scout.*	
708	*Air Cadet.*	
709	*Marine.*	
710	*Boxer* (with robe). Molded hair only.	
711	*Cub Scout.*	
712	*Cowboy.*	
713	*Boxer* (without robe). Molded hair only.	
714	*Hunter.*	
715	*Bellhop.*	
716	*Jockey.*	
717	*Clown.* Painted face; fabric hat.	
718	*Sport Outfit.* Fabric hat.	

Illustration 132. 10½in (26.7cm) *Mickey, the All-American Boy,* circa 1960. All-vinyl and fully-jointed. Molded hair and molded hats; painted blue eyes. Left to right: *Baseball Player,* No. 701; *Football Player,* No. 702; *Policeman,* No. 703; *Soldier,* No. 704; and *Sailor,* No. 707. *Photograph courtesy of Al Kirchof.*

Illustration 133. 10½in (26.7cm) *Mickey, the All-American Boy,* circa 1960. Left to right: *Fireman,* No. 706; *Boy Scout,* No. 707; *Air Cadet,* No. 708; *Marine,* No. 709; and *Boxer* without robe, No. 713. *Photograph courtesy of Al Kirchof.*

Illustration 134. 10½in (26.7cm) *Mickey, the All-American Boy,* as *Cowboy,* No. 712; and *Boxer* with robe, No. 710; circa 1960. *Photograph courtesy of Al Kirchof.*

Illustration 135. 11in (27.9cm) *Mickey, the All-American Boy*, No. 708, circa 1960. All-vinyl and fully-jointed. Molded hair and hat; blue painted eyes. The hat is gray; the uniform is dark blue. Head marked: "MICKEY// EFFANBEE." *Patricia Gardner Collection.*

Illustration 136. Original box for *Mickey, the All-American Boy*, in *Illustration 135. Patricia Gardner Collection.*

Mary Jane   Vinyl head with rooted Saran hair;   32in (81.3cm)
flirty sleep eyes. Plastic body
with walking mechanism.

7854   Dressed in red organdy dress.

7851   Dressed in embossed cotton dress.

7857   Dressed in nurse's uniform.

Dolls and Bassinette Combination 3085/841
     32in (81.3cm) *Mary Jane* and 16in (40.6cm) *Lil Darlin* (sic).
     Retailed for $41.00.
Trimmed bassinette only with pillow, mattress and blanket. 30/85
     Retailed for $15.98.
Bassinette and baby doll. 3085
     Retailed for $22.98.

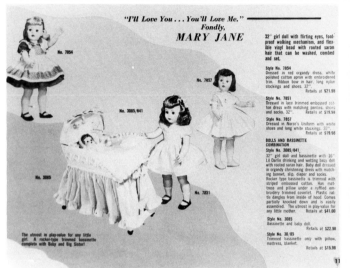

Illustration 137. Mary Jane from the Effanbee Doll Corporation catalog,
circa 1960. *Courtesy of Al Kirchof.*

Illustration 138. 32in (81.3cm) *Mary Jane*, No. 7854, circa 1960. All-vinyl
and fully-jointed. Blonde rooted Saran hair; sleep eyes with lashes; walking
mechanism. The dress is red organdy with a white polished cotton apron.
Photograph courtesy of Al Kirchof.

Illustration 140. 16in (40.6cm) *Lil Darlin* and bassinette, No. 3085, circa 1960. All-vinyl and fully-jointed. Rooted Saran hair; sleep eyes; open mouth nurser. She is dressed in an organdy christening dress with a matching bonnet. The bassinette is trimmed with embossed cotton and has a mattress and pillow under the coverlet. *Photograph courtesy of Al Kirchof.*

Illustration 141. Dolls and Bassinette Combination, No. 3085/841, circa 1960. The girl is *Mary Jane*; the baby is *Lil Darlin. Photograph courtesy of Al Kirchof.*

Illustration 142. Li l Darlin in Bassi-nette, No. 3085, with *Mary Jane* as a nurse, No. 7857, circa 1960. *Mary Jane* is 32in (81.3cm) and she wears a nurse's uniform and white shoes and long stockings. *Photo-graph courtesy of Al Kirchof.*

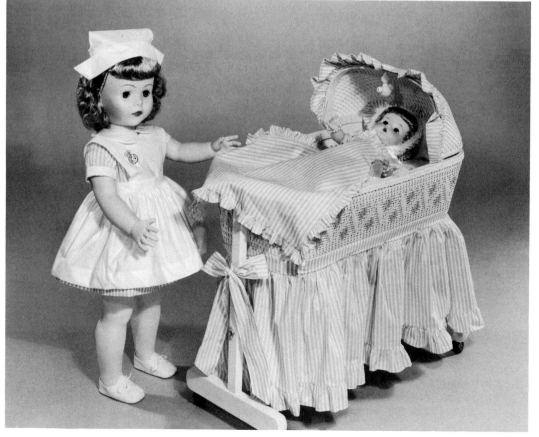

Dy-Dee Baby		Plastic head with rubber ears; jointed vinyl body. A drink and wet doll that "cried real tears." She could keep her eyes closed in an upright position and keep her eyes open in a reclining position.	
5162	Molded hair	Came with a layette and accessories.	12in (30.5cm)
5362	Molded hair	Came with a layette and accessories.	17in (43.2cm)
5762	Molded hair	Came with a layette and accessories.	21in (53.3cm)
5192	Lamb's wool hair	Came with a layette and accessories.	12in (30.5cm)
5392	Lamb's wool hair	Came with a layette and accessories.	17in (43.2cm)
5792	Lamb's wool hair	Came with a layette and accessories.	21in (53.3cm)

CATALOG II

Sugar Baby and *My Fair Baby*		All-vinyl and fully-jointed with sleep eyes; cry voice. Came with identification bracelet and nursing bottle.	
		Sugar Baby had a tiltable head.	
4451	Molded hair	*Fair Baby* dressed in zippered fleecy bunting and hood.	14in (35.6cm)
4471	Rooted hair	Dressed in zippered fleecy bunting and hood.	14in (35.6cm)
4651	Molded hair	*Sugar Baby* dressed in zippered fleecy bunting and hood.	18in (45.7cm)
4671	Rooted hair	Dressed in zippered fleecy bunting and hood.	18in (45.7cm)
4442	Molded hair	*Fair Baby* dressed in long organdy dress.	14in (35.6cm)
4642	Molded hair	*Sugar Baby* dressed in long organdy dress.	18in (45.7cm)
4456	Molded hair	*Fair Baby* dressed in short organdy dress.	14in (35.6cm)
4476	Rooted hair	*Fair Baby* dressed in short organdy dress.	14in (35.6cm)
4656	Molded hair	*Sugar Baby* dressed in short organdy dress.	18in (45.7cm)
4676	Rooted hair	*Sugar Baby* dressed in short organdy dress.	18in (45.7cm)
Sugar Pie		All-vinyl and fully-jointed with rooted hair.	
4684		Wears taffeta-lined fleece coat.	18in (45.7cm)
Sugar Baby		All-vinyl and fully-jointed. Sleep eyes; drink and wet; squeeze cry voice. Came with identification bracelet; nursing bottle.	18in (45.7cm)
4652	Molded hair	In lacy zippered quilted bunting.	
4672	Rooted hair	In lacy zippered quilted bunting with satin binding.	
4673	Rooted hair	In zippered flannel bunting.	
4679	Rooted hair	In long lace-trimmed fleece coat.	
4659	Molded hair	In long lace-trimmed fleece coat.	

Illustration 143. 18in (45.7cm) *Suzie Sunshine*, designed by Eugenia Dukas, 1961. All-vinyl and fully-jointed. Rooted hair; sleep eyes with lashes; freckles across the bridge of the nose. This example is redressed. *Patricia Schoonmaker Collection. Photograph by John Schoonmaker.*

Illustration 145. 23in (58.4cm) *Alyssa* and 15in (38.1cm) *Patsy Ann* from the Effanbee Doll Corporation catalog, circa 1961. *Courtesy of Eugenia Dukas.*

Twinkie	All-vinyl and fully-jointed. Sleep eyes; molded hair; tiltable head; cry voice. Drinks and wets.	16in (40.6cm)
2543	Dressed in wool fleece sacque.	
2544	Dressed in organdy dress.	
2545	Dressed in lace-trimmed gingham dress.	
0537	Dressed in embroidered sacque set. Layette box has extra outfits.	
Sweetie Pie	All-vinyl and fully-jointed. Sleep eyes; rooted Saran hair; tiltable head; Mama voice. Drinks and wets.	22in (55.9cm)
4876	In organdy dress with matching cap.	
4884	In taffeta-lined fleece coat and hood.	
Mary Jane	Vinyl head with rooted Saran hair; plastic body with walking mechanism.	32in (81.3cm)
7872	Wears polished cotton dress and apron.	
7874	Wears red organdy dress and white apron.	
Suzette	All-vinyl and fully-jointed with rooted Saran hair.	15in (38.1cm)
911	Dressed in short cotton dress.	
913	Dressed in broadcloth dress.	
914	Dressed in gingham checked slacks; sunglasses.	
915	Dressed in red, white and blue sailor dress.	
925	Dressed as *Bo Peep*.	
926	Dressed in printed cotton dress; straw hat.	
927	Dressed as a bride in nylon net.	
Suzie Sunshine	All-vinyl and fully-jointed with rooted hair and flirty eyes.	18in (45.7cm)
1812	Dressed in snowsuit.	
1813	Dressed in cotton tunic dress.	
1814	Dressed in cotton top and slacks.	
1815	Dressed in sun dress.	
1817	Dressed in plaid pinafore.	
1818	Dressed in cotton dress and pantaloons.	
1819	Wears polished cotton dress and pinafore.	
1821	Dressed in cotton dress and coat.	
1822	Dressed in white pique dress and coat set.	
My Precious Baby	Vinyl head, arms and legs; soft vinyl covered nylon body filled with kapok. Drinks and wets; has sleep eyes and a cryer mechanism. Short rooted hair.	22in (55.9cm)
9712	Dressed in jacket, hat and leggings set.	
9713	Wearing gingham dress and romper.	
9714	Wears printed cotton dress and bonnet.	
9716	Wears organdy baby dress.	
9717P	Wears plush bunny suit; lies on satin pillow.	
9717	Same as the above without the pillow.	
9718	In long christening dress on ruffled pillow.	

Alyssa	All-vinyl and fully-jointed, including elbows. Rooted Saran hair; sleep eyes.	23in (58.4cm)
7781	Wears polished cotton dress and cobbler apron.	
7788	Wears plaid taffeta jumper.	
Little Lady	All-vinyl and fully-jointed. Rooted Saran hair; sleep eyes.	20in (50.8cm)
8673	Dressed as a bride.	
Patsy Ann	All-vinyl and fully-jointed with rooted Saran hair and sleep eyes.	15in (38.1cm)
637	*Official Brownie Scout.*	
638	*Official Girl Scout.*	
0636	Boxed set. Wears organdy dress and has extra outfits.	
Fluffy	All-vinyl and fully-jointed toddler. Rooted Saran hair; sleep eyes.	11in (27.9cm)
1121	Dressed in chemise, shoes and socks.	
1131	Wears checked gingham dress and panties.	
1132	Flower print sun dress and panties.	
1133	Print cotton school dress and panties.	
1134	Print sun dress and panties.	
1135	Playsuit with babushka and pants.	
L'il Darlin'	All-vinyl and fully-jointed baby. Sleep eyes. Drinks and wets.	13in (33cm)
3331	Molded hair	In organdy christening dress.
3372	Rooted hair	In gingham play outfit with matching bonnet.
3373	Rooted hair	In polished cotton play dress with matching bonnet.
3374	Rooted hair	In trimmed polished cotton dress with matching bonnet.

Illustration 146. 11in (27.9cm) *Mickey* and 11in (27.9cm) *Happy Boy* from the Effanbee Doll Corporation catalog, circa 1961. *Courtesy of Eugenia Dukas.*

Mickey, the All-American Boy	All-vinyl and fully-jointed. Painted eyes; molded hair; molded hats.	11in (27.9cm)	1959-1963

701   *Baseball Player.*

702   *Football Player.*

703   *Policeman.*

704   *Soldier.*

705   *Sailor.*

706   *Fireman.*

707   *Boy Scout.*

708   *Air Cadet.*

709   *Marine.*

710   *Boxer* (with robe). Molded hair only.

711   *Cub Scout.*

712   *Cowboy.*

713   *Boxer* (without robe). Molded hair only.

714   *Hunter.*

715   *Bellhop.*

716   *Jockey.*

717   *Clown.* Painted face; fabric hat.

718   *Sport Outfit.*

721   *Johnny Reb.*

722   *Yankee Boy.*

Happy Boy	All-vinyl and fully-jointed. Painted eyes; molded hair.	11in (27.9cm)

801   Dressed in overalls.

802   Dressed in a nightshirt.

803   Dressed as a boxer.

Babykin	All-vinyl and fully-jointed with sleep eyes and molded hair. Drinks and wets.	8in (20.3cm)

2151   Wears long organdy christening dress.

2152   Wears lace-trimmed gingham dress.

2153   Dressed in print play skirt and top.

2154   Dressed in one-piece bunny suit.

2155   Wears pique trapeze dress and cap.

Tiny Tubber	All-vinyl and fully-jointed. Sleep eyes. Drinks and wets.	10½in (26.7cm)

2312   Molded hair   Dressed in diaper, booties and blanket.

2372   Rooted hair   Dressed in play outfit.

2373   Rooted hair   Wears play dress.

Dy-Dee Baby	Hard plastic head; fully-jointed vinyl body. Drinks and wets. In suitcase with layette.	17in (43.2cm)

5391   Tousle wig

5371   Molded hair

Sugar Baby in Bassinette 3086   18in (45.7cm)

My Precious Baby in Trimmed Basket 9786   22in (55.9cm)

Trimmed Bassinette 30/86

Trimmed Basket 97/86

Mary Jane 7873	In nurse's uniform.	32in (81.3cm)

Boudoir Doll	Vinyl head, arms and legs;
	    vinyl covered nylon body.
	    Rooted Saran hair; sleep eyes.
		28in (71.1cm)

2911	Dressed in lounging outfit of tunic and slacks.	
2912	Wears cotton print gypsy outfit.	

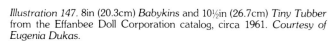

Illustration 147. 8in (20.3cm) *Babykins* and 10½in (26.7cm) *Tiny Tubber* from the Effanbee Doll Corporation catalog, circa 1961. *Courtesy of Eugenia Dukas.*

Illustration 148. Sugar Baby, Mary Jane and the 28in (71.1cm) *Boudoir Doll* from the Effanbee Doll Corporation catalog, circa 1961. The *Boudoir Doll* has a vinyl head with rooted hair, sleep eyes and vinyl arms and legs. The body is nylon covered with vinyl. *Courtesy of Eugenia Dukas.*

Illustration 149. Effanbee dolls from Kravitz & Rothbard, Inc. catalog, 1961. This illustration shows how many dolls have several, often confusing, names. Catalog companies give the dolls different names than the manufacturer did originally. The 19in (48.3cm) doll in the "Musical Cradle" is the 18in (45.7cm) *Sugar Baby*. The "Official Brownie Scout" is *Patsy Ann*. "Pixie Baby" is 16in (40.6cm) *L'il Darlin'*. "Christening Dolly" is listed at 19in (48.3cm) but she is 22in (55.9cm) *Sweetie Pie*. 18in (45.7cm) "Sugar Pie" is *Sugar Baby*. 16in (40.6cm) *Twinkie* is identified correctly.

CATALOG III

My Baby		Vinyl head, arms and legs; kapok stuffed body. Painted eyes; rooted hair; cry voice.	14in (35.6cm)
9331		Dressed in nylon tricot shirt and diaper.	
9332		Dressed in flannel pajamas; has teddy bear.	
9333		Dressed in fleece bunting.	
9335		Dressed in sleeping sacque. Lying on flannel pillow with pocket.	
9336		Dressed in organdy christening dress.	
9341W		Dressed in cotton romper. Has wiggle mechanism.	
My Baby		Vinyl head, arms and legs; kapok stuffed body. Sleep eyes; rooted hair; cry voice.	18in (45.7cm)
9521		Dressed in nylon tricot sacque, shirt and diaper.	
9523		Dressed in gingham play dress.	
9524		Dressed in fleece bunting.	
9525		Dressed in flannel pajamas. Holds plush teddy bear.	
9526		Dressed in nylon coat and hat.	
9558		Dressed in organdy dress.	
9541W		Dressed in cotton romper. Has wiggle mechanism.	
My Baby		Vinyl head, arms and legs; kapok stuffed body. Sleep eyes; rooted hair; cry voice.	24in (61cm)
9851		Dressed in nylon tricot sacque, shirt and diaper.	
9852		Dressed in gingham play dress.	
9854		Dressed in nylon hat and coat.	
9857		Dressed in organdy lined Dacron batiste overdress.	
9858		Dressed in organdy dress.	
Twinkie		All-vinyl and fully-jointed. Sleep eyes. Drinks and wets.	
2531	Molded hair	Dressed in flannel sacque and diaper.	16in (40.6cm)
2532	Molded hair	Dressed in nylon dress, cap and panties.	
2572	Rooted hair	Dressed in nylon dress, cap and panties. Has matching pillow.	
0538	Molded hair	Dressed in flannel pajamas. Has layette with extra outfits.	
Tiny Tubber		All-vinyl and fully-jointed with sleep eyes. Drinks and wets.	
2375	Rooted hair	Wears broadcloth dress with ribbon trim.	10in (25.4cm)
2376	Rooted hair	In flannel hood, sacque, diaper and blanket.	
2377	Rooted hair	Broadcloth dress.	
2312	Molded hair	Dressed in diaper, booties and blanket.	

81

Suzie Sunshine	All-vinyl and fully-jointed toddler with rooted hair and sleep eyes.	18in (45.7cm)
1841	Dressed in gingham dress.	
1842	Dressed in broadcloth school dress.	
1843	Dressed in polished cotton school dress.	
1844	Dressed in gingham dress and apron.	
1845	Dressed in striped cotton dress.	
1846	Dressed in print dress with coat.	
Gum Drop	All-vinyl and fully-jointed toddler with sleep eyes and rooted hair.	16in (40.6cm)
1621	Dressed in polka dot play dress.	
1622	Dressed in slack set and babushka.	
1623	Dressed in romper and pinafore.	
1624	Dressed in organdy party dress.	
1626	Dressed in cotton dress, coat and hat.	
Suzette	All-vinyl and fully-jointed girl with rooted hair and sleep eyes.	15in (38.1cm)
941	Dressed in checked school dress.	
942	Dressed in plaid school dress.	
944	Dressed in taffeta party dress.	
945	*Bride.* Wears gown of nylon lace and net.	
947	*Official Blue Bird* uniform	
948	*Official Camp Fire Girl* uniform.	
957	*Official Brownie Scout* uniform.	
958	*Official Girl Scout* uniform.	

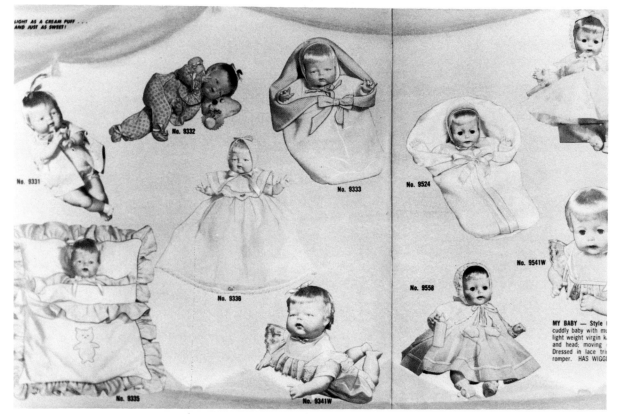

Illustration 150. 14in (35.6cm) and 18in (45.7cm) *My Baby* from the Effanbee Doll Corporation catalog, circa 1962. See catalog listings for descriptions. *Courtesy of Arthur Keller.*

Illustration 151. 18in (45.7cm) *Sweetie Pie,* 1962. All-vinyl and fully-jointed. Blonde rooted hair; blue sleep eyes with lashes; open mouth nurser; cry voice in body. Note the careful modeling of the arms and legs. Head marked: " © // EFFANBEE // 1962." *Patricia Schoonmaker Collection. Photograph by John Schoonmaker.*

Illustration 152. 15in (38.1cm) *Suzette* from the Effanbee Doll Corporation catalog, circa 1962. All-vinyl and fully-jointed with rooted hair and sleep eyes. *Courtesy of Arthur Keller.*

Fluffy	All-vinyl and fully-jointed toddler with rooted hair and sleep eyes.	11in (27.9cm)
1121	Dressed in chemise, shoes and socks.	
1141	Dressed in cotton dress.	
1142	Dressed in cotton dress.	
1143	Dressed in cotton print dress.	
1144	Dressed in red print cotton dress.	
1145	Dressed in polka dot play dress and babushka.	
1146	Dressed in floral print cotton dress.	

Babykin	All-vinyl and fully-jointed baby with sleep eyes and molded hair. Drinks and wets.	8in (20.3cm)
2151	Dressed in organdy christening dress.	
2152	Dressed in gingham check dress.	
2154	Dressed in snowsuit and hat.	
2155	Dressed in pique trapeze dress and cap.	
2156	Dressed in fleece sacque with hood.	

Mickey, the All-American Boy		All-vinyl and fully-jointed boy with molded hair and painted eyes. Has molded hats.	10½in (26.7cm)
701		*Baseball Player.*	
702		*Football Player.*	
705		*Sailor.*	
706		*Fireman.*	
707		*Boy Scout.*	
710		*Fighter* (with robe). Molded hair only.	
711		*Cub Scout.*	
712		*Cowboy.*	
713		*Fighter* (without robe). Molded hair only.	
721		*Johnny Reb.*	
722		*Yankee Boy.*	
Happy Boy		All-vinyl and fully-jointed boy with molded hair and painted eyes. Open/closed mouth with one molded tooth.	10½in (26.7cm)
801		Wears overalls.	
802		Wears a nightshirt.	
803		*Boxer.*	
Sweetie Pie		All-vinyl and fully-jointed baby with rooted hair, sleep eyes and a cry voice.	
4485	Rooted hair	Dressed in polished cotton dress.	14in (35.6cm)
4471	Rooted hair	Dressed in bunting and hood.	14in (35.6cm)
4451	Molded hair	Dressed in bunting and hood.	14in (35.6cm)
4651	Molded hair	Dressed in bunting and hood.	19in (48.3cm)
4681	Rooted hair	Wears organdy dress.	18in (45.7cm)
4481	Rooted hair	Wears organdy dress.	14in (35.6cm)
4684	Rooted hair	Wears checked cotton dress, hat and coat.	18in (45.7cm)
4660	Rooted hair	Dressed in pajamas and has layette and pillow. Packaged "with an entertaining record explaining the 'How' and 'Why' of a doll mother's love and tenderness."	18in (45.7cm)

Combination Rocking Bassinette With My Baby Infant Doll and Suzie Sunshine Big Sister Doll.

9386/18 *My Baby*   14in (35.6cm)   *Suzie Sunshine*   18in (45.7cm)
9386   *My Baby in Bassinette*
1886   *Suzie Sunshine*

The above dolls wear flannel pajamas.

New for 1962:

Belle Telle and Her Talking Telephone	Vinyl head with rooted hair; sleep eyes with lashes. The doll holds a telephone and says 11 sentences and is operated with a "D" battery. The left hand is sculpted to hold the phone receiver and other objects.	18in (45.7cm)

New for 1963:

Mary Jane	All-vinyl and fully-jointed toddler. Rooted hair; sleep eyes with lashes; freckles across nose.	13in (33cm)

Illustration 153. 11in (27.9cm) *Fluffy* and 8in (20.3cm) *Babykin* from the Effanbee Doll Corporation catalog, circa 1962. Both dolls are all-vinyl and fully-jointed. *Courtesy of Arthur Keller.*

Illustration 154. 10½in (26.7cm) *Mickey, the All-American Boy* and *Happy Boy* from the Effanbee Doll Corporation catalog, circa 1962. Note the reduction in models for *Mickey* from the previous year. *Courtesy of Arthur Keller*

Illustration 155. Page from *Sears Christmas 1962.* The dolls shown are *Belle Telle, My Baby* with *Suzie Sunshine, Suzie Sunshine* (No. 1846), *Suzette* in Blue Bird uniform (No. 947), *Suzette* in Girl Scout uniform (No. 958), *Fluffy, Tiny Tubber* and *Mickey.*

Illustration 156. Catalog page from *Sears Christmas 1963.* This is the first time that Effanbee dolls were grouped in a "theme" with coordinated costumes. The dolls are all-vinyl and fully-jointed with rooted hair and sleep eyes. They are: (1) 18in (45.7cm) *Suzie Sunshine,* (2) 15in (38.1cm) *Gumdrop* [sic], (3) 15in (38.1cm) *Twinkie,* (4) 13in (33cm) *Mary Jane* and (5) 15in (38.1cm) *Twinkie.*

1964-1969

For the years 1964 through 1969 there are catalogs from the Effanbee Doll Corporation showing the line for each year. Sometimes the names of the various dolls can be confusing. This is because when the dolls were shown in catalogs from other companies they were sometimes given different names. An example of this is *Sugar Baby*, who was called "Sugar Pie" by Kravitz & Rothbard, Inc., in their catalog. (See *Illustration 149*.)

From 1964 to 1969 most of the Effanbee dolls were babies and toddlers, with very few girl dolls. *Mickey* and *Happy* were the only dolls in the line for which a mold was made that clearly depicted a male character. There are some attractive dolls in these years, but there is no outstanding original design. In 1967 black dolls were introduced and they were called "colored" dolls. By 1968 the black dolls were called a "Negro" doll.

1964 Catalog

My Baby		Vinyl head, arms and legs; soft kapok stuffed body. Sleep eyes; rooted hair; mama voice in torso.	18in (45.7cm)
9521		Dressed in lace-trimmed organdy dress.	
9523		Dressed in striped cotton dress.	
9527		Dressed in velvet dress.	
9528		Wears organdy dress, crocheted cap and sweater.	
9529P		Wears lace-trimmed organdy christening dress. Lies on organdy pillow.	
My Baby		Vinyl head, arms and legs; soft kapok stuffed body. Sleep eyes; rooted hair; mama voice in torso.	24in (61cm)
9842		Wears organdy dress.	
9843		Wears polished cotton dress.	
9845		Dressed in three-piece fleece snowsuit.	
9847		Wears velvet dress.	
9848		Wears organdy dress; crocheted cap, sweater and booties.	
My Fair Baby		All-vinyl and fully-jointed. Drinks and wets. Sleep eyes.	14in (35.6cm)
4461	Molded hair	Dressed in zippered fleecy bunting and hood.	
4481	Rooted hair	Dressed in zippered fleecy bunting and hood.	
4483		Dressed in polished cotton dress.	
4484		Dressed in print checked cotton dress.	
My Fair Baby		All-vinyl and fully-jointed. Drinks and wets. Sleep eyes and rooted hair.	18in (45.7cm)
4661		Dressed in two-tone organdy dress.	
4643		Dressed in velveteen dress.	
Patricia		All-vinyl and fully-jointed toddler. Sleep eyes; rooted hair.	13in (33cm)
6441		Wears two-tier dotted swiss dress.	
6443		Dressed in solid cotton dress with ruffles.	
6448		Boy doll in blue cotton sailor suit.	
6449		Girl doll in blue cotton sailor dress.	

Cup Cake		All-vinyl and fully-jointed baby. Rooted hair; open mouth; cry voice.	12in (30.5cm)
6332		Wears gingham checked dress.	
6334		Wears lace and embroidery-trimmed cotton dress.	
6335		Dressed in bikini bathing suit and sunglasses.	
Baby Winkie		All-vinyl and fully-jointed. Sleep eyes; molded hair; drinks and wets.	12in (30.5cm)
2431		Dressed in flannel sacque and diaper.	
2432		Dressed in gingham checked dress.	
2434		Dressed in organdy dress.	
Twinkie		All-vinyl and fully-jointed baby. Sleep eyes; cry voice; drinks and wets.	16in (40.6cm)
2541	Molded hair	Dressed in flocked dotted taffeta dress. Has matching pillow.	
2571	Rooted hair	Dressed in flocked dotted taffeta dress. Has matching pillow.	
2561	Molded hair	Dressed in flannel sacque and diaper.	
2576	Rooted hair	Dressed in fleecy hood, sacque and diaper.	
2577	Rooted hair	Dressed in lace-trimmed organdy dress.	

Illustration 157. 12in (30.5cm) *Cup Cake*, 1964. All-vinyl and fully-jointed. Dark auburn rooted hair; blue sleep eyes with lashes. Head and back marked: "EFFANBEE // 19 © 63."

Illustration 158. Effanbee advertisement from *Playthings*, February 1964. At the top is *Cup Cake*, No. 6335; in the center is *Twinkie*; at the bottom is *Susie Sunshine* with *Babykin*, No. 1886.

Susie Sunshine	All-vinyl and fully-jointed toddler. Sleep eyes; freckles across nose; long rooted hair.	18in (45.7cm)
1851	Dressed in velvet-trimmed white cotton dress.	
1853	Dressed in flared cotton percale dress.	
1886	Dressed in flannel nightgown. Carries 8in (20.3cm) vinyl baby.	
Bettina	All-vinyl and fully-jointed toddler. Sleep eyes; rooted hair.	18in (45.7cm)
1972	Dressed in gingham checked dress with solid color top.	
1973	Dressed in organdy dress.	
1975	Dressed in velvet skirt with attached organdy top.	
1981	Dressed in "A-line" dress with nautical buttons.	
Gum Drop	All-vinyl and fully-jointed toddler. Sleep eyes; long rooted Saran hair.	16in (40.6cm)
1631	Wears striped cotton dress with velvet bodice.	
1651	Wears lace-trimmed gingham checked dress.	
1653	Wears velveteen dress.	
1655	Dressed in printed cotton dress and velvet pinafore.	
1666	Dressed in flannel nightgown. Holds an 8in (20.3cm) all-vinyl baby. (*Babykin.*)	
Little Gum Drop	All-vinyl and fully-jointed toddler. Sleep eyes and long rooted hair.	14in (35.6cm)
1422	Dressed in gingham checked dress.	
1424	Wears gingham checked dress with eyelet apron.	
1426	Dressed as Dutch girl with lace apron and cap.	

Illustration 159. 16in (40.6cm) *Gum Drop* from the Effanbee Doll Corporation catalog, 1964. *Courtesy of Eugenia Dukas.*

Illustration 160. 14in (35.6cm) *Little Gum Drop* from the Effanbee Doll Corporation catalog, 1964. *Courtesy of Eugenia Dukas.*

Illustration 161. 18in (45.7cm) *Bettina* from the Effanbee Doll Corporation catalog, 1964. *Courtesy of Eugenia Dukas.*

Fluffy		All-vinyl and fully-jointed toddler. Sleep eyes; rooted hair.	11in (27.9cm)
1161		Striped dress with rickrack trim.	
1162		Striped dress with solid color yoke.	
1163		Gingham dress with large collar.	
1164		Wears nautical print dress with babushka.	
Official Brownie Scout 667		All-vinyl and fully-jointed girl. Sleep eyes; rooted hair.	16in (40.6cm)
Official Girl Scout 668		All-vinyl and fully-jointed girl. Sleep eyes; rooted hair.	16in (40.6cm)
Patsy		All-vinyl and fully-jointed toddler. Sleep eyes; rooted hair.	11in (27.9cm)
1310		Wears "A-line" dress.	
1311		Dressed in velvet dress.	
Tiny Tubber		All-vinyl and fully-jointed baby. Sleep eyes. Drinks and wets.	10½in (26.7cm)
2312	Molded hair	Dressed in diaper, booties and blanket.	
2385	Rooted hair	Dressed in cotton dress.	
2386	Rooted hair	Has flannel hood, sacque, diaper and blanket.	
2387	Rooted hair	Wears striped polished cotton dress.	

Babykin		All-vinyl and fully-jointed baby. Sleep eyes; drinks and wets.	8in (20.3cm)
2161	Molded hair	Wears organdy dress and cap; blanket.	
2162	Molded hair	Wears gingham check dress and cap.	
2163	Molded hair	Wears solid cotton dress and cap.	
2164	Molded hair	Dressed in fleece bunting with cap.	
2174	Rooted hair	Wears lace-trimmed organdy dress.	
Mickey, the All-American Boy		All-vinyl and fully-jointed boy. Molded hair; painted eyes.	11in (27.9cm)
701		*Baseball Player*. Molded cap.	
702		*Football Player*. Molded helmet.	
705		*Sailor*. Molded cap.	
713		*Fighter* (without robe).	
704		Wears knee pants and shirt.	
721		*Johnny Reb*. Molded cap.	
Happy		All-vinyl and fully-jointed boy. Molded hair; painted eyes.	11in (27.9cm)
801		In denim overalls.	
802		In nightshirt.	
803		*Boxer*.	
226	*Tidy-Hidy*	All-cloth girl doll.	size not known
225	*Floppy doll*	All-cloth clown.	21in (53.3cm)
Combination Set			
1900/21		18in (45.7cm) *Bettina* in coat and carrying print umbrella. Baby in wicker carriage is 8in (20.3cm) *Babykin* with molded hair.	

Illustration 162. 11in (27.9cm) *Fluffy* from the Effanbee Doll Corporation catalog, 1964. *Courtesy of Eugenia Dukas.*

Illustration 163. 16in (40.6cm) *Official Brownie Scout* and *Official Girl Scout* from the Effanbee Doll Corporation catalog, 1964. *Courtesy of Eugenia Dukas.*

PATSY

11" Soft, flexible vinyl toddler, fully jointed with moving eyes and rooted hair.

#1310 —Dressed in solid color "A" line style dress with gingham check and ric rac trim; gingham check panties, shoes and socks. Ribbon bow in hair.   Retail —$4.00

#1311 —Dressed in lace and ric rac trimmed velvet "A" line style dress; lace trimmed taffeta panties; shoes and socks. Matching velvet ribbon in hair.   Retail —$4.00

Illustration 164. 11in (27.9cm) *Patsy* from the Effanbee Doll Corporation catalog, 1964. *Courtesy of Eugenia Dukas.*

HAPPY

11" All vinyl Boy Doll. Fully jointed. Painted eyes, molded hair. All clothes removable. Has shoes, socks.

HAPPY BOY

#801 —In denim overalls.	Retail —$3.00	
#802 —Nightshirt.	Retail —$3.00	
#803 —Boxer.	Retail —$3.00	

Illustration 166. 11in (27.9cm) *Happy* from the Effanbee Doll Corporation catalog, 1964. *Courtesy of Eugenia Dukas.*

MICKEY *The All American Boys*

EFFANBEE DURABLE DOLLS

11" All vinyl Boy Doll. Fully jointed. Painted eyes, molded hair. All clothes removable. Has shoes, socks. Molded hats.

MICKEY

#701 —Baseball Player.	Retail —$3.00
#702 —Football Player.	Retail —$3.00
#705 —Sailor.	Retail —$3.00
#713 —Fighter without robe.	Retail —$3.00
#704 —Knee pants and shirt.	Retail —$3.00
#721 —Johnny Reb. (not ill.)	Retail —$3.00

The Profit-Protected Line

Illustration 165. 11in (27.9cm) *Mickey, the All-American Boy* from the Effanbee Doll Corporation catalog, 1964. *Courtesy of Eugenia Dukas.*

1965 Catalog

Thumkin		Vinyl head, arms and legs; soft kapok filled body. Sleep eyes; rooted hair.	18in (45.7cm)
9551		Wears organdy dress.	
9554		Wears polished cotton dress and pinafore.	
9555		Wears velveteen overdress.	
9558		Wears polished cotton dress.	
Precious Baby		Vinyl head, arms and legs; soft kapok filled body. Sleep eyes; rooted hair.	24in (61cm)
9861		Wears lace-trimmed organdy dress.	
9862		Wears flocked polka dot organdy dress with velveteen overdress.	
9845		Wears three-piece fleece snowsuit.	
9848		Wears organdy dress; crocheted cap, sweater and booties.	
L'il Darlin'		Vinyl head, arms and legs; Soft kapok filled body. Sleep eyes and rooted hair.	18in (45.7cm)
9684		Wears organdy christening dress; crocheted cap, sweater and booties. Lies on a ruffled pillow.	
9685		Wears embroidered organdy christening dress, capelet and cap. Has embroidered pillow.	
Baby Winkie		All-vinyl and fully-jointed baby. Sleep eyes and molded hair. Drinks and wets.	12in (30.5cm)
2431		In flannel sacque and diaper.	
2432		In dress and cap on pillow.	
2433		In rayon plaid dress on matching pillow.	
Twinkie		All-vinyl and fully-jointed baby. Sleep eyes; drinks and wets; cry voice.	16in (40.6cm)
2561	Molded hair	In flannel sacque and diaper.	
2541	Molded hair	In flocked dotted taffeta dress and cap.	
2543	Rooted hair	In flocked dotted nylon dress and cap.	
2546	Rooted hair	In eyelet lace cotton dress on red velveteen pillow with organdy ruffle.	
2545		In crepe coat; organdy dress. On ruffled organdy-trimmed pillow.	
My Fair Baby		All-vinyl and fully-jointed baby. Sleep eyes; open mouth.	14in (35.6cm)
4461	Molded hair	In zippered fleecy bunting and hood.	
4481	Rooted hair	In zippered fleecy bunting and hood.	
4483	Rooted hair	In cotton dress.	
4484	Rooted hair	In cotton dress.	

Cup Cake		All-vinyl and fully-jointed baby. Sleep eyes; rooted hair; drinks and wets.	12in (30.5cm)
6332		In gingham checked cotton dress.	
6334		In solid color cotton dress.	
Patricia		All-vinyl and fully-jointed toddler. Sleep eyes; rooted hair.	13in (33cm)
6441		In dotted swiss dress.	
6443		In cotton dress with ruffled lace.	
6445		In red velveteen coat and hat.	
6446		In white cotton sailor dress.	
6346		Boy dressed in two-piece cotton sailor suit.	
Official Brownie Scout 667		All-vinyl and fully-jointed girl. Sleep eyes and rooted hair.	16in (40.6cm)
Official Girl Scout 668		All-vinyl and fully-jointed girl. Sleep eyes and rooted hair.	16in (40.6cm)
Patsy		All-vinyl and fully-jointed toddler. Sleep eyes and rooted hair.	11in (27.9cm)
1311		Wears trimmed velveteen dress.	
1313		Wears trimmed velveteen dress.	
1314		Wears long flannel nightie.	
Tiny Tubber		All-vinyl and fully-jointed baby. Sleep eyes; drinks and wets.	11in (27.9cm)
2312	Molded hair	Dressed in diaper and blanket.	
2371	Rooted hair	Dressed in sacque with flannel hood.	
2372	Rooted hair	Dressed in printed cotton dress.	
2373	Rooted hair	Dressed in embroidered cotton dress.	
Babykin		All-vinyl and fully-jointed baby. Sleep eyes; drinks and wets.	8in (20.3cm)
2161	Molded hair	Wears organdy dress; wrapped in blanket.	
2162	Molded hair	Wears gingham checked dress and cap.	
2163	Molded hair	Wears solid cotton dress.	
2164	Molded hair	Dressed in fleece bunting and cap.	
2165	Molded hair	Wears long organdy dress and cap. Has lace-trimmed pillow.	
2174	Rooted hair	In lace-trimmed organdy dress.	
Mickey, the All-American Boy		All-vinyl and fully-jointed boy. Molded hair; painted eyes.	11in (27.9cm)
701	Molded hat	*Baseball Player.*	
702	Molded helmet	*Football Player.*	
704		Wears knee pants and shirt.	
705	Molded cap	*Sailor.*	
713		*Fighter.*	

Fluffy	All-vinyl and fully-jointed toddler. Sleep eyes; rooted hair.	11in (27.9cm)
1161	Wears checked gingham dress.	
1162	Wears print dress with head scarf.	
1163	Wears dotted cotton dress.	
1164	Wears flowered cotton dress.	
Little Gum Drop	All-vinyl and fully-jointed toddler. Sleep eyes; rooted hair.	14in (35.6cm)
1421	Wears striped cotton dress.	
1422	Wears red velveteen jumper.	
1424	Wears gingham dress and apron.	
1426	Dressed as Dutch girl.	
1428	Carries 8in (20.3cm) *Babykin* "piggy back." Both wear checked gingham outfits.	
Gum Drop	All-vinyl and fully-jointed toddler. Sleep eyes; long rooted hair.	16in (40.6cm)
1631	Wears striped cotton dress with velvet bodice.	
1641	Wears velveteen jumper.	
1644	Wears solid cotton "A-line" dress.	
1645	Wears cotton dress and smock.	
1666	Wears flannel nightie and carries 8in (20.3cm) *Babykin* in matching sleeping bag.	

Illustration 167. 11in (27.9cm) *Fluffy* and 14in (35.6cm) *Little Gum Drop* from the 1965 Effanbee Doll Corporation catalog. *Courtesy of Eugenia Dukas.*

94

EFFANBEE
DURABLE
DOLLS

Gum Drop

16" All vinyl toddler, fully jointed with moving eyes and long rooted hair that can be washed and combed. All with shoes & socks, ribbon bow in hair.

#1631 — Striped cotton dress wih velvet bodice; matching panties.   Retail $6.00

#1641 — Velveteen jumper with white cotton blouse; white cotton panties. Retail $7.00

#1644 — Solid cotton "A" line dress with polka dot trim; matching panties. Retail $7.00

#1645 — Striped cotton dress with solid color overdress; matching panties. Retail $7.00

#1666 — Flannel nitie with matching panties and bedroom scuffs. Holds 8" Babykin dressed in flannel sleeping bag.   Retail $8.00

#1666

#1631

#1641

#1644

#1645

Illustration 168. 16in (40.6cm) *Gum Drop* from the 1965 Effanbee Doll Corporation catalog. *Courtesy of Eugenia Dukas.*

11

Chips

EFFANBEE
DURABLE
DOLLS

17" All vinyl girl doll, fully jointed with side glance moving eyes and rooted hair that can be washed and combed.

#1731

#1731 — In polka dot shift with ruffled hem; ankle boots. Retail $8.00

#1734 — Black velveteen "A" line dress with ruffled lace sleeves; taffeta panties, long textured stockings and velvet slippers. Retail $9.00

#1735 — Solid color broadcloth dress with striped jacket & boots. Solid color jockey cap with striped trim & matching solid color panties. Retail $10.00

#1737 — Cotton shift and matching coat with polka dot trim; matching polka dot headscarf and high boots. Retail $10.00

#1734

#1735

#1737

Illustration 169. 17in (43.2cm) *Chips* from the 1965 Effanbee Doll Corporation catalog. *Courtesy of Eugenia Dukas.*

#1738 — Checked slacks with white pique Rajah coat; high black boots. Retail $10.00

#1739 — Lace and velvet trimmed nylon bridesmaid gown; taffeta slip & crinoline; long textured stockings and satin slippers; ribbon bow in hair. Retail $12.00

#1740 — Lace trimmed nylon bridal gown with taffeta slip and crinoline, panties. Long textured stockings, satin slippers and blue garter. Bridal veil. Retail $12.00

#1740 —

#1738

#1739

The Profit Protected Line

13

Illustration 170. 17in (43.2cm) *Chips* from the 1965 Effanbee Doll Corporation catalog. *Courtesy of Eugenia Dukas.*

Bettina
18" All vinyl toddler, fully jointed with moving eyes and rooted hair that can be washed and combed. All with shoes and socks.

#1941 —

#1944 —

#1945 —

#1946 —

#1948 —

#1941 — Velvet "A" line dress with eyelet lace trim around yoke; matching velvet panties. Retail $9.00

#1944 — Velvet "A" line dress with multi-color braid and button trim; organdy collar and sleeves. Matching panties. Retail $9.00

#1945 — Cotton polka dot dress with solid color over-dress; matching polka dot panties Retail $9.00

#1946 — Velveteen hat and coat set with solid color cotton dress underneath; cotton panties and low boots. Retail $10.00

#1948 — Flocked dotted organdy dress with solid color cotton bodice; attached taffeta half slip and panties. She carries a matching polka dot umbrella. Retail $12.00

4

Illustration 171. 18in (45.7cm) *Bettina* from the 1965 Effanbee Doll Corporation catalog. *Courtesy of Eugenia Dukas.*

Illustration 172. 18in (45.7cm) *Suzie Sunshine* from the 1965 Effanbee Doll Corporation catalog. *Courtesy of Eugenia Dukas.*

Text within the illustration:

EFFANBEE DURABLE DOLLS

Suzie Sunshine
18" All vinyl toddler, fully pointed with moving eyes and long rooted hair that can be washed and combed. All with shoes & socks.

The Profit Protected Line

#1822

#1866

#1823

#1824

#1822 — Broadcloth dress with pleated trim around sleeves, neck and hemline. Matching panties. Retail $8.00

#1823 — Gingham checked taffeta dress with velvet weskit; gingham checked panties; velvet band in hair. Retail $9.00

#1824 — Velvet dress with panel front and ribbon trim; matching panties. Retail $9.00

#1866 — Checked flannel nightgown with matching panties & bedroom scuffs. She holds and 8" all vinyl baby, fully jointed with moving eyes and molded hair; dressed in matching flannel sleeping bag. Retail $10.00

15

Chips	All-vinyl and fully-jointed girl. Sleep eyes; rooted hair.	17in (43.2cm)
1731	Dressed in polka dot shift.	
1734	Wears black velveteen "A-line" dress.	
1735	Wears broadcloth dress.	
1737	Wears cotton shift with matching coat.	
1738	Wears slacks and Rajah coat.	
1739	Wears lace and velvet-trimmed nylon bridesmaid gown.	
1740	Wears lace-trimmed bridal gown.	
Bettina	All-vinyl and fully-jointed toddler. Sleep eyes and rooted hair.	18in (45.7cm)
1941	Wears velvet "A-line" dress.	
1944	Wears velvet "A-line" dress.	
1945	Wears cotton polka dot dress.	
1946	Wears velveteen coat and hat set.	
1948	Wears flocked dotted organdy dress and carries matching umbrella.	
Suzie Sunshine	All-vinyl and fully-jointed toddler. Sleep eyes; long rooted hair.	18in (45.7cm)
1822	Wears broadcloth dress.	
1823	Wears checked taffeta dress.	
1824	Wears velvet dress.	
1866	Wears flannel nightgown. Carries 8in (20.3cm) *Babykin* in matching sleeping bag.	
Set 1800/36	18in (45.7cm) *Suzie Sunshine*, 11in (27.9cm) *Patsy* and 8in (20.3cm) *Babykin*, all in flannel nightgowns. The baby is in a wicker rocker.	

♥ EFFANBEE DOLLS
—The perfect gift the year 'round!

D O L L S
—The perfect gift the year 'round!

#65—WIRE DISPLAY RACK
(Dolls not included)
$7.50 each

#1800/36 — 18" All vinyl toddler, fully jointed with moving eyes and long rooted hair that can be washed and combed. In checked flannel nightgown with matching panties & bedroom scuffs.

11" Flexible all vinyl toddler, fully jointed with moving eyes and rooted hair. Dressed in matching outfit, as above.

Ribbon trimmed rocking wicker cradle with mattress and pillow on which lies an 8" flexible vinyl drink and wet baby with moving eyes and molded hair; fully jointed. Dressed in checked flannel sleeping bag.

Retail $20.00

16 **Effanbee Doll Corp.** 200 Fifth Avenue, New York, N. Y. 10016

Illustration 173. Special set for 1965 from the Effanbee Doll Corporation catalog. This is 18in (45.7cm) *Suzie Sunshine*, 11in (27.9cm) *Patsy* and 8in (20.3cm) *Babykin.* At the left is a display rack that doll dealers could purchase from Effanbee. *Courtesy of Eugenia Dukas.*

Illustration 174. 15in (38.1cm) *Chipper,* 1966. All-vinyl and fully-jointed. Blonde rooted hair; blue sleep eyes with lashes. Head marked: "EFFANBEE // 19 © 66." The costume is a replacement.

OPPOSITE PAGE: Illustration 175. 11in (27.9cm) *Half Pint,* 1966. All-vinyl and fully-jointed. Bright red rooted hair; brown side-glancing sleep eyes with lashes. Head marked: "EFFANBEE // 19 © 66."

98

99

Miss Chips

17" All vinyl girl doll, fully jointed with side glance moving eyes and rooted hair that can be washed and combed. Available colored.

#1752 — Oatmeal slack suit with pink cotton blouse; black patent belt and shoes. Retail $8.00

#1753 — Lineen dress and hat with matching panties; textured hose. Retail $9.00

#1754 — White vinyl rain coat with polka dot trim; polka dot dress with matching panties; polka dot boots and babushka. Retail $10.00

#1756 — Striped blazed jacket over white cotton dress with pleated skirt; matching panties and hat; textured hose. Retail $10.00

#1757 — Nylon bridesmaid gown with rosebud trim; taffeta slip and panties; crinoline; long textured hose. Retail $12.00

#1758 — Lace trimmed tulle bridal gown with taffeta slip and panties; crinoline, long textured stockings. Bridal veil. Retail $13.00

#1756

#1757

#1758

#1752

#1753

#1754

Illustration 176. 17in (43.2cm) *Miss Chips* from the 1966 Effanbee Doll Corporation catalog. *Courtesy of Eugenia Dukas.*

EFFANBEE DURABLE DOLLS

Pun'kin

11" All vinyl toddler, fully jointed with moving eyes and rooted hair that can be washed and combed.

#1315 — Velveteen dress with matching panties. Retail $4.00

#1317 — Long flannel nitie with matching panties. Retail $4.00

#1318 — Lace trimmed organdy party dress with cotton slip and panties. Retail $5.00

#1319 — Checked coat and hat over cotton dress and panties. Retail $5.00

#1319

#1315

#1317

#1318

Illustration 177. 11in (27.9cm) *Pun'kin* from the 1966 Effanbee Doll Corporation catalog. *Courtesy of Eugenia Dukas.*

Illustration 178. 14in (35.6cm) *Little Gum Drop* and 16in (40.6cm) *Gum Drop* from the 1966 Effanbee Doll Corporation catalog. *Courtesy of Eugenia Dukas.*

Little Gum Drop

#1428 — 14" All vinyl toddler with moving eyes and rooted hair; fully jointed. Shoes and socks. 8" vinyl Babykin; drinks and wets; bottle. Both in checked gingham. Retail $7.00

Gum Drop

16" All vinyl toddler, fully jointed with moving eyes and long rooted hair that can be washed and combed. All with shoes and socks, ribbon bow in hair. Available colored.

#1631 — Striped cotton dress with velvet bodice; matching panties. Retail $6.00

#1641 — Velveteen jumper with white cotton blouse and white cotton panties. Retail $7.00

#1642 — Navy and white polka dot cotton dress; White pique pinafore with red trim; polka dot panties. Retail $7.00

#1646 — Flannel nitey with matching panties and bedroom scuffs. She holds an 8" Babykin dressed in flannel sleeping bag. Retail $8.00

EFFANBEE DURABLE DOLLS

#1428

#1646

#1631

#1641

#1642

14

Suzie Sunshine

18" All vinyl toddler, fully jointed with moving eyes and long rooted hair that can be washed and combed. All with shoes and socks.

#1941 — Velvet "A" line dress with eyelet lace trim around yoke; matching velvet panties. Retail $9.00

#1861 — Red, white and blue velveteen dress with velveteen panties. Retail $8.00

#1864 — Two-tone printed cotton dress with matching cap and panties. Retail $9.00

#1866 — Flannel nightgown with matching panties and bedroom scuffs. She holds an 8" all vinyl baby, fully jointed with moving eyes and molded hair; dressed in matching flannel sleeping bag. Retail $10.00

#1868 — Velvet trimmed organdy party dress with cotton slip and panties; textured hose. Retail $10.00

#1941

#1868

#1861

#1864

#1866

Illustration 179. Designer Eugenia Dukas' favorite doll: 18in (45.7cm) *Suzie Sunshine* from the 1966 Effanbee Doll Corporation catalog. *Courtesy of Eugenia Dukas.*

15

1966 Catalog

Precious Baby		Vinyl head, arms and legs; kapok filled body. Sleep eyes; rooted hair; cry voice.	24in (61cm)
9832		Wears striped cotton dress.	
9833		Wears printed cotton dress.	
9834		Wears "lineen" dress with daisy trim.	
9835		Wears lace and embroidery-trimmed dress.	
9836		Wears "lineen" coat and hat.	
9837		Wears three-piece fleece garment.	
9838		Wears organdy dress with crocheted sweater, cap and booties.	
L'il Darlin'		Vinyl head, arms and legs; kapok filled body. Sleep eyes and rooted hair.	18in (45.7cm)
9684		Wears lace-trimmed organdy christening dress; crocheted cap and sweater. Has ruffled trimmed pillow.	
Thumkin		Vinyl head, arms and legs; kapok stuffed body. Sleep eyes; rooted hair.	18in (45.7cm)
9510		Dressed in fleece bunting.	
9511		Wears striped cotton batiste dress.	
9512		Wears print cotton dress.	
9513		Wears pique dress with polka dot panels.	
9514		Wears organdy dress and crocheted sweater.	
9515		Wears "lineen" dress with organdy pinafore.	
9517		Wears embroidery-trimmed organdy dress.	
Peaches		Vinyl head, arms and legs; kapok stuffed body. Sleep eyes and rooted hair. Baby.	16in (40.6cm)
9320		Wears satin-trimmed bunting.	
9321		Wears batiste dress.	
9322		Wears cotton dress.	
9323		Wears organdy dress.	
Twinkie		All-vinyl and fully-jointed baby. Sleep eyes; drinks and wets; has cry voice.	16in (40.6cm)
2531	Molded hair	Dressed in flannel sacque and diaper.	
2552	Molded hair	Wears "lineen" dress and hat.	
2585	Rooted hair	Wears eyelet lace cotton dress. Has red velveteen pillow with lace trim.	
2586	Rooted hair	Wears lace-trimmed organdy dress. On pink velveteen pillow.	
2587	Rooted hair	Wears eyelet embroidered organdy dress. On gingham checked pillow.	
2588	Rooted hair	Wears crepe coat and cap. On ruffle-trimmed organdy pillow.	

Illustration 168. 16in (40.6cm) *Gum Drop* from the 1965 Effanbee Doll Corporation catalog. *Courtesy of Eugenia Dukas.*

EFFANBEE DURABLE DOLLS

Gum Drop

16" All vinyl toddler, fully jointed with moving eyes and long rooted hair that can be washed and combed. All with shoes & socks, ribbon bow in hair.

#1631 — Striped cotton dress wih velvet bodice; matching panties.   Retail $6.00

#1641 — Velveteen jumper with white cotton blouse; white cotton panties. Retail $7.00

#1644 — Solid cotton "A" line dress with polka dot trim; matching panties. Retail $7.00

#1645 — Striped cotton dress with solid color overdress; matching panties. Retail $7.00

#1666 — Flannel nitie with matching panties and bedroom scuffs. Holds 8" Babykin dressed in flannel sleeping bag.   Retail $8.00

#1666

#1631

#1641

#1644

#1645

Illustration 169. 17in (43.2cm) *Chips* from the 1965 Effanbee Doll Corporation catalog. *Courtesy of Eugenia Dukas.*

EFFANBEE DURABLE DOLLS

Chips

17" All vinyl girl doll, fully jointed with side glance moving eyes and rooted hair that can be washed and combed.

#1731 — In polka dot shift with ruffled hem; ankle boots.   Retail $8.00

#1734 — Black velveteen "A" line dress with ruffled lace sleeves; taffeta panties, long textured stockings and velvet slippers.   Retail $9.00

#1735 — Solid color broadcloth dress with striped jacket & boots. Solid color jockey cap with striped trim & matching solid color panties.   Retail $10.00

#1737 — Cotton shift and matching coat with polka dot trim; matching polka dot headscarf and high boots.   Retail $10.00

#1731

#1734

#1735

#1737

#1738 — Checked slacks with white pique Rajah coat; high black boots.   Retail $10.00

#1739 — Lace and velvet trimmed nylon bridesmaid gown; taffeta slip & crinoline; long textured stockings and satin slippers; ribbon bow in hair.   Retail $12.00

#1740 — Lace trimmed nylon bridal gown with taffeta slip and crinoline, panties. Long textured stockings, satin slippers and blue garter. Bridal veil.   Retail $12.00

— #1740 —

The Profit Protected Line

#1738

#1739

13

Illustration 170. 17in (43.2cm) *Chips* from the 1965 Effanbee Doll Corporation catalog. *Courtesy of Eugenia Dukas.*

Bettina

18" All vinyl toddler, fully jointed with moving eyes and rooted hair that can be washed and combed. All with shoes and socks.

— #1941 —

— #1946 —

— #1948 —

#1944 —

— #1945 —

#1941 — Velvet "A" line dress with eyelet lace trim around yoke; matching velvet panties.   Retail $9.00

#1944 — Velvet "A" line dress with multi-color braid and button trim; organdy collar and sleeves. Matching panties.   Retail $9.00

#1945 — Cotton polka dot dress with solid color overdress; matching polka dot panties   Retail $9.00

#1946 — Velveteen hat and coat set with solid color cotton dress underneath; cotton panties and low boots.   Retail $10.00

#1948 — Flocked dotted organdy dress with solid color cotton bodice; attached taffeta half slip and panties. She carries a matching polka dot umbrella.   Retail $12.00

4

Illustration 171. 18in (45.7cm) *Bettina* from the 1965 Effanbee Doll Corporation catalog. *Courtesy of Eugenia Dukas.*

Chips	All-vinyl and fully-jointed girl. Sleep eyes; rooted hair.	17in (43.2cm)
1731	Dressed in polka dot shift.	
1734	Wears black velveteen "A-line" dress.	
1735	Wears broadcloth dress.	
1737	Wears cotton shift with matching coat.	
1738	Wears slacks and Rajah coat.	
1739	Wears lace and velvet-trimmed nylon bridesmaid gown.	
1740	Wears lace-trimmed bridal gown.	
Bettina	All-vinyl and fully-jointed toddler. Sleep eyes and rooted hair.	18in (45.7cm)
1941	Wears velvet "A-line" dress.	
1944	Wears velvet "A-line" dress.	
1945	Wears cotton polka dot dress.	
1946	Wears velveteen coat and hat set.	
1948	Wears flocked dotted organdy dress and carries matching umbrella.	
Suzie Sunshine	All-vinyl and fully-jointed toddler. Sleep eyes; long rooted hair.	18in (45.7cm)
1822	Wears broadcloth dress.	
1823	Wears checked taffeta dress.	
1824	Wears velvet dress.	
1866	Wears flannel nightgown. Carries 8in (20.3cm) *Babykin* in matching sleeping bag.	
Set 1800/36	18in (45.7cm) *Suzie Sunshine,* 11in (27.9cm) *Patsy* and 8in (20.3cm) *Babykin,* all in flannel nightgowns. The baby is in a wicker rocker.	

EFFANBEE
DURABLE
DOLLS

EFFANBEE DOLLS
—The perfect gift the year 'round!

D O L L S
—The perfect gift the year 'round!

#65—WIRE DISPLAY RACK
(Dolls not included)
$7.50 each

#1800/36 — 18" All vinyl toddler, fully jointed with moving eyes and long rooted hair that can be washed and combed. In checked flannel nightgown with matching panties & bedroom scuffs.

11" Flexible all vinyl toddler, fully jointed with moving eyes and rooted hair. Dressed in matching outfit, as above.

Ribbon trimmed rocking wicker cradle with mattress and pillow on which lies and 8" flexible vinyl drink and wet baby with moving eyes and molded hair; fully jointed. Dressed in checked flannel sleeping bag.

Retail $20.00

Effanbee Doll Corp. 200 Fifth Avenue, New York, N. Y. 10016

Illustration 173. Special set for 1965 from the Effanbee Doll Corporation catalog. This is 18in (45.7cm) *Suzie Sunshine*, 11in (27.9cm) *Patsy* and 8in (20.3cm) *Babykin*. At the left is a display rack that doll dealers could purchase from Effanbee. *Courtesy of Eugenia Dukas.*

Illustration 174. 15in (38.1cm) *Chipper*, 1966. All-vinyl and fully-jointed. Blonde rooted hair; blue sleep eyes with lashes. Head marked: "EFFANBEE // 19 © 66." The costume is a replacement.

OPPOSITE PAGE: Illustration 175. 11in (27.9cm) *Half Pint*, 1966. All-vinyl and fully-jointed. Bright red rooted hair; brown side-glancing sleep eyes with lashes. Head marked: "EFFANBEE // 19 © 66."

98

Miss Chips

17" All vinyl girl doll, fully jointed with side glance moving eyes and rooted hair that can be washed and combed. Available colored.

#1752 — Oatmeal slack suit with pink cotton blouse; black patent belt and shoes. Retail $8.00

#1753 — Lineen dress and hat with matching panties; textured hose. Retail $9.00

#1754 — White vinyl rain coat with polka dot trim; polka dot dress with matching panties; polka dot boots and babushka. Retail $10.00

#1756 — Striped blazed jacket over white cotton dress with pleated skirt; matching panties and hat; textured hose. Retail $10.00

#1757 — Nylon bridesmaid gown with rosebud trim; taffeta slip and panties; crinoline; long textured hose. Retail $12.00

#1758 — Lace trimmed tulle bridal gown with taffeta slip and panties; crinoline, long textured stockings. Bridal veil. Retail $13.00

#1756

#1757

#1758

#1752   #1753   #1754

Illustration 176. 17in (43.2cm) *Miss Chips* from the 1966 Effanbee Doll Corporation catalog. *Courtesy of Eugenia Dukas.*

EFFANBEE DURABLE DOLLS

Pun'kin

11" All vinyl toddler, fully jointed with moving eyes and rooted hair that can be washed and combed.

#1315 — Velveteen dress with matching panties. Retail $4.00

#1317 — Long flannel nitie with matching panties. Retail $4.00

#1318 — Lace trimmed organdy party dress with cotton slip and panties. Retail $5.00

#1319 — Checked coat and hat over cotton dress and panties. Retail $5.00

#1319

#1315   #1317   #1318

Illustration 177. 11in (27.9cm) *Pun'kin* from the 1966 Effanbee Doll Corporation catalog. *Courtesy of Eugenia Dukas.*

100

Illustration 178. 14in (35.6cm) *Little Gum Drop* and 16in (40.6cm) *Gum Drop* from the 1966 Effanbee Doll Corporation catalog. *Courtesy of Eugenia Dukas.*

Illustration 179. Designer Eugenia Dukas' favorite doll: 18in (45.7cm) *Suzie Sunshine* from the 1966 Effanbee Doll Corporation catalog. *Courtesy of Eugenia Dukas.*

1966 Catalog

Precious Baby		Vinyl head, arms and legs; kapok filled body. Sleep eyes; rooted hair; cry voice.	24in (61cm)
9832		Wears striped cotton dress.	
9833		Wears printed cotton dress.	
9834		Wears "lineen" dress with daisy trim.	
9835		Wears lace and embroidery-trimmed dress.	
9836		Wears "lineen" coat and hat.	
9837		Wears three-piece fleece garment.	
9838		Wears organdy dress with crocheted sweater, cap and booties.	
L'il Darlin'		Vinyl head, arms and legs; kapok filled body. Sleep eyes and rooted hair.	18in (45.7cm)
9684		Wears lace-trimmed organdy christening dress; crocheted cap and sweater. Has ruffled trimmed pillow.	
Thumkin		Vinyl head, arms and legs; kapok stuffed body. Sleep eyes; rooted hair.	18in (45.7cm)
9510		Dressed in fleece bunting.	
9511		Wears striped cotton batiste dress.	
9512		Wears print cotton dress.	
9513		Wears pique dress with polka dot panels.	
9514		Wears organdy dress and crocheted sweater.	
9515		Wears "lineen" dress with organdy pinafore.	
9517		Wears embroidery-trimmed organdy dress.	
Peaches		Vinyl head, arms and legs; kapok stuffed body. Sleep eyes and rooted hair. Baby.	16in (40.6cm)
9320		Wears satin-trimmed bunting.	
9321		Wears batiste dress.	
9322		Wears cotton dress.	
9323		Wears organdy dress.	
Twinkie		All-vinyl and fully-jointed baby. Sleep eyes; drinks and wets; has cry voice.	16in (40.6cm)
2531	Molded hair	Dressed in flannel sacque and diaper.	
2552	Molded hair	Wears "lineen" dress and hat.	
2585	Rooted hair	Wears eyelet lace cotton dress. Has red velveteen pillow with lace trim.	
2586	Rooted hair	Wears lace-trimmed organdy dress. On pink velveteen pillow.	
2587	Rooted hair	Wears eyelet embroidered organdy dress. On gingham checked pillow.	
2588	Rooted hair	Wears crepe coat and cap. On ruffle-trimmed organdy pillow.	

Charlee		All-vinyl and fully-jointed toddler. Sleep eyes and rooted hair.	13in (33cm)
6431		Wears striped cotton dress.	
6434		Wears plaid percale dress.	
6436		Wears printed flannel pajamas and cap.	
Half Pint		All-vinyl and fully-jointed toddler. Sleep eyes; rooted hair.	11in (27.9cm)
6211		Wears printed cotton dress.	
6212		Wears velveteen dress.	
6213		Wears printed batiste dress.	
My Fair Baby		All-vinyl and fully-jointed baby. Sleep eyes; cry voice; drinks and wets.	14in (35.6cm)
4461	Molded hair	In zippered fleecy bunting and hood.	
4481	Rooted hair	In zippered fleecy bunting and hood.	
4482	Rooted hair	Wears cotton dress and cap.	
4483	Rooted hair	Wears printed cotton dress and cap.	
Baby Winkie		All-vinyl and fully-jointed baby. Sleep eyes; molded hair; drinks and wets.	12in (30.5cm)
2431		In flannel sacque and diaper.	
2432		In printed cotton dress.	
Babykin		All-vinyl and fully-jointed baby. Sleep eyes; drinks and wets.	8in (20.3cm)
2161	Molded hair	Wears long organdy dress.	
2162	Molded hair	Wears gingham checked dress and cap.	
2164	Molded hair	In fleece bunting and cap.	
2165	Molded hair	In long organdy dress and cap. On lace-- trimmed pillow.	
2174	Rooted hair	In lace-trimmed organdy dress and cap.	
Mickey, the All-American Boy		All-vinyl and fully-jointed boy. Molded hair; painted eyes.	11in (27.9cm)
701	Molded cap	*Baseball Player.*	
702	Molded cap	*Football Player.*	
705	Molded cap	*Sailor.*	
713	Molded cap	*Fighter.*	
*Tiny Tubber.**		All-vinyl and fully-jointed baby. Sleep eyes; drinks and wets.	11in (27.9cm)
2312	Molded hair	Dressed in diaper and blanket.	
2382	Rooted hair	Dressed in flannel sacque and hood.	
2384	Rooted hair	In printed cotton dress.	
2385	Rooted hair	In gingham checked dress.	
Chipper		All-vinyl and fully-jointed girl. Sleep side-glance eyes; rooted hair.	15in (38.1cm)
1531		Dressed in percale dress and hat.	
1532		Dressed in cotton dress with textured hose.	
1535		In lace-trimmed tulle bridal gown.	

*Beginning in 1966 *Tiny Tubber* had the same head mold as *Pun'kin*.

Miss Chips	All-vinyl and fully-jointed girl. Sleep side-glance eyes; rooted hair.	17in (43.2cm)
1752	In slack suit with blouse.	
1753	In "lineen" dress and hat.	
1754	In white vinyl rain coat; boots; babushka.	
1756	In jacket over white cotton dress.	
1757	In nylon bridesmaid gown.	
1758	In tulle bridal gown.	
Pun'kin	All-vinyl and fully-jointed toddler. Sleep eyes and rooted hair.	11in (27.9cm)
1315	In velveteen dress.	
1317	In long flannel nightie.	
1318	In lace-trimmed party dress.	
1319	In checked coat and hat over cotton dress.	
Little Gum Drop	All-vinyl and fully-jointed toddler. Sleep eyes and rooted hair.	14in (35.6cm)
1428	Carries 8in (20.3cm) *Babykin*. Both wear checked gingham outfits.	
Gum Drop	All-vinyl and fully-jointed toddler. Sleep eyes; long rooted hair.	16in (40.6cm)
1631	Dressed in striped cotton dress.	
1641	Dressed in velveteen jumper.	
1642	In navy and white polka dot cotton dress.	
1646	In flannel nightie and holding 8in (20.3cm) *Babykin* in flannel sleeping bag.	
Suzie Sunshine	All-vinyl and fully-jointed toddler. Sleep eyes and long rooted hair.	18in (45.7cm)
1941	Dressed in velvet "A-line" dress.	
1861	In velveteen dress.	
1864	In cotton dress and cap.	
1866	In flannel nightgown and holding 8in (20.3cm) *Babykin* in matching sleeping bag.	
1868	Dressed in velvet-trimmed organdy party dress.	

Precious Baby	Vinyl head, arms and legs; kapok stuffed body. Sleep eyes; rooted hair; cry voice in body.	24in (61cm)
9881	Wears printed Dacron dress.	
9882	Wears permanent pleated nylon dress.	
9883	Wears gingham checked cotton dress with organdy pinafore.	
9885	Wears organdy dress; bib.	
9888	Wears organdy dress; sweater.	
9889	Wears fleece coat and hat; Dacron and cotton dress.	
L'il Darlin'	Vinyl head, arms and legs; kapok stuffed body. Sleep eyes; rooted hair; cry voice in body.	18in (45.7cm)
9683	Wears knit coat and hat; cotton dress.	
9684	Wears organdy christening dress; has ruffle-trimmed organdy pillow.	

Illustration 180. Advertisement from *Playthings*, March 1967, showing Effanbee's 24in (61cm) *Precious Baby*.

Illustration 181. 18in (45.7cm) *Honey Bun* from the 1967 Effanbee Doll Corporation catalog. *Courtesy of Eugenia Dukas.*

Illustration 182. At the left: 11in (27.9cm) *Pun'kin* from the 1967 Effanbee Doll Corporation catalog. *Courtesy of Eugenia Dukas.*

Honey Bun	Vinyl head, arms and legs; kapok stuffed body. Sleep eyes; rooted hair; cry voice in body.	18in (45.7cm)
9550	Dressed in fleece bunting.	
9552	Wears Dacron dress.	
9553	Wears gingham checked cotton dress.	
9553N	Same as the above in "colored" version.	
9554	Wears organdy dress with lace hem.	
9555	Wears organdy dress and cap.	
9556	Wears permanent pleated nylon dress.	
9557	Wears three-piece fleece suit.	
9558	Wears organdy dress with hand-crocheted sweater.	
9558N	Same as the above in "colored" version.	
Baby Cuddles	Vinyl head, arms and legs; kapok stuffed body. Sleep eyes; rooted hair; cry voice in body.	16in (40.6cm)
9330	In quilted fleece bunting.	
9332	In lace-trimmed crepe dress.	
9333	In lace-trimmed organdy dress.	
9334	In organdy christening dress on lace-trimmed organdy pillow.	
9335	In organdy christening dress with wide lace hem on lace-trimmed organdy pillow.	
9336	Wears velvet coat, hat and muff.	

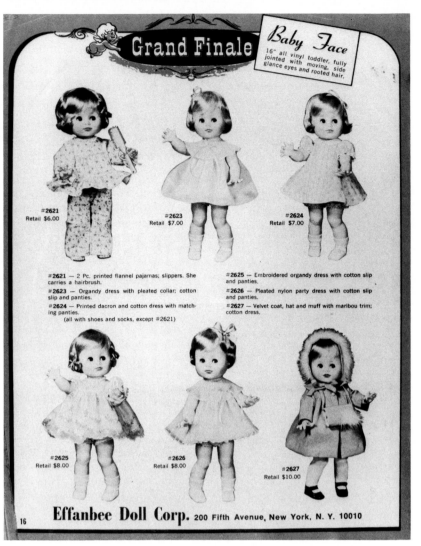

Illustration 183. Above: 11in (27.9cm) *Half Pint;* below; 18in (45.7cm) *Suzie Sunshine.* Effanbee Doll Corporation catalog, 1967. *Courtesy of Eugenia Dukas.*

Illustration 184. 16in (40.6cm) *Baby Face* from the 1967 Effanbee Doll Corporation catalog. *Courtesy of Eugenia Dukas.*

My Fair Baby		All-vinyl and fully-jointed baby. Sleep eyes; drinks and wets.	14in (35.6cm)
4461	Molded hair	In zippered bunting and hood.	
4481	Rooted hair	In zippered bunting and hood.	
4482	Rooted hair	In cotton dress and cap.	
Baby Winkie		All-vinyl and fully-jointed baby. Sleep eyes; molded hair; drinks and wets.	12in (30.5cm)
2431		In flannel sacque and diaper.	
2432		In printed cotton dress and cap on matching pillow.	
Twinkie		All-vinyl and fully-jointed baby. Sleep eyes; cry voice; drinks and wets.	16in (40.6cm)
2521	Rooted hair	In printed cotton quilted blanket, sacque and diaper.	
2522	Molded hair	In crepe dress.	
2523	Rooted hair	In long organdy dress with velvet bodice.	

2523N	Rooted hair	Same as the above in "colored" version.	
2524	Rooted hair	In long, lace-trimmed christening dress.	
2524N	Rooted hair	Same as the above in "colored" version.	
2525	Rooted hair	In embroidered organdy dress on organdy pillow.	
2526	Rooted hair	In fleece coat with lace-trimmed collar.	
2531	Molded hair	In flannel sacque and diaper.	
2531N	Molded hair	Same as the above in "colored" version.	
Little Gum Drop		All-vinyl and fully-jointed toddler. Rooted hair; sleep eyes.	14in (35.6cm)
1422		In velveteen jumper and cotton blouse.	
Gum Drop		All-vinyl and fully-jointed "negro" toddler. Sleep eyes; rooted hair.	16in (40.6cm)
1662N		In velveteen and eyelet lace dress.	
Charlee		All-vinyl and fully-jointed baby. Rooted hair; sleep eyes.	13in (33cm)
6441		In flannel pajamas and slippers.	
6442		In flannel snowsuit and hood.	
6443		In knit dress with matching cap.	
Twinkie in Suitcase		All-vinyl and fully-jointed baby. Rooted hair; sleep eyes; drinks and wets.	16in (40.6cm)
025		Packaged in suitcase with layette.	
Chipper		All-vinyl and fully-jointed girl. Rooted hair; side-glancing sleep eyes.	15in (38.1cm)
1521		In printed Dacron dress.	
1522		In printed flannel nightgown.	
1528		In lace bridal gown.	
Miss Chips		All-vinyl and fully-jointed girl. Rooted hair; side-glancing sleep eyes.	17in (43.2cm)
1754		In vinyl raincoat with polka dot trim.	
1754N		Same as the above in "colored" version.	
1761		In knitted mini dress.	
1767		In allover lace formal.	
1768		In allover lace bridal gown.	
1768N		Same as the above in "colored" version.	
Babykin		All-vinyl and fully-jointed baby. Sleep eyes; drinks and wets.	8in (20.3cm)
2161	Molded hair	In long organdy dress.	
2162	Molded hair	In gingham checked dress and cap.	
2163	Molded hair	In fleece jacket and hood.	
2164	Molded hair	In fleece bunting with cap.	
2165	Molded hair	In long organdy dress on pillow.	
2174	Rooted hair	In lace-trimmed organdy dress and cap.	
Mickey, the All-American Boy		All-vinyl and fully-jointed boy. Molded hair and painted eyes.	11in (27.9cm)
701	Molded cap	*Baseball Player.*	
702	Molded helmet	*Football Player.*	
705	Molded cap	*Sailor.*	
713		*Fighter.*	

Tiny Tubber		All-vinyl and fully-jointed baby. Sleep eyes; drinks and wets.	11in (27.9cm)
2312	Molded hair	In diaper, booties and blanket.	
2382	Rooted hair	In flannel sacque and hood.	
2384	Rooted hair	In printed cotton dress.	
2385	Rooted hair	In gingham checked dress.	
Pun'kin		All-vinyl and fully-jointed toddler. Rooted hair; sleep eyes.	11in (27.9cm)
1315		In velveteen dress.	
1317		In long flannel nightgown.	
1319		In nylon pleated dress.	
Half Pint		All-vinyl and fully-jointed toddler. Rooted hair; sleep eyes.	11in (27.9cm)
6210		Boy in velveteen suit.	
6210N		"Colored" boy in velveteen suit.	
6212		In lace-trimmed velveteen dress.	
6212N		Same as the above in "colored" version.	
6216		In printed cotton dress.	
6217		In printed flannel pajamas.	
6218		In long nylon formal.	
6218N		Same as the above in "colored" version.	
Suzie Sunshine		All-vinyl and fully-jointed toddler. Long rooted hair; sleep eyes.	18in (45.7cm)
1866		In printed flannel nightgown; carries 8in (20.3cm) baby (*Babykin*) in matching sleeping bag.	
1871		In knitted jersey dress.	
1873		In knit dress with wide lace hem.	
1875		In long velveteen hostess gown.	
Baby Face		All-vinyl and fully-jointed toddler. Rooted hair; side-glance sleep eyes.	16in (40.6cm)
2621		In flannel pajamas.	
2623		In organdy dress.	
2624		In printed Dacron and cotton dress.	
2625		In embroidered organdy dress.	
2626		In pleated nylon party dress.	
2627		In velvet coat, hat and muff.	

To love and to cherish...

Dy Dee Darlin' by Effanbee

Dy Dee Darlin' — the latest arrival at Effanbee Doll . . . she is a real sweetheart, and will capture the heart of every little girl the country over.

Dy Dee is an all soft vinyl drinking and wetting doll with a delightfully different face. A face that is more realistic than ever before seen on any baby doll yet.

Dy Dee is 18" tall from the tip of her toes to the top of her rooted hair . . . that's not all, she is fully jointed and comes dressed in three different beautiful outfits.

We love her; we feel sure you'll love her too!

SEPT. 1967

EFFANBEE Doll Corporation
The profit protected line • **200 FIFTH AVENUE, NEW YORK, N.Y. 10010**

EFFANBEE DURABLE DOLLS

Illustration 185. Effanbee Doll Corporation advertisement from *Playthings*, September 1967, showing 18in (45.7cm) *Dy Dee Darlin'*. This doll was shown in the 1968 catalog as *Dy-Dee Darlin'*.

110

1968 Catalog

Button Nose		Vinyl head and hands; kapok stuffed body. Sleep eyes; cry voice.	16in (40.6cm)
8311	Molded hair	Covered with gingham checked cotton fabric and dressed in matching dress.	
8312	Molded hair	In sheer white voile infant dress.	
8314	Molded hair	In rayon crepe christening dress.	
8325	Rooted hair	Dressed in flannel pajamas and in sleeping bag with plush teddy bear.	
8326	Rooted hair	In gingham checked overalls with white cotton pullover.	

Illustration 186. 11in (27.9cm) *Mickey, the All-American Boy,* No. 721 *Baseball Player,* 1968. All-vinyl and fully-jointed. Molded hair with molded hat; blue painted eyes. Head marked: "MICKEY // EFFANBEE." *Marjorie Smith Collection.*

Illustration 187. 11in (27.9cm) *Mickey, the All-American Boy* as *Basketball Player, Football Player* and *Sailor,* 1960s. All-vinyl and fully-jointed. Molded hair and molded hats; blue painted eyes; freckles across nose. Heads marked: "MICKEY // EFFANBEE." *Marjorie Smith Collection.*

Honey Bun		Vinyl head, arms and legs; kapok stuffed body. Rooted hair; sleep eyes; cry voice.	18in (45.7cm)
9561		In gingham checked cotton dress.	
9561N		Same as the above as a "Negro."	
9562		In silk broadcloth dress.	
9563		In snowsuit.	
9564		In gingham checked cotton dress.	
9565		In organdy dress.	
9568		In organdy dress with crocheted sweater.	
9568N		Same as the above as a "Negro."	
9569		In cotton dress; fleece coat, hat and muff.	
9571		In organdy dress with lace hem.	
L'il Darlin'		Vinyl head, arms and legs; kapok stuffed body. Sleep eyes; cry voice.	18in (45.7cm)
8542	Molded hair	In long lace-trimmed coat dress.	
8584	Rooted hair	In organdy christening dress on organdy pillow.	
Precious Baby		Vinyl head, arms and legs; kapok filled body. Rooted hair; sleep eyes; cry voice.	24in (61cm)
9872		In silk broadcloth dress.	
9872N		Same as the above as a "Negro."	
9873		In three-piece snowsuit.	
9874		In gingham checked cotton dress.	
9876		In organdy dress with crocheted sweater.	
9877		In cotton dress and corded fleece coat, hat and muff.	
9878		In embroidered organdy dress.	
My Fair Baby		All-vinyl and fully-jointed baby. Sleep eyes; drinks and wets; "coo voice."	14in (35.6cm)
4461	Molded hair	Dressed in bunting and hood.	
4461N	Molded hair	Same as the above as a "Negro."	
4481	Rooted hair	Same as the above No. 4461.	
4481N	Rooted hair	Same as the above as a "Negro."	
4466	Molded hair	Twins in fleece sacques. One is dressed in blue; the other in pink. Both are placed in a fleece bunting.	
Baby Cuddles		Vinyl head, arms and legs; kapok filled body. Rooted hair; sleep eyes; cry voice.	16in (40.6cm)
9340		In satin-trimmed fleece bunting.	
9341		In lace-trimmed crepe dress.	
9341N		Same as the above as a "Negro."	
9343		In embroidered organdy dress.	
9343N		Same as the above as a "Negro."	
9344		In Dacron dress.	

9345		In long, lace-trimmed organdy dress. Lies on a matching lace and organdy pillow.	
9347		In organdy christening dress on lace and organdy pillow.	
Cookie		All-vinyl and fully-jointed baby. Sleep eyes; drinks and wets; "coo voice."	16in (40.6cm)
2831	Molded hair	In flannel sacque and diaper.	
2831N	Molded hair	Same as the above as a "Negro."	
2832	Molded hair	In zippered fleece bunting and hood.	
2853	Rooted hair	In flannel diaper and lace-trimmed nylon robe.	
2855	Rooted hair	In organdy dress on organdy pillow.	
2855N	Rooted hair	Same as the above as a "Negro."	
Baby Winkie		All-vinyl and fully-jointed baby. Molded hair; sleep eyes; drinks and wets.	12in (30.5cm)
2411		Dressed in sacque and diaper; wrapped in fleece blanket.	
2412		In checked cotton dress on matching pillow.	
Dy-Dee Darlin'		All-vinyl and fully-jointed baby. Rooted hair; sleep eyes; drinks and wets.	18in (45.7cm)
5360		Dressed in gingham checked overalls.	
5361		Dressed in bunting, jacket and cap.	
5361N		Same as the above as a "Negro."	
5363		In crepe christening dress on matching pillow.	
5365		In long crepe christening dress on crepe pillow with nylon and lace ruffle.	

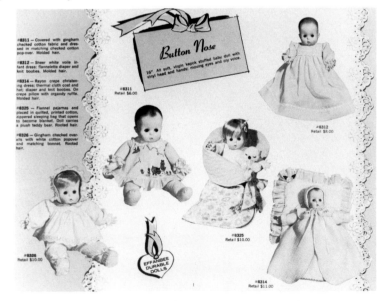

Illustration 189. 16in (40.6cm) *Button Nose* from the 1968 Effanbee Doll Corporation catalog. *Courtesy of Eugenia Dukas.*

Illustration 188. 18in (45.7cm) *Dy-Dee Darlin'* from an advertisement in *Playthings*, March 1968.

Half Pint	All-vinyl and fully-jointed toddler. Rooted hair; sleep eyes.	11in (27.9cm)
6210	Boy dressed in velveteen suit.	
6210N	Same as the above as a "Negro."	
6211	Girl dressed in flannel pajamas.	
6211N	Same as the above as a "Negro."	
6212	In lace-trimmed velveteen dress.	
6212N	Same as the above as a "Negro."	
6213	Boy in dotted pants and striped shirt.	
6214	Girl in dress that matches boy of No. 6213.	
6215	In printed cotton dress.	
Toddletot	All-vinyl and fully-jointed toddler. Molded hair; sleep eyes; drinks and wets.	13in (33cm)
6321	In bikini pants and bib.	
6323	In cotton dress.	
6324	In cotton dress with matching coat and hat.	
Baby Face	All-vinyl and fully-jointed toddler. Rooted hair; side-glancing sleep eyes.	16in (40.6cm)
2631	In flannel pajamas.	
2633	In broadcloth dress.	
2633N	Same as the above as a "Negro."	
2634	In long nightgown.	
2634N	Same as the above as a "Negro."	
2635	In organdy party dress.	
2636	In embroidered party dress.	
Suzie Sunshine	All-vinyl and fully-jointed toddler. Long rooted hair; sleep eyes.	18in (45.7cm)
1861	In granny gown with pinafore.	
1862	In printed flannel nightgown with 8in (20.3cm) baby (*Babykin*) in matching sleeping bag.	
1863	In gingham checked cotton skirt and white organdy blouse.	
Miss Chips	All-vinyl and fully-jointed girl. Rooted hair; side-glancing sleep eyes.	17in (43.2cm)
1742	In plaid jumper and white blouse.	
1742N	Same as the above as a "Negro."	
1743	In printed voile dress.	
1743N	Same as the above as a "Negro."	
1745	In cotton dress; velveteen coat and hat.	
1746	In vinyl raincoat.	
1748	In lace and tulle bridal gown.	
1748N	Same as the above as a "Negro."	

Baby Cuddles

16" Light, cuddly baby with kapok filled body. Soft vinyl arms, legs and head; moving eyes and rooted hair that can be washed and combed. Cry voice.

#9343N
Available negro
Retail $10.00

#9340 — Satin trimmed fleece bunting with satin and lace trimmed hood with cape collar.

#9341 — Lace trimmed crepe dress with matching panties; shoes and socks.

#9341N — Same as above. NEGRO.

#9343 — Embroidered organdy dress and cap, lace trimmed cotton slip and panties; shoes and socks.

#9343 — Same as above. NEGRO.

#9344 — Dacron dress & matching panties, fleece coat and hat; shoes and socks.

#9345 — Long, lace trimmed organdy dress w/stitched tucks at hemline; cotton slip, flannel diaper and booties. On a matching organdy and lace pillow w/stitched tucking on the sides.

#9347 — Lace trimmed organdy christening dress, lace cap, crepe slip and diaper; booties. On crepe pillow w/organdy and lace ruffle.

#9347
Retail $13.00

#9345
Retail $12.00

#9344
Retail $11.00

#9343
Retail $10.00

Illustration 190. 16in (40.6cm) *Baby Cuddles* from the 1968 Effanbee Doll Corporation catalog. *Courtesy of Eugenia Dukas.*

#6212
Retail $5.00

Half Pint

11" All vinyl toddler, fully jointed with moving eyes and rooted hair that can be washed and combed.

#6210 — Velveteen suit with white cotton blouse.

#6210N — Same as above — NEGRO.

#6211 — 2 pc. printed flannel pajamas.

#6211N — Same as above — NEGRO.

#6212 — Lace trimmed velveteen dress with taffeta panties.

#6212N — Same as above — NEGRO.

#6213 — Striped cotton pants and dotted cotton blouse.

#6214 — Striped and dotted cotton dress and matching panties.

#6215 — Printed cotton dress with matching panties.

#6210
Retail $5.00

#6210N
Available negro
Retail $5.00

#6212N
Available negro
Retail $5.00

#6215
Retail $5.00

#6214
Retail $5.00

#6213
Retail $5.00

#6211N
Available negro
Retail $5.00

#6211
Retail $5.00

Illustration 191. 11in (27.9cm) *Half Pint* from the 1968 Effanbee Doll Corporation catalog. *Courtesy of Eugenia Dukas.*

115

Chipper		All-vinyl and fully-jointed girl. Rooted hair; side-glance sleep eyes.	15in (38.1cm)
1551		In party dress.	
1552		In printed cotton dress.	
1554		In lace and tulle bridal gown.	
1555		In printed voile dress.	
Pun'kin		All-vinyl and fully-jointed toddler. Sleep eyes.	11in (27.9cm)
1310	Molded hair	In plaid cotton dress.	
1311	Rooted hair	In long flannel nightgown.	
1312	Rooted hair	In dotted cotton dress.	
1319	Rooted hair	In nylon pleated dress.	
Mickey, the All-American Boy		All-vinyl and fully-jointed. Molded hair; painted eyes.	11in (27.9cm)
721	Molded cap	*Baseball Player.*	
721N	Molded cap	Same as the above as a "Negro" doll.	
722	Molded helmet	*Football Player.*	
722N	Molded helmet	Same as the above as a "Negro" doll.	
723		*Prize Fighter.*	
723N		*Prize Fighter* as a "Negro" doll.	
724		*Basketball Player.*	
724N		Same as the above as a "Negro" doll.	
725	Molded cap	*Sailor.*	
725N	Molded cap	Same as the above as a "Negro" doll.	
Tiny Tubber		All-vinyl and fully-jointed baby. Sleep eyes; drinks and wets.	11in (27.9cm)
2322	Molded hair	In diaper, sacque and blanket.	
2322N	Molded hair	Same as the above as a "Negro."	
2333	Rooted hair	In diaper, sacque and blanket.	
2334	Rooted hair	In printed cotton dress.	
2335	Rooted hair	In eyelet embroidered dress.	
2335N	Rooted hair	Same as the above as a "Negro."	
Babykin		All-vinyl and fully-jointed baby. Molded hair; sleep eyes; drinks and wets.	8in (20.3cm)
2161		Wears long organdy dress, cap and slip.	
2162		In short printed dress and cap.	
2163		In fleece jacket and hood.	
2164		In fleece bunting with cap.	
2166		Twins in flannel jacket with hood in flannel bunting.	
Cookie in Suitcase		All-vinyl and fully-jointed baby. Rooted hair; sleep eyes; drinks and wets.	16in (40.6cm)
025		In suitcase with layette.	

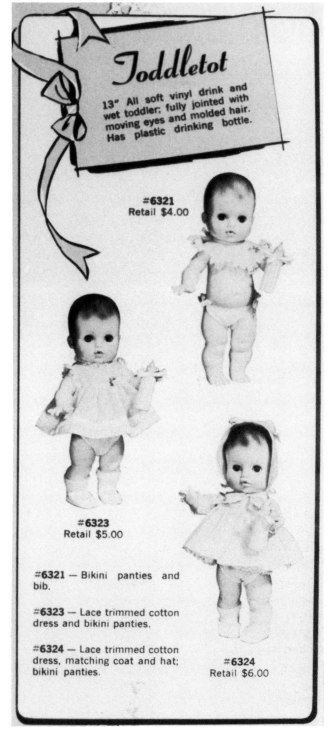

Toddletot

13" All soft vinyl drink and wet toddler; fully jointed with moving eyes and molded hair. Has plastic drinking bottle.

#6321
Retail $4.00

#6323
Retail $5.00

#6321 — Bikini panties and bib.

#6323 — Lace trimmed cotton dress and bikini panties.

#6324 — Lace trimmed cotton dress, matching coat and hat; bikini panties.

#6324
Retail $6.00

Illustration 192. 13in (33cm) Toddletot from the 1968 Effanbee Doll Corporation catalog. Courtesy of Eugenia Dukas.

Chipper

15" All vinyl girl doll, fully jointed with side glance eyes and rooted hair that can be washed and combed. All with knee socks and shoes except #1554 Bride.

#1551 — Ruffled voile party dress with matching panties.

#1552 — Printed cotton dress with lace trimmed pinafore and matching panties; straw hat.

#1554 — Lace and tulle bridal gown over taffeta slip and panties; crinoline, stockings and satin shoes. Lace trimmed bridal veil with flowers on crown.

#1555 — Printed voile dress with tucked bodice; cotton slip and panties.

#1551
Retail $7.00

#1552
Retail $8.00

#1554
Retail $9.00

#1555
Retail $7.00

Illustration 193. 15in (38.1cm) Chipper from the 1968 Effanbee Doll Corporation catalog. Courtesy of Eugenia Dukas.

Pun'kin

11" All vinyl toddler, fully jointed with moving eyes. All with shoes and socks. All with rooted hair except 1310.

#1310
Retail $4.00

#1319
Retail $5.00

#1310 — Plaid cotton dress with matching panties and hat. MOLDED HAIR.
#1311 — Long flannel nities with matching panties.
#1312 — Dotted cotton dress with matching panties.
#1319 — Nylon pleated dress with cotton slip and panties.

#1311
Retail $4.50

#1312
Retail $4.50

Illustration 194. 11in (27.9cm) Pun'kin from the 1968 Effanbee Doll Corporation catalog. Courtesy of Eugenia Dukas.

1969 Catalog

Cookie		All-vinyl and fully-jointed baby. Sleep eyes; "coo voice;" drinks and wets.	16in (40.6cm)
025	Rooted hair	In suitcase with layette.	
2531	Molded hair	In flannel sacque and diaper.	
2531N	Molded hair	Same as the above as a "Negro."	
2842	Rooted hair	In crepe dress on matching pillow.	
2843	Rooted hair	In embroidered organdy dress.	
2843N	Rooted hair	Same as the above as a "Negro."	
2844	Rooted hair	In "chinchilla" cloth pram suit on matching pillow.	
Dy-Dee Baby		All-vinyl and fully-jointed baby. Rooted hair; sleep eyes; drinks and wets.	18in (45.7cm)
5573		In cotton romper, jacket, hat and bunting.	
5574		In organdy dress.	
5575		In christening dress on matching pillow.	
Butter Ball		All-vinyl and fully-jointed baby. Sleep eyes; "coo voice;" drinks and wets.	13in (33cm)
6592	Molded hair	In cotton bib and diaper in blanket.	
6592N	Molded hair	Same as the above as a "Negro."	
6594	Rooted hair	In organdy dress and hat on round pillow.	
066	Rooted hair	In suitcase with layette.	
Fair Baby		All-vinyl and fully-jointed. Sleep eyes; "coo voice;" drinks and wets.	14in (35.6cm)
4461	Molded hair	In zippered bunting and hood.	
4461N	Molded hair	Same as the above as a "Negro."	
4481	Rooted hair	Same as No. 4461 with rooted hair.	
4481N	Rooted hair	Same as No. 4461 with rooted hair as a "Negro."	
4466	Molded hair	Twins in bunting. One has a pink outfit; the other is in blue.	
4483	Rooted hair	Rayon crepe christening dress.	
Baby Winkie		All-vinyl and fully-jointed. Sleep eyes; drinks and wets.	12in (30.5cm)
2421	Molded hair	Dressed in flannel sacque and diaper.	
2433	Rooted hair	Wears crepe dress, coat and hat.	
Sweetie Pie		Vinyl head, arms and legs; kapok filled body. Rooted hair; sleep eyes; cry voice.	17in (43.2cm)
9431		In "lineen" dress.	
9431N		Same as the above as a "Negro."	
9432		In crepe dress.	
9434		In "chinchilla" cloth snowsuit.	
9435		In white organdy dress.	
9436		In rayon crepe dress and crocheted sweater, hat and booties.	
9436N		Same as the above as a "Negro."	

#2843N
Retail $13.00

#2843
Retail $13.00

#2844
Retail $13.00

Dy-Dee Baby

18" All soft vinyl drink and wet baby, fully jointed with moving eyes and rooted hair that can be washed and combed. All have plastic bottle.

#5573 — Cotton romper and lace trimmed fleece jacket, hat and bunting.

#5574 — Embroidered organdy dress, organdy cap; slip and panties; shoes and socks.

#5575 — All lace christening dress w/ lace and organdy cap, slip, diaper and booties. On lace trimmed organdy pillow.

#5574
Retail $13.00

#5575
Retail $14.00

#5573
Retail $12.00

3

ABOVE: Illustration 195. 16in (40.6cm) *Cookie* from the 1969 Effanbee Doll Corporation catalog. *Courtesy of Eugenia Dukas.*

Illustration 196. 18in (45.7cm) *Dy-Dee Baby* from the 1969 Effanbee Doll Corporation catalog. *Courtesy of Eugenia Dukas*

Butter Ball

13" All soft vinyl drink and wet chubby baby, fully jointed with moving eyes. Coo voice, plastic drinking bottle and I.D. bracelet.

#6594
Retail $9.00

RIGHT: Illustration 197. 13in (33cm) *Butter Ball* from the 1969 Effanbee Doll Corporation catalog. *Courtesy of Eugenia Dukas.*

#6592 — Lace trimmed cotton bib and diaper — in lace trimmed fleece blanket. Molded hair.

#6592N — as above — NEGRO.

#6594 — Organdy dress w/3 tiers of lace; matching organdy hat and diaper. On round lace trimmed organdy pillow. Rooted hair.

#066 — Dressed in lace trimmed organdy jacket and diaper — tied in lace bound flannel blanket. Rooted hair. Layette consists of dotted organdy dress and cap, printed flannel pajamas, baby powder and soap, wash cloth, Q-tips and powder puffs.

#6592
Retail $6.00

#6592N
Retail $6.00

#066
Retail $13.00

Button Nose		Vinyl head and hands. Kapok stuffed body. Sleep eyes; cry voice.	16in (40.6cm)
8321	Molded hair	Covered with printed cotton fabric and dressed in matching "pop-over" and bonnet.	
8321N	Molded hair	Same as the above as a "Negro."	
8333	Rooted hair	In cotton infant dress with cap.	
Sugar Plum		Vinyl head, arms and legs; kapok filled body. Rooted hair; sleep eyes; cry voice.	20in (50.8cm)
9641		In gingham checked playsuit.	
9642		In "lineen" dress.	
9642N		Same as the above as a "Negro."	
9643		In cotton dress.	
9645		In organdy dress.	
9645N		Same as the above as a "Negro."	
9646		In long christening dress with crocheted sweater, cap and booties. On organdy pillow with lace ruffle.	
9646N		Same as the above as a "Negro."	
9647		In "chinchilla" cloth coat, hat and leggings.	
9648		In organdy dress and cap.	

Illustration 198. 25in (63.5cm) Precious Baby from the 1969 Effanbee Doll Corporation catalog. Courtesy of Eugenia Duka

Illustration 199. 14in (35.6cm) *Miss Chips* and 15in (38.1cm) *Chipper* from the 1969 Effanbee Doll Corporation catalog. *Courtesy of Eugenia Dukas.*

Precious Baby	Vinyl head, arms and legs. Kapok filled body. Rooted hair; sleep eyes; "Mama" voice.	25in (63.5cm)
9952	In printed batiste dress.	
9954	In heavy lace cotton dress.	
9955	In organdy dress.	
9956	In lace and organdy dress; crocheted sweater.	
9957	In "chinchilla" cloth coat, hat and leggings.	
Miss Chips	All-vinyl and fully-jointed girl. Rooted hair; side-glance sleep eyes.	17in (43.2cm)
1724	In organdy bridal gown.	
1724N	Same as the above as a "Negro."	
1725	In organdy bridesmaid gown.	
Chipper	All-vinyl and fully-jointed girl. Rooted hair; side-glance sleep eyes.	15in (38.1cm)
1513	Long granny gown with pinafore.	
1514	In organdy bridal gown.	
Toddletot	All-vinyl and fully-jointed toddler. Molded hair; sleep eyes; drinks and wets.	13in (33cm)
6313	Boy in "lineen" suit and cap.	
6314	Girl in cotton voile dress, hat and coat.	

Illustration 200. 13in (33cm) *Toddletot* and 16in (40.6cm) *Baby Face* from the 1969 Effanbee Doll Corporation catalog. *Courtesy of Eugenia Dukas.*

Baby Face	All-vinyl and fully-jointed toddler. Rooted hair; side-glance sleep eyes.	16in (40.6cm)
2642	In crepe and nylon tutu.	
2642N	Same as the above as a "Negro."	
2644	In gingham checked nightgown. Has plastic hair brush.	
2647	In cotton dress.	
Suzie Sunshine	All-vinyl and fully-jointed toddler. Rooted hair; sleep eyes.	18in (45.7cm)
1821	Wears long granny gown and pinafore.	
1822	In flannel nightgown. Carries 8in (20.3cm) baby (*Babykin*) in matching flannel sleeping bag.	
1944	In coat, hat, leggings and muff.	
Half Pint	All-vinyl and fully-jointed toddler. Rooted hair; sleep eyes.	11in (27.9cm)
6220	Boy in velveteen suit.	
6220N	Same as the above as a "Negro."	
6221	Girl in long nightgown.	
6221N	Same as the above as a "Negro."	
6222	In lace-trimmed velveteen dress.	
6222N	Same as the above as a "Negro."	
6225	In cotton overalls and eyelet top.	
6225N	Same as the above as a "Negro."	

Illustration 201. 18in (45.7cm) *Suzie Sunshine* from the 1969 Effanbee Doll Corporation catalog. *Courtesy of Eugenia Dukas.*

6226		In organdy party dress and bonnet.	
6227		In ballerina costume.	
Tiny Tubber		All-vinyl and fully-jointed baby. Sleep eyes; drinks and wets.	11in (27.9cm)
2322	Molded hair	In diaper, sacque and blanket.	
2322N	Molded hair	Same as the above as a "Negro."	
2334	Rooted hair	In batiste party dress.	
2335	Rooted hair	In gingham checked dress.	
2335N	Rooted hair	Same as the above as a "Negro."	
2336	Molded hair	Twins in flannel jacket and hood in bunting.	
2336N	Molded hair	Same as the above as "Negro" twins.	
Pun'kin		All-vinyl and fully-jointed toddler. Rooted hair; sleep eyes.	11in (27.9cm)
1321		In long flannel nightgown.	
1321N		Same as the above as a "Negro."	
1323		In gingham dress.	
1324		In pleated nylon dress.	
Babykin		All-vinyl and fully-jointed baby. Molded hair; sleep eyes; drinks and wets.	8in (20.3cm)
2161		In long organdy dress and cap.	
2162		In short printed dress and cap.	
2163		In fleece jacket and hood.	

Within the illustration:

Half Pint

11" All vinyl toddler, fully jointed with moving eyes and rooted hair that can be washed and combed.

#6221N
Retail $6.00

#6227
Retail $7.00

#2322N
Retail $3.50

#6220 — Velveteen suit with white cotton blouse. Shoes and socks.

#6220N — Same as above — NEGRO.

#6221 — Lace trimmed long gingham checked nitie w/matching panties; shoes.

#6221N — Same as above — NEGRO.

#6222 — Lace trimmed velveteen dress with taffeta panties. Shoes and socks.

#6222N — Same as above — NEGRO.

#6225 — Eyelet lace pop-over, long cotton overalls and matching bonnet; shoes and socks.

#6225N — As above — NEGRO.

#6226 — Lace trimmed organdy party dress w/matching bonnet; panties, shoes and socks.

#6227 — Ballerina costume w/ crepe top and nylon tulle tutu, stretch tights and satin slippers.

#6221
Retail $6.00

#6222N
Available negro
Retail $6.00

#6226
Retail $7.00

#2322
Retail $3.50

#6225N
Retail $7.00

#6225
Retail $7.00

#6222
Retail $6.00

#6220N
Retail $6.00

#6220
Retail $6.00

#2366N
Retail $8.00

14

Illustration 202. 11in (27.9cm) *Half Pint* from the 1969 Effanbee Doll Corporation catalog. *Courtesy of Eugenia Dukas.*

2164		In gingham checked overalls.	
2165		In gingham checked top and overalls.	
2167		In lace-trimmed party dress.	
Mickey, the All-American Boy		All-vinyl and fully-jointed. Molded hair; painted eyes.	11in (27.9cm)
721	Molded cap	*Baseball Player.*	
721N	Molded cap	Same as the above as a "Negro."	
722	Molded helmet	*Football Player.*	
722N	Molded helmet	Same as the above as a "Negro."	
723		*Prize Fighter.*	
723N		Same as the above as a "Negro."	
724		*Basketball Player.*	
724N		Same as the above as a "Negro."	
725	Molded cap	*Sailor.*	
725N	Molded cap	Same as the above as a "Negro."	

1970-1979

During the 1970s the Effanbee Doll Corporation changed greatly. By 1979 Effanbee dolls were no longer primarily babies and toddlers as they had been at the beginning of the decade. During the 1970s there were more and more girl and boy dolls; more lady dolls dressed in elegant costumes; dolls that came in a series, such as the *International Collection;* and dolls of special appeal to collectors. Beginning in 1971 Effanbee dolls came in a matching group, with various dolls dressed in similar costumes. The first of these was the *Frontier Series,* with eight different doll designs dressed in printed calico costumes, reminiscent of the early years of America.

The reason for the change was that in 1971 Effanbee was purchased by Leroy Fadem and Roy R. Raizen. From this point on Effanbee dolls were more interesting, more appealing, and were of a higher quality in design and execution. The new dolls that were introduced each year were original concepts, as Effanbee dolls had been in the 1920s and 1930s. The costumes, reflecting the artistry of designer Eugenia Dukas, were more fashionable and elaborate. The new owners of the company exercised a more personal artistic control over the product, placing Effanbee in the forefront of American doll manufacture. No longer was Effanbee a follower of trends in doll designing; Effanbee set the trends that other doll companies copied.

From the 1970s the Effanbee dolls that are of special interest to collectors are those from the *Historical Collection,* the *Four Seasons Collection,* the *Grandes Dames Collection,* the *Currier and Ives Collection,* the *Passing Parade Collection* and *Through the Years with Gigi.* Adding to the collectibility and desirability of Effanbee dolls was the fact that they were still play dolls, as Effanbee dolls had always been.

1970 Catalog

Chipper	All-vinyl and fully-jointed girl. Rooted hair; side-glance sleep eyes.	14in (35.6cm)
1525	Dressed in lace bridal gown.	
Miss Chips	All-vinyl and fully-jointed girl. Rooted hair; sleep eyes.	17in (43.2cm)
1741	In long cotton dress with bonnet.	
1742	In long cotton gown with felt hat.	
1743	In long dress with apron and dust cap.	
1743N	Same as the above as a "Negro."	
1745	Dressed in lace bridal gown.	
1745N	Same as the above as a "Negro."	
1746	In bell-bottom pants and blouse.	
1747	In velvet-trimmed coat over a mini dress.	
Gum Drop	All-vinyl and fully-jointed toddler. Long rooted hair; sleep eyes.	16in (40.6cm)
1621	In white cotton nightie.	
1621N	Same as the above as a "Negro."	
1623	In cotton skirt and blouse.	
1625	In "granny dress" and dust cap.	
1625N	Same as the above as a "Negro."	
Suzie Sunshine	All-vinyl and fully-jointed toddler. Long rooted hair; sleep eyes.	18in (45.7cm)
1851	In printed flannel nightgown. Holds 8in (20.3cm) baby (*Babykin*) in matching sleeping bag.	
1852	In long cotton robe over cotton nightie.	
1853	In long "granny gown."	
1854	In patchwork "granny gown."	

Illustration 203. Photographed during an informal moment at the factory of the Effanbee Doll Corporation: President Roy R. Raizen, left, and Chairman of the Board Leroy Fadem, right.

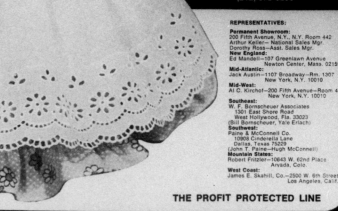

Talk about Quality— you talk about EFFANBEE!

For a long time now—over 61 years, in fact— we've been talking about Effanbee Dolls— the dolls that have everything...all the quality features that add up to saleability and profits. Isn't it about time you proved it to yourself? Visit us at the Toy Fair—we're in

Room 442

(200 FIFTH AVENUE, of course)!

EFFANBEE
DOLL CORPORATION

EFFANBEE DURABLE DOLLS

200 Fifth Ave., New York, N.Y. 10010
(212) 675-5650

THE PROFIT PROTECTED LINE

(Circle No. 131 on Reader Inquiry Card)

MARCH, 1970—PLAYTHINGS   12

Illustration 204. 18in (45.7cm) *Suzie Sunshine* from an Effanbee advertisement in *Playthings*, March 1970.

#1971
Retail $10.00

#1972
Retail $11.00

Luv

18" All vinyl toddler, fully jointed with moving eyes and rooted hair that can be washed and combed.

Illustration 205. 18in (45.7cm) *Luv*, Style No. 1971 and No. 1972, from the Effanbee Doll Corporation catalog, 1970. *Courtesy of Al Kirchof.*

Luv		All-vinyl and fully-jointed toddler. Rooted hair; sleep eyes.	18in (45.7cm)	1970 Catalog
1971		In "lineen" jump suit.		
1972		In eyelet cotton dress.		
1973		In coat, hat, leggings and muff.		
Baby Button Nose		Vinyl head and hands; kapok stuffed body. Sleep eyes; cry voice.	12in (30.5cm)	
8121	Molded hair	Body covered in checked cotton fabric with matching dress.		
8122	Rooted hair	Body covered with cotton fabric with dress in reverse print.		
Button Nose		Vinyl head and hands; kapok stuffed body. Sleep eyes; cry voice. Baby.	16in (40.6cm)	
8341	Molded hair	In helecana knit sacque.		
8341N	Molded hair	Same as the above as a "Negro."		
8344	Rooted hair	Body covered with printed cotton fabric and dressed in matching "granny dress."		
Baby Winkie		All-vinyl and fully-jointed baby. Sleep eyes; drinks and wets.	12in (30.5cm)	
2421	Molded hair	Wears flannel sacque.		
2422	Rooted hair	In lace-trimmed cotton dress.		
2423	Rooted hair	In gingham pants and top with matching bonnet.		
Fair Baby		All-vinyl and fully-jointed baby. Sleep eyes; "coo voice."	14in (35.6cm)	
4442	Molded hair	Dressed in bunting.		
4442N	Molded hair	Same as the above as a "Negro."		
4443	Rooted hair	Same as No. 4442 with rooted hair.		
4443N	Rooted hair	Same as No. 4442N with rooted hair.		
4446	Rooted hair	In embroidered dress with hat.		
Dy-Dee Baby		All-vinyl and fully-jointed baby. Rooted hair; sleep eyes; drinks and wets.	18in (45.7cm)	
5573		Wears cotton romper, jacket and hat; in bunting.		
Toddletot		All-vinyl and fully-jointed toddler. Molded hair; sleep eyes; drinks and wets.	13in (33cm)	
6321		Boy with gingham suit.		
6322		Girl in cotton dress with gingham coat and hat.		
Butter Ball		All-vinyl and fully-jointed baby. Sleep eyes; drinks and wets; "coo voice."	13in (33cm)	
6592	Molded hair	In lace-trimmed bib and diaper on fleece blanket.		
6592N	Molded hair	Same as the above as a "Negro."		
6595	Rooted hair	In organdy dress on organdy pillow.		
6595N	Rooted hair	Same as the above as a "Negro."		
067	Rooted hair	In a suitcase with a layette and accessories.		

Baby Button Nose

12" All soft, virgin kapok stuffed baby doll with vinyl head and hands; moving eyes and cry voice.

#1974
Retail $13.00

#8121
Retail $5.00

#8122
Retail $6.00

LEFT: Illustration 206. 12in (30.5cm) *Baby Button Nose,* Style No. 1974, from the 1970 Effanbee Doll Corporation catalog. *Courtesy of Al Kirchof.*

RIGHT: Illustration 207. 12in (30.5cm) *Baby Button Nose,* Style No. 8121 and No. 8122, from the Effanbee Doll Corporation catalog, 1970. *Courtesy of Al Kirchof.*

Fair Baby

14" Soft, vinyl drink and wet baby, fully jointed with moving eyes. Coo voice. Has plastic drinking bottle.

#4442 — fleece bunting w/ heavy cotton lace trim; matching jacket & bonnet. Flannel diaper —molded hair.

#4442N — same as above NEGRO.

#4443 — same as #4442 but with rooted hair.

#4443N — same as above NEGRO

#4446 — white eyelet embroidered dress w/ hat, flannel diaper & knit booties. Rooted hair.

#4443N
Retail $8.00

#4443
Retail $8.00

#4446
Retail $8.00

#4442
Retail $7.00

#4442N
Retail $7.00

Dy-Dee Baby

18" All soft vinyl drink and wet baby, fully j with moving eyes and rooted hair- that c washed and combed. All have plastic bottle

#5573
Retail $13.00

Illustration 208. 14in (35.6cm) *Fair Baby* from the 1970 Effanbee Doll Corporation catalog. *Courtesy of Al Kirchof.*

Illustration 209. 18in (45.7cm) *Dy-Dee Baby* from the 1970 Effanbee Doll Corporation catalog. *Courtesy of Al Kirchof.*

128

Illustration 210. 13in (33cm) *Toddletot* from the 1970 Effanbee Doll Corporation catalog. *Courtesy of Al Kirchof.*

Twinkie		All-vinyl and fully-jointed baby. Sleep eyes; drinks and wets; "coo voice."	16in (40.6cm)
2531	Molded hair	In flannel sacque and diaper.	
2531N	Molded hair	Same as the above as a "Negro."	
2533	Rooted hair	In "lineen" jacket, hat and leggings.	
2537	Rooted hair	In long organdy christening dress on organdy pillow.	
2537N	Rooted hair	Same as the above as a "Negro."	
2539	Rooted hair	In eyelet dress, wrapped in hand crocheted blanket.	
Sweetie Pie		Vinyl head, arms and legs; kapok filled body. Rooted hair; sleep eyes; cry voice. Baby.	17in (43.2cm)
9421		Dressed in flannel pajamas.	
9422		In cotton jump suit.	
9423		In cotton dress with lace trim.	
9423N		Same as the above as a "Negro."	
9425		In white organdy dress.	
9427		In "chinchilla" snowsuit and cap.	
9428		In crocheted sweater, cap and leggings.	
9428N		Same as the above as a "Negro."	
9429		Boy dressed in short pants and cotton shirt.	
9436		In rayon crepe dress.	
9438		In christening dress on matching pillow.	
Little Luv		Vinyl head, arms and legs; kapok filled body. Sleep eyes; cry voice. Baby.	14in (35.6cm)
9310	Molded hair	In long cotton christening dress.	
9311	Rooted hair	In printed cotton dress.	
9312	Rooted hair	In cotton dress and pinafore.	

Illustration 211. 13in (33cm) *Butterball* (or *Butter Ball*), No. 6592N, 1970. All-vinyl and fully-jointed. *Marjorie Smith Collection.*

Precious Baby

25" Cuddly, light weight baby, virgin kapok filled body, vinyl arms, legs and head; moving eyes and rooted hair that can be washed and combed. MAMA voice. (All with shoes & socks except #9971 and 9976)

#9971 — 2 Pc. printed flannel pajamas. Baby carries an 8" all vinyl, fully jointed drink and wet baby dressed in matching saque.

#9972 — Gingham checked cotton dress with lace inserts, matching panties; shoes and socks.

#9973 — All-over embroidered organdy dress with matching cap, cotton slip and panties; shoes and socks.

#9975 — Nylon fleece hat and coat set trimmed with wool braid, cotton dress and panties; leotards and shoes. LONG HAIR.

#9976 — Lace and organdy dress, cotton slip & panties! hand crocheted sweater, cap and booties.

#9971 Retail $16.00

#9975 Retail $21.00

#9973 Retail $18.00

#9976 Retail $18.00

#9972 Retail $16.00

Illustration 212. 25in (63.5cm) *Precious Baby* from the 1970 Effanbee Doll Corporation catalog. *Courtesy of Al Kirchof.*

Sugar Plum		Vinyl head, arms and legs; kapok filled body. Sleep eyes; cry voice. Baby.	20in (50.8cm)
9631	Molded hair	In long cotton christening dress.	
9646	Rooted hair	In christening dress; crocheted sweater and cap; on pillow.	
9646N	Rooted hair	Same as the above as a "Negro."	
9652	Rooted hair	In gingham checked cotton dress.	
9652N	Rooted hair	Same as the above as a "Negro."	
9656	Rooted hair	In white organdy dress.	
9657	Rooted hair	In batiste dress.	
9658	Rooted hair	In cotton dress with nylon hat and coat.	
Precious Baby		Vinyl head, arms and legs; kapok filled body. Rooted hair; sleep eyes; "Mama voice."	25in (63.5cm)
9971		In two-piece flannel pajamas with 8in (20.3cm) baby (*Babykin*) in matching sacque.	
9972		In gingham checked cotton dress.	
9973		In embroidered organdy dress.	
9975		In cotton dress and nylon fleece coat and hat.	
9976		In lace and organdy dress and crocheted sweater, cap and booties.	

Pun'kin		All-vinyl and fully-jointed toddler. Rooted hair; sleep eyes.	11in (27.9cm)
1321		In flannel nightie.	
1321N		Same as the above as a "Negro."	
1322		In gingham dress with organdy apron.	
1322N		Same as the above as a "Negro."	
1324		In nylon dress.	
Half Pint		All-vinyl and fully-jointed toddler. Rooted hair; sleep eyes.	11in (27.9cm)
6220		Boy with velveteen suit.	
6221		In long gingham checked nightie.	
6221N		Same as the above as a "Negro."	
6222		In velveteen dress trimmed with lace.	
6222N		Same as the above as a "Negro."	
6223		In printed cotton dress.	
6225		In cotton overalls, top and hat.	
6243		In dotted organdy party dress.	
6244		In tulle and lace bridal gown.	
013		In gingham checked dress and packaged with extra clothing and accessories.	
Tiny Tubber		All-vinyl and fully-jointed baby. Sleep eyes; drinks and wets.	11in (27.9cm)
2322	Molded hair	In diaper, sacque and blanket.	
2322N	Molded hair	Same as the above as a "Negro."	
2334	Rooted hair	In batiste party dress.	
2335	Rooted hair	Wears gingham checked dress.	
2335N	Rooted hair	Same as the above as a "Negro."	
2366	Molded hair	Twins in flannel jackets with hood and placed in a bunting.	
023	Rooted hair	Wears gingham dress and packaged with extra clothing and accessories.	
Babykin		All-vinyl and fully-jointed baby. Sleep eyes; drinks and wets.	8in (20.3cm)
2161	Molded hair	In long organdy dress.	
2163	Molded hair	In fleece jacket and hood in bunting.	
2165	Molded hair	In gingham topper, overalls, hat.	
2167	Molded hair	In lace-trimmed party dress.	
021	Rooted hair	In cotton dress with layette and accessories.	
Mickey, the All-American Boy		All-vinyl and fully-jointed. Molded hair; painted eyes.	11in (27.9cm)
721	Molded hat	*Baseball Player.*	
721N	Molded hat	Same as the above as a "Negro."	
722	Molded helmet	*Football Player.*	
722N	Molded helmet	Same as the above as a "Negro."	
723		*Prizefighter.*	
723N		Same as the above as a "Negro."	
724		*Basketball Player.*	
724N		Same as the above as a "Negro."	
725	Molded cap	*Sailor.*	
725N	Molded cap	Same as the above as a "Negro."	

Illustration 213. 11in (27.9cm) *Half Pint* with layette from the 1970 Effanbee Doll Corporation catalog. *Courtesy of Al Kirchof.*

Illustration 214. 11in (27.9cm) *Half Pint* from the 1970 Effanbee Doll Corporation catalog. *Courtesy of Al Kirchof.*

#013
Retail $13.00

Half Pint

#6222 N
Retail $6.00

#6221N
Retail $6.00

#6223
Retail $7.00

#6222
Retail $6.00

#6221
Retail $6.00

#6244
Retail $8.00

#6220
Retail $6.00

Half Pint

11" All vinyl toddler, fully jointed with moving eyes and rooted hair that can be washed and combed.

#6243
Retail $8.00

#6220 — Velveteen suit with white cotton blouse. Shoes and socks.

#6221 — Lace trimmed long gingham checked nitie w/matching panties; shoes.

#6221N — Same as above — NEGRO.

#6222 — Lace trimmed velveteen dress with taffeta panties. Shoes and socks.

#6222N — Same as above — NEGRO.

#6223 — Printed cotton dress, helenca tights and "spats".

#6225 — Eyelet lace pop-over, long cotton overalls and matching bonnet; shoes and socks.

#6243—Dotted organdy party dress, straw hat, helenca stretch tights and "spats".

#6244—Tulle & lace bridal gown w/ cotton slip & panties; net ruffled tiara & bridal veil; satin shoes.

#6225
Retail $7.00

22

1971 Catalog

Frontier Series		Baby dolls, toddlers and girls all dressed in printed calico cotton dresses, aprons and bonnets. All-vinyl and fully-jointed. Rooted hair and sleep eyes.	
1344		*Pun'kin*	11in (27.9cm)
9323		*Little Luv*	14in (35.6cm)
1538		*Chipper*	15in (38.1cm)
1643		*Gum Drop*	16in (40.6cm)
1754		*Miss Chips*	17in (43.2cm)
1824		*Suzie Sunshine*	18in (45.7cm)
9639		*Sugar Plum*	20in (50.8cm)
9984		*Precious Baby*	25in (63.5cm)
Baby Winkie		All-vinyl and fully-jointed baby. Sleep eyes; drinks and wets.	12in (30.5cm)
6132	Molded hair	Dressed in flannel sacque and diaper; wrapped in a blanket.	
6134	Rooted hair	In tricot dress and bonnet.	
Baby Button Nose		Vinyl head and hands; kapok filled body. Sleep eyes; cry voice.	12in (30.5cm)
8122	Rooted hair	Body is covered with gingham checked cotton; dressed in matching pop-over.	
8123	Molded hair	Body is covered with flesh colored cotton; dressed in fleece pajamas.	
Button Nose		Vinyl head and hands; kapok filled body. Molded hair; sleep eyes; cry voice. Baby.	16in (40.6cm)
8331		Dressed in fleece sacque.	
8331B		Same as the above as a black doll.	
Butter Ball		All-vinyl and fully-jointed baby. Sleep eyes; drinks and wets; "coo voice."	13in (33cm)
6551	Molded hair	In lace-trimmed knit dress.	
6592	Molded hair	In cotton bib and diaper.	
6592B	Molded hair	Same as the above as a black doll.	
6553	Rooted hair	In eyelet lace dress.	
6555	Rooted hair	In cotton dress and fleece coat and bonnet.	
6595	Rooted hair	In tricot dress on pillow.	
6595B	Rooted hair	Same as the above as a black doll.	
Fair Baby		All-vinyl and fully-jointed baby. Sleep eyes; "coo voice."	14in (35.6cm)
4442	Molded hair	In fleece bunting, jacket and bonnet.	
4442B	Molded hair	Same as the above as a black doll.	
4443	Rooted hair	Same as No. 4442.	
4443B	Rooted hair	Same as No. 4442B.	

Illustration 215. Frontier Series dolls from the 1971 Effanbee Doll Corporation catalog. The dolls are dressed in printed calico cotton dresses, aprons and bonnets. Courtesy of Al Kirchof.

Illustration 216. The complete line of Miss Chips and Chipper dolls for 1971 from the Effanbee Doll Corporation catalog. Courtesy of Al Kirchof.

Twinkie		All-vinyl and fully-jointed baby. Sleep eyes; drinks and wets; "coo voice."	16in (40.6cm)
2531	Molded hair	Dressed in sacque and diaper.	
2531B	Molded hair	Same as the above as a black doll.	
2533	Rooted hair	In christening dress on crocheted blanket.	
2534	Rooted hair	In christening dress on pillow.	
2534B	Rooted hair	Same as the above as a black doll.	
Dy-Dee Darlin'		All-vinyl and fully-jointed baby. Sleep eyes; drinks and wets.	18in (45.7cm)
5681	Molded hair	In embroidered dress and cap.	
5682	Rooted hair	In crocheted sweater, cap and leggings.	
5683	Rooted hair	In organdy dress.	
Little Luv		Vinyl head, arms and legs; kapok filled body. Sleep eyes; cry voice. Baby.	14in (35.6cm)
9321	Molded hair	In denim overalls and knit shirt.	
9322	Rooted hair	In gingham dress.	
9322B	Rooted hair	Same as the above as a black doll.	
9324	Rooted hair	In organdy dress.	
Sweetie Pie		Vinyl head, arms and legs; kapok filled body. Baby with sleep eyes and cry voice.	17in (43.2cm)
9428	Rooted hair	Crocheted sweater, cap and leggings.	
9429B	Rooted hair	Same as the above as a black doll.	
9431	Molded hair	In long christening dress.	
9442	Rooted hair	In denim jump suit.	
9442B	Rooted hair	Same as the above as a black doll.	
9443	Rooted hair	Pink and blue gingham checked dress.	
9444	Rooted hair	In tricot dress with lace trim.	
9445	Rooted hair	In white bunting with matching jacket and bonnet.	
9447	Rooted hair	In christening dress with crocheted sweater, cap and booties; on organdy pillow.	
9447B	Rooted hair	Same as the above as a black doll.	
Sugar Plum		Vinyl head, arms and legs; kapok filled body. Baby with sleep eyes and cry voice.	20in (50.8cm)
9631	Molded hair	Dressed in long christening gown.	
9631B	Molded hair	Same as the above as a black doll.	
9632	Rooted hair	In flannel pajamas with lace trim.	
9633	Rooted hair	In gingham checked cotton dress.	
9633B	Rooted hair	Same as the above as a black doll.	
9635	Rooted hair	In fleece snowsuit.	
9637	Rooted hair	In organdy dress.	
9638	Rooted hair	In gingham checked dress with pinafore.	

Precious Baby	Vinyl head, arms and legs; kapok filled body. Baby with rooted hair; sleep eyes; "Mama voice."	25in (63.5cm)
9982	In organdy dress.	
9983	In cotton dress and fleece coat with matching bonnet.	
Miss Chips	All-vinyl and fully-jointed girl. Rooted hair; sleep eyes.	17in (43.2cm)
1751	In fleece nightie and organdy cap.	
1752	In long cotton dress with apron and dust cap.	
1753	In long cotton gown.	
1755	In lace bridal gown.	
Chipper	All-vinyl and fully-jointed girl. Rooted hair; sleep eyes.	15in (38.1cm)
1531	In fleece nightie with organdy cap.	
1532	In polka dot pinafore.	
1533	In solid cotton dress.	
1533B	Same as the above as a black doll.	
1534	In printed cotton dress with apron.	
1534B	Same as the above as a black doll.	
1535	In skirt, blouse, bolero jacket and bonnet.	
1539	In eyelet lace bridal gown.	
1539B	Same as the above as a black doll.	
Suzie Sunshine	All-vinyl and fully-jointed toddler. Long rooted hair; sleep eyes.	18in (45.7cm)
1821	In flannel nightgown and holding 8in (20.3cm) baby (*Babykin*) in matching sleeping bag.	
1822	In long "granny gown" and pinafore.	
1823	In long gingham "granny gown" with organdy pinafore.	
Gum Drop	All-vinyl and fully-jointed toddler. Long rooted hair; sleep eyes.	6in (40.6cm)
1642	In long "granny gown" with patchwork pinafore.	
1642B	Same as the above as a black doll.	
Butter Ball in Suitcase	All-vinyl and fully-jointed baby. Rooted hair; sleep eyes.	13in (33cm)
072	Dressed in infant outfit with extra clothing and accessories.	
Pun'kin	All-vinyl and fully-jointed toddler. Rooted hair; sleep eyes.	11in (27.9cm)
1341	In long flannel nightie.	
1341B	Same as the above as a black doll.	
1342	In dotted cotton dress with organdy apron.	
1342B	Same as the above as a black doll.	
1343	In pleated nylon dress.	

Half Pint	All-vinyl and fully-jointed toddler. Rooted hair and sleep eyes.	11in (27.9cm)
6230	Boy in red velveteen suit.	
6230B	Same as the above as black boy with Afro hair.	
6231	Girl with red velveteen jumper.	
6231B	Same as the above as a black doll.	
6232	Wearing cotton nightie.	
6233	In printed cotton dress and straw hat.	
6234	In gingham checked dress with straw hat.	
6234B	Same as the above as a black doll.	
Babykin	All-vinyl and fully-jointed baby. Sleep eyes; drinks and wets.	8in (20.3cm)
2162 Molded hair	Wears long checked dress and cap.	
2164 Molded hair	In fleece jacket and hood in fleece bunting.	
2166 Rooted hair	In checked dress and diaper.	

Illustration 217. The complete line of *Pun'kin and Half Pint* dolls from the 1971 Effanbee Doll Corporation catalog. *Courtesy of Al Kirchof.*

Tiny Tubber		All-vinyl and fully-jointed baby. Sleep eyes; drinks and wets.	11in (27.9cm)
2322	Molded hair	In diaper, sacque and blanket.	
2322B	Molded hair	Same as the above as a black doll.	
2334	Rooted hair	In batiste party dress.	
2334B	Rooted hair	Same as the above as a black doll.	
2335	Rooted hair	In gingham checked dress.	
2335B	Rooted hair	Same as the above as a black doll.	
2336	Molded hair	In cotton christening dress.	
Mickey, the All-American Boy		All-vinyl and fully-jointed. Molded hair; painted eyes.	11in (27.9cm)
721	Molded cap	*Baseball Player.*	
721B	Molded cap	Same as the above as a black doll.	
722	Molded helmet	*Football Player.*	
722B	Molded helmet	Same as the above as a black doll.	
723		*Prize Fighter.*	
723B		Same as the above as a black doll.	
724		*Basketball Player.*	
724B		Same as the above as a black doll.	
725	Molded cap	*Sailor.*	
725B	Molded cap	Same as the above as a black doll.	
Educational Doll		All-vinyl and fully-jointed baby. Water-tight joints; sleep eyes; molded hair. Recommended for "pre-natal education..child care centers and the Red Cross all over the world."	20in (50.8cm)
5700		Dressed in cotton shirt and diaper. Has bottle, spoon, pacifier and Q-tips.	
5700B		Same as the above as a black doll.	

1972 Catalog

Doll	Description	Size
Babykin	All-vinyl and fully-jointed baby. Rooted or molded hair; sleep eyes; drinks and wets.	8in (20.3cm)
Tiny Tubber	All-vinyl and fully-jointed baby. Rooted or molded hair; sleep eyes; drinks and wets.	10in (25.4cm)
Mickey	All-vinyl and fully-jointed boy. Molded hair; painted eyes.	11in (27.9cm)
Pun'kin	All-vinyl and fully-jointed toddler. Rooted hair; sleep eyes.	11in (27.9cm)
Half Pint	All-vinyl and fully-jointed toddler. Rooted hair and sleep eyes.	11in (27.9cm)
Baby Winkie	All-vinyl and fully-jointed baby. Molded hair; sleep eyes; drinks and wets; cry voice.	12in (30.5cm)
Baby Button Nose	Vinyl head and hands; kapok filled body. Molded hair; sleep eyes; cry voice.	12in (30.5cm)
Butter Ball	All-vinyl and fully-jointed baby. Rooted hair; sleep eyes; drinks and wets; cry voice.	13in (33cm)
Fair Baby	All-vinyl and fully-jointed baby. Molded or rooted hair; sleep eyes; drinks and wets; cry voice.	14in (35.6cm)
Sissy	All-vinyl and fully-jointed toddler. Rooted hair; sleep eyes.	14in (35.6cm)
Little Luv	Vinyl head, arms and legs; kapok filled body. Rooted hair; sleep eyes; cry voice. Baby.	14in (35.6cm)
Chipper	All-vinyl and fully-jointed girl. Rooted hair; sleep eyes.	15in (38.1cm)
Twinkie	All-vinyl and fully-jointed baby. Rooted or molded hair; sleep eyes; drinks and wets; cry voice.	16in (40.6cm)
Gum Drop	All-vinyl and fully-jointed girl. Rooted hair; sleep eyes.	16in (40.6cm)
Sweetie Pie	Vinyl head, arms and legs; kapok filled body. Rooted hair; sleep eyes; cry voice.	17in (43.2cm)
Dy Dee Baby	All-vinyl and fully-jointed baby. Rooted hair; sleep eyes; drinks and wets; cry voice.	18in (45.7cm)
Miss Chips	All-vinyl and fully-jointed girl. Rooted hair; sleep eyes.	18in (45.7cm)
Suzie Sunshine	All-vinyl and fully-jointed girl. Rooted hair; sleep eyes.	18in (45.7cm)
Sugar Plum	Vinyl head; arms and legs; kapok stuffed body. Rooted or molded hair; sleep eyes; cry voice.	20in (50.8cm)

Dy Dee Educational Doll	All-vinyl and fully-jointed baby. Molded hair; sleep eyes.	20in (50.8cm)
Precious Baby	Vinyl head, arms and legs; kapok filled body. Rooted hair; sleep eyes; cry voice.	25in (63.5cm)

Party Time Collection

1793	Miss Chips	Embroidered nylon gown; organdy hat.
1593	Chipper	Same as the above.
1593B	Chipper	Same as the above as a black doll.
1592	Chipper	Pleated nylon gown; pleated headpiece.
1792	Miss Chips	Same as the above.
1392	Pun'kin	Dressed as flower girl; same as the above.
1795	Chipper	Organdy and lace bridal gown.
1795B	Chipper	Same as the above as black doll.
1791	Miss Chips	Gingham gown; organdy hat.
1595	Chipper	Organdy and lace bridal gown.
1595B	Chipper	Same as the above as black doll.
1591	Chipper	Gingham gown; organdy hat.

Daffy Dot Collection

All dressed in multi-colored daffy dot cotton print dresses, bonnets and pillows for babies.

1839	Suzie Sunshine	2539	Twinkie
9339	Little Luv	1639	Gum Drop
1739	Miss Chips	6539	Butter Ball
9639	Sugar Plum	1339	Pun'kin
9939	Precious Baby		

Illustration 218. The *Daffy Dot Collection* from the 1972 Effanbee Doll Corporation catalog. Each doll is dressed in multi-colored cotton print dresses, bonnets and has a pillow as shown. *Courtesy of Al Kirchof.*

Pajama Kids Collection

All are dressed in soft printed flannel sleep wear.

1874	*Suzie Sunshine*	9474	*Sweetie Pie*
1374	*Pun'kin*	9474B	*Sweetie Pie* (black)
1374B	*Pun'kin* (black)	2174	*Babykin*
2374	*Tiny Tubber*		

Strawberry Patch Collection

All the dolls are dressed in pink and white gingham
check outfits in strawberry print or "patch" motif.

1611	*Gum Drop*	6511	*Butterball*
9411	*Sweetie Pie*	6511B	*Butterball* (black)
1311	*Pun'kin*	2511	*Twinkie*
1811	*Suzie Sunshine*		

Illustration 219. 8in (20.3cm) *Babykin*, No. 2174, 1972. All-vinyl and fully-jointed with blonde rooted hair and blue sleep eyes. She is from the *Pajama Kids Collection* and is wearing flowered two-piece flannel pajamas. *Patricia N. Schoonmaker Collection. Photograph by John Schoonmaker.*

Illustration 220. Part of the *Baby Classics Collection* from the 1972
Effanbee Doll Corporation catalog. *Courtesy of Al Kirchof.*

Baby Classics Collection

9663	*Sugar Plum*	Fleece snowsuit.
9662	*Sugar Plum*	"Lineen" dress with organdy yoke.
9662B	*Sugar Plum*	Same as the above as a black doll.
9963	*Precious Baby*	Organdy dress with yoke.
9964	*Precious Baby*	Organdy dress; shag coat and hat.
9664	*Sugar Plum*	Dotted swiss dress.
9666	*Sugar Plum*	Cotton dress; pique coat and hat.
9661	*Sugar Plum*	Dotted swiss christening dress.
2566	*Twinkie*	Flocked christening dress; pillow.
2566B	*Twinkie*	Same as the above as a black doll.
2565	*Twinkie*	Diaper set; hand-crocheted blanket.
2561	*Twinkie*	In diaper and fleece blanket.
2561B	*Twinkie*	Same as the above as a black doll.
2567	*Twinkie*	Embroidered christening dress; pillow.
9461	*Sweetie Pie*	In lined bunting.
9464	*Sweetie Pie*	In organdy and gingham dress.
9465	*Sweetie Pie*	In organdy dress; crocheted sweater set.
9465B	*Sweetie Pie*	Same as the above as a black doll.
5665	*Dy Dee Baby*	Three-piece crocheted legging set.
5666	*Dy Dee Baby*	Embroidered organdy dress.
9364	*Little Luv*	"Lineen" dress.
9365	*Little Luv*	Hand-crocheted dress.
9363	*Little Luv*	Snowsuit and hood.
9366	*Little Luv*	Embroidered organdy dress.

Baby Classics Collection continued

9366B	*Little Luv*	Same as the above as a black doll.
4461	*Fair Baby*	Flannel bunting.
4461B	*Fair Baby*	Same as the above as a black doll.
4462	*Fair Baby*	Same as No. 4461, with rooted hair.
1661	*Gum Drop*	Floral flocked dress.
1661B	*Gum Drop*	Same as the above as a black doll.
6561	*Butter Ball*	Floral flocked dress.
6262	*Half Pint*	Velveteen dress (girl).
6262B	*Half Pint*	Same as the above as a black doll.
6261	*Half Pint*	Velveteen suit (boy).
6261B	*Half Pint*	Same as the above as a black doll.
6562	*Butter Ball*	Embroidered dress and pillow.
6562B	*Butter Ball*	Same as the above as a black doll.
6566	*Butter Ball*	Christening dress and pillow.
6263	*Half Pint*	Flocked dress and straw hat.
6565	*Butter Ball*	Two-piece crocheted outfit.
8161	*Baby Button Nose*	Fleece pajamas.
8161B	*Baby Button Nose*	Same as the above as a black doll.
2162	*Babykin*	Gingham infant gown and blanket.
2166	*Babykin*	Gingham checked dress.
2164	*Babykin*	Fleece bunting and hood.
6161	*Baby Winkie*	Diaper set and blanket.
721	*Mickey*	*Baseball Player.*
721B	*Mickey*	Same as the above as a black doll.
725	*Mickey*	*Sailor.*
725B	*Mickey*	Same as the above as a black doll.
723	*Mickey*	*Boxer.*
723B	*Mickey*	Same as the above as a black doll.
722	*Mickey*	*Football Player.*
722B	*Mickey*	Same as the above as a black doll.
2365	*Tiny Tubber*	Hand-crocheted dress and booties.
2362	*Tiny Tubber*	Checked gingham dress.
2362B	*Tiny Tubber*	Same as the above as a black doll.
2363	*Tiny Tubber*	Floral flocked dress.
2361	*Tiny Tubber*	Diaper set and blanket.
2361B	*Tiny Tubber*	Same as the above as a black doll.

Bedtime Story Collection

All the dolls wear bright red sleep wear.

9373	*Little Luv*		1873	*Suzie Sunshine*
1473	*Sissy*		1373	*Pun'kin*
8173	*Baby Button Nose*		6573	*Butter Ball*

Anchors Aweigh Collection

The dolls are dressed in a red, white and blue nautical motif.

1780	*Miss Chips*		8180	*Baby Button Nose*
9680	*Sugar Plum*		1580	*Chipper*
9980	*Precious Baby*			

Illustration 221. 11in (27.9cm) *Half Pint,* No. 6263, from the *Baby Classics Collection,* 1972. All-vinyl and fully-jointed. Brown rooted hair; black pupilless sleep eyes. The dress is a muted flowered design in pale pink and is trimmed with white eyelet. The straw hat and the leotards are white. Head marked: "EFFANBEE // 19 © 66." *Patricia Gardner Collection.*

Special Dolls for 1972

5700	*Dy Dee Educational Doll*	Dressed in cotton shirt and diaper.
5700B	*Dy Dee Educational Doll*	Same as the above as a black doll.
6505	*Butter Ball Layette in Wicker Hamper*	Dressed in organdy christening dress and lies on organdy pillow. Has layette and accessories.
2505	*Twinkie Layette in Wicker Hamper*	Same as the above.
6501	*Butter Ball in Suitcase with Layette*	Dressed in flannel infant outfit with layette and accessories.

1973 Catalog

Doll	Description	Size
Pun'kin	All-vinyl and fully-jointed toddler. Rooted hair; sleep eyes.	11in (27.9cm)
Chipper	All-vinyl and fully-jointed girl. Rooted hair; sleep eyes.	15in (38.1cm)
Miss Chips	All-vinyl and fully-jointed girl. Rooted hair; sleep eyes.	18in (45.7cm)
Suzie Sunshine	All-vinyl and fully-jointed girl. Rooted hair; sleep eyes.	19in (48.3cm)
Babykin	All-vinyl and fully-jointed baby. Rooted or molded hair; sleep eyes; drinks and wets.	9in (22.9cm)
Tiny Tubber	All-vinyl and fully-jointed baby. Rooted or molded hair; sleep eyes; drinks and wets.	11in (27.9cm)
Twinkie	All-vinyl and fully-jointed baby. Rooted or molded hair; sleep eyes; drinks and wets; cry voice.	17in (43.2cm)
Baby Face	All-vinyl and fully-jointed girl. Rooted hair; sleep eyes.	16in (40.6cm)
Sunny	All-vinyl and fully-jointed girl. Rooted or molded hair; sleep eyes.	19in (48.3cm)
Fair Baby	All-vinyl and fully-jointed baby. Rooted or molded hair; sleep eyes; drinks and wets; cry voice.	13in (33cm)
Dy Dee	All-vinyl and fully-jointed baby. Rooted hair; sleep eyes; drinks and wets; cry voice.	18in (45.7cm)
Baby Winkie	All-vinyl and fully-jointed baby. Rooted hair; sleep eyes; drinks and wets; cry voice.	12in (30.5cm)
Half Pint	All-vinyl and fully-jointed toddler. Rooted hair; sleep eyes.	11in (27.9cm)
Buttercup	All-vinyl and fully-jointed toddler. Rooted hair; sleep eyes; drinks and wets; cry voice.	13in (33cm)
Butter Ball	All-vinyl and fully-jointed baby. Rooted or molded hair; sleep eyes; drinks and wets; cry voice.	13in (33cm)
Baby Button Nose	Vinyl head and hands; kapok filled body. Baby. Molded hair; sleep eyes; cry voice.	14in (35.6cm)
Lil' Darlin'	Vinyl head; arms and legs; kapok filled body. Baby. Rooted or molded hair; sleep eyes; cry voice.	13in (33cm)
Little Luv	Vinyl head, arms and legs; kapok filled body. Baby. Rooted hair sleep eyes; cry voice.	15in (38.1cm)

Sweetie Pie	Vinyl head, arms and legs; kapok filled body. Rooted hair; sleep eyes; cry voice. Baby.	18in (45.7cm)
Sugar Plum	Vinyl head, arms and legs; kapok filled body. Rooted or molded hair; sleep eyes; cry voice. Baby.	20in (50.8cm)
Dy Dee Educational Doll	All-vinyl and fully-jointed baby. Molded hair; sleep eyes.	20in (50.8cm)
Precious Baby	Vinyl head, arms and legs; kapok filled body. Rooted hair; sleep eyes; cry voice. Baby.	25in (63.5cm)

Note: The sizes of many of the dolls are listed as different than these same dolls were in previous years.

Bridal Suite Collection

1397	Pun'kin	Ring boy in satin pants.
1398	Pun'kin	Flower girl in embroidered gown.
1399	Pun'kin	Organdy and lace bridal gown.
1399B	Pun'kin	Same as the above as a black doll.
1598	Chipper	Bridesmaid in nylon gown.
1598B	Chipper	Same as the above as a black doll.
1599	Chipper	Organdy and lace bridal gown.
1599B	Chipper	Same as the above as a black doll.
1798	Miss Chips	Bridesmaid in nylon gown.
1798B	Miss Chips	Same as the above as a black doll.
1799	Miss Chips	Organdy and lace bridal gown.
1799B	Miss Chips	Same as the above as a black doll.

Illustration 222. Bridal Suite Collection from the 1973 Effanbee Doll Corporation catalog. In the top row are No. 1798, 18in (45.7cm) Miss Chips; No. 1598, 15in (38.1cm) Chipper; No. 1799, Miss Chips; and No. 1598B, Chipper as a black doll. In the front row are No. 1399B, 11in (27.9cm) Pun'kin as a bride; Pun'kin as a ring boy, No. 1397; No. 1399, Pun'kin as a bride as a white doll; No. 1398 Pun'kin as a flower girl; and No. 1799B 18in (45.7cm) Miss Chips as a black doll dressed as a bride. Courtesy of Patricia N. Schoonmaker.

ABOVE LEFT: Illustration 223. 15in (38.1cm) Chipper, No. 1599B, 1973. All-vinyl and fully-jointed. Black rooted hair; brown sleep eyes with lashes. The bridal gown is white organdy and lace. Patricia Gardner Collection.

ABOVE RIGHT: Illustration 225. Pajama Kids Collection from the 1973 Effanbee Doll Corporation catalog. Each tot is dressed in a soft print flannel sleeping outfit. At the top are No. 1354, 11in (27.9cm) Pun'kin and No. 2654, 16in (40.6cm) Baby Face carrying an 8in (20.3cm) baby in a sleeping bag. In the center row are No. 9354, 15in (38.1cm) Little Luv, No. 6454, 13in (33cm) Buttercup; and No. 5654, 18in (45.7cm) Dydee holding an 8in (20.3cm) baby. In the front row are No. 2154, 9in (22.9cm) Babykin and No. 1354B, 11in (27.9cm) Pun'kin. Courtesy of Patricia N. Schoonmaker.

LEFT: Illustration 224. Over the Rainbow Collection from the 1973 Effanbee Doll Corporation catalog. On the top shelf are No. 9415, 18in (45.7cm) Sweetie Pie and No. 2615, 16in (40.6cm) Baby Face. On the middle shelf are No. 1315, 11in (27.9cm) Pun'kin; No. 9115, 13in (33cm) Lil Darlin' (also called L'il Darlin', Li'l Darlin' and Lil' Darlin'); and No. 1815, 19in (48.3cm) Suzie Sunshine. At the bottom are No. 6115, 12in (30.5cm) Baby Winkie and No.6515, 13in (33cm) Butter Ball (also called Butterball). Each doll is dressed in a checked print cotton dress of pastel pink, blue and lavender. Courtesy of Patricia N. Schoonmaker.

148

Over the Rainbow Collection

All of the dolls wear pastel pink, blue and lavender
costumes.

1315	Pun'kin	6115	Baby Winkie
1815	Suzie Sunshine	6515	Butter Ball
1815B	Suzie Sunshine (black)	9115	Lil Darlin'
2615	Baby Face	9415	Sweetie Pie
2615B	Baby Face (black)		

Highland Fling Collection

All of the dolls are dressed in matching costumes
of red plaid trimmed in organdy.

1377	Pun'kin	6577	Butter Ball
1777	Miss Chips	9377	Little Luv
1877	Suzie Sunshine	9677	Sugar Plum
2677	Baby Face		

Crochet Classics Collection

All of the dolls are wearing hand-crocheted outfits.

2375	Tiny Tubber	6275	Half Pint
2875	Sunny	6575	Butter Ball
4475	Fair Baby	9375	Little Luv
4475B	Fair Baby (black)	9475	Sweetie Pie
4675	Dydee (sic)	9475B	Sweetie Pie (black)

Sweet Nostalgia Collection

All of the dolls are wearing long dresses of pastel
prints trimmed in ruffles.

1333	Pun'kin	2633	Baby Face
1833	Suzie Sunshine	9333	Little Luv
2533	Twinkie		

Baby Classics Collection

9441	Sweetie Pie	In patchwork check dress.
9441B	Sweetie Pie	Same as the above as a black doll.
9442	Sweetie Pie	In plaid and organdy dress.
9641	Sugar Plum	Striped infant dress.
9641B	Sugar Plum	Same as the above as a black doll.
9642	Sugar Plum	Multi-colored gingham dress.
9642B	Sugar Plum	Same as the above as a black doll.
9643	Sugar Plum	Organdy dress with gingham trim.
9645	Sugar Plum	Striped dress; knit hat and coat.
9941	Precious Baby	Striped pants; white cotton blouse.
9942	Precious Baby	Plaid baby dress.

Baby Classics Collection continued from page 149.

6541	*Butter Ball*	In diaper and fleece blanket.
6541B	*Butter Ball*	Same as the above as a black doll.
6542	*Butter Ball*	Plaid baby dress.
6543	*Butter Ball*	Lace-trimmed gingham dress; on pillow.
6543B	*Butter Ball*	Same as the above as a black doll.
9341	*Little Luv*	Lace-trimmed gingham dress.
9341B	*Little Luv*	Same as the above as a black doll.
9342	*Little Luv*	Fleece snowsuit and hood.
9343	*Little Luv*	Fleece bunting with plaid trim.
9344	*Little Luv*	Gingham dress with embroidery.
9345	*Little Luv*	Striped dress; knit hat and coat.
2541	*Twinkie*	In diaper and fleece blanket.
2541B	*Twinkie*	Same as the above as a black doll.
2542	*Twinkie*	In striped infant dress.
2543	*Twinkie*	Crepe christening dress; on pillow.
9141	*Lil' Darlin'*	Cotton christening dress with nylon trim.
9142	*Lil' Darlin'*	Patchwork check dress.
9143	*Lil' Darlin'*	Striped dress.
9143B	*Lil' Darlin'*	Same as the above as a black doll.
9144	*Lil' Darlin'*	In plaid baby dress.
1541	*Chipper*	In patchwork check dress.
1841	*Suzie Sunshine*	In patchwork check dress.
1841B	*Suzie Sunshine*	Same as the above as a black doll.
2645	*Baby Face*	Striped dress; knit coat; straw hat.
2645B	*Baby Face*	Same as the above as a black doll.
2841	*Sunny*	In striped pants; cotton blouse; bonnet.
4441	*Fair Baby*	In nylon christening dress on pillow.
4441B	*Fair Baby*	Same as the above as a black doll.
6141	*Baby Winkie*	In lace-trimmed flannel bunting.
6141B	*Baby Winkie*	Same as the above as a black doll.
6142	*Baby Winkie*	Same as No. 6141 with rooted hair.
6143	*Baby Winkie*	In nylon christening dress on pillow.
6145	*Baby Winkie*	In long dress; long coat; bonnet; on pillow.
6445	*Buttercup*	In striped dress; knit coat and bonnet.
1341	*Pun'kin*	In patchwork check dress.
1341B	*Pun'kin*	Same as the above as a black doll.
2141	*Babykin*	In gingham gown and blanket.
2142	*Babykin*	In fleece bunting and hood.
2143	*Babykin*	In gingham dress.
2341	*Tiny Tubber*	In diaper and knit blanket.
2341B	*Tiny Tubber*	Same as the above as a black doll.
2342	*Tiny Tubber*	In infant dress and bonnet on pillow.
2342B	*Tiny Tubber*	Same as the above as a black doll.
2343	*Tiny Tubber*	In bunting with diaper and hood.
2343B	*Tiny Tubber*	Same as the above as a black doll.
2344	*Tiny Tubber*	In lace-trimmed dress.
2344B	*Tiny Tubber*	Same as the above as a black doll.

6241	*Half Pint*	In multi-colored gingham dress.
6241B	*Half Pint*	Same as the above as a black doll.
6242	*Half Pint*	In plaid dress and bonnet.
8141	*Baby Button Nose*	In fleece pajamas.

Candy Land Collection

Each doll is dressed in a red and white striped dress.

1322	*Pun'kin*	6422	*Buttercup*
1522	*Chipper*	6522	*Butter Ball*
1722	*Miss Chips*	9322	*Little Luv*

Pajama Kids Collection

Each doll is wearing print flannel night wear.

1354	*Pun'kin*	5654	*Dydee* (with *Babykin*)
1354B	*Pun'kin* (black)	6454	*Buttercup*
2154	*Babykin*	9354	*Little Luv*
2654	*Baby Face* (with *Babykin*)	9354B	*Little Luv* (black)

Travel Time Collection

Each doll has extra clothing, a layette and accessories.
   Twinkie and *Baby Winkie* are in a wicker hamper;
   Butter Ball is in a suitcase.

2506	*Twinkie*
6106	*Baby Winkie*
6506	*Butter Ball* Crocheted carriage blanket and organdy pillow only.

| 5700 | *Dy Dee Educational Doll* Dressed in cotton shirt and diaper. |
| 5700B | *Dy Dee Educational Doll* Same as the above as a black doll. |

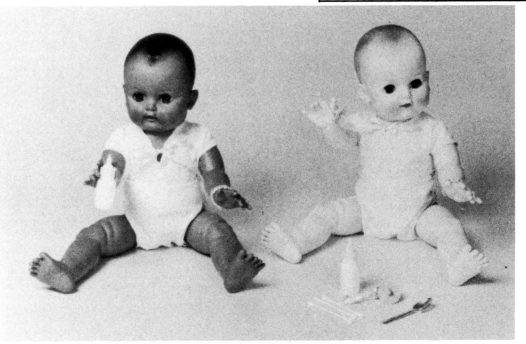

Illustration 226. 20in (50.8cm) *Dy Dee Educational Doll* from the 1973 Effanbee Doll Corporation catalog. All-vinyl and fully-jointed with air-tight joints and valves. Molded hair; sleep eyes with lashes. This doll was offered from 1971 to 1976 as "the perfect doll for pre-natal education and is being used by child-care centers and the Red Cross all over the world." The doll could drink from her bottle or be spoon-fed "just like a real baby." *Courtesy of Patricia N. Schoonmaker.*

1974 Catalog

The basic dolls were the same as they were in 1973, except that the following were discontinued:

19in (48.3cm) *Sunny*
13in (33cm) *Fair Baby*
13in (33cm) *Buttercup*
25in (63.5cm) *Precious Baby*

Bridal Suite Collection

1386	*Pun'kin*	Ring boy in velveteen pants.
1387	*Pun'kin*	Flower girl in organdy gown.
1587	*Chipper*	Bridesmaid in organdy gown.
1587B	*Chipper*	Same as the above as a black doll.
1588	*Chipper*	Bride in organdy gown.
1588B	*Chipper*	Same as the above as a black doll.
1787	*Miss Chips*	Bridesmaid in organdy gown.
1788	*Miss Chips*	Bride in organdy gown.
1788B	*Miss Chips*	Same as the above as a black doll.

Illustration 227. 18in (45.7cm) *Miss Chips* bride as a black doll. All-vinyl and fully-jointed. Dark brown rooted hair; brown sleep eyes with lashes. The white bridal gown is organdy and lace. This doll is part of the *Bridal Suite Collection* of 1974. Head marked: "EFFANBEE // 19 © 65 // 1700." *Patricia Gardner Collection.*

OPPOSITE PAGE: Illustration 228. From the 1974 *Bridal Suite Collection:* No. 1386, 11in (27.9cm) *Pun'kin* as the ring boy. All-vinyl and fully-jointed. Red rooted hair; green sleep eyes with molded lashes; freckles on the cheeks. The pants and the pillow are rust colored velveteen. The shirt is white organdy and is trimmed with lace, as is the pillow, which holds a "gold" ring. The white shoes are cloth with a satin finish. Head marked: "EFFANBEE // 19 © 66."

I AM
Pun'kin
An
EFFANBEE
DURABLE
DOLL

Enchanted Garden Collection

All of the dolls are dressed in a pastel floral print
trimmed with organdy and lace.

1059	A child's pillow that matches the doll costumes.	12in (30.5cm) x 12in (30.5cm)

1359	*Pun'kin*	6559	*Butter Ball*
1559	*Chipper*	9159	*Li'l Darlin'*
1859	*Suzie Sunshine*	9459	*Sweetie Pie*
2559	*Twinkie*		

Carousel Collection

All of the dolls are dressed in white gowns
trimmed with a bright multi-colored stripe
that is printed on the bias.

1349	*Pun'kin*	1749	*Miss Chips*
2649	*Baby Face*	1849	*Suzie Sunshine*
9349	*Little Luv*	9649	*Sugar Plum*

Charming Checks Collection

Each doll, except *Baby Winkie*, is dressed in a pale
pink or blue checked gingham gown with an embroidered
white apron. *Baby Winkie* is on a gingham pillow.

1018	A child's pillow that matches the collection. One side is pink; the other side is blue.	12in (30.5cm) x 12in (30.5cm)

1318	*Pun'kin*	2618B	*Baby Face* (black)
1818	*Suzie Sunshine*	6118	*Baby Winkie*
1818B	*Suzie Sunshine* (black)	6518	*Butter Ball*
2618	*Baby Face*	9418	*Sweetie Pie*

Country Cousins Collection

Each doll is dressed in a bright cotton dress that
has the "country look."

1005	A child's pillow that matches the collection. One side is a red print; the other is blue.	12in (30.5cm) x 12in (30.5cm)

1305	*Pun'kin*	6505	*Butter Ball*
1705	*Miss Chips*	9305	*Little Luv*
1805	*Suzie Sunshine*	9605	*Sugar Plum*
2605	*Baby Face*		

Baby Classics Collection

2523	*Twinkie*	In diaper set and blanket.
2523B	*Twinkie*	Same as the above as a black doll.
2524	*Twinkie*	Infant dress with pink lace.
2525	*Twinkie*	In lace-trimmed fleece bunting.

Carousel Collection

These darling young ladies attired in their eye appealing swirl dresses with brilliant, flashing multi-colors, offset by gleaming white are reminiscent of the whirling Carousel.

Illustration 229. The *Carousel Collection* from the 1974 Effanbee Doll Corporation catalog. Each of the young ladies wears a dress that is white organdy with a bright striped panel trim. At the top are: No. 1849, 19in (48.3cm) *Suzie Sunshine;* No. 2649, 16in (40.6cm) *Baby Face;* and No. 1749, 18in (45.7cm) *Miss Chips.* On the bottom are: No. 1349, 11in (27.9cm) *Pun'kin;* No. 9649, 20in (50.8cm) *Sugar Plum;* and No. 9349, 15in (40.6cm) *Little Luv. Courtesy of Patricia N. Schoonmaker.*

Country Cousins Collection

EFFANBEE, the fashion leader of the doll industry is right up to date with this popular collection that is today's rage. . . the country look. Return to those wonderful days of hay rides, square dances and the easy country life with these lovely lasses.

Illustration 230. The *Country Cousins Collection* from the 1974 Effanbee Doll Corporation catalog. Each doll wears a multi-colored costume. At the top are No. 9305, 15in (38.1cm) *Little Luv;* No. 1705, 18in (45.7cm) *Miss Chips;* and No. 9605, 20in (50.8cm) *Sugar Plum.* At the bottom are No. 1805, 19in (48.3cm) *Suzie Sunshine;* No. 1305, 11in (27.9cm) *Pun'kin;* No. 6505, 13in (33cm) *Butter Ball;* and No. 2605, 16in (40.6cm) *Baby Face. Courtesy of Patricia N. Schoonmaker.*

Illustration 231. Part of the *Baby Classics Collection* from the 1974 Effanbee Doll Corporation catalog. On the top shelf are No. 1324, 11in (27.9cm) *Pun'kin* and No. 1323, *Pun'kin*. On the middle shelf are No. 2624, 16in (40.6cm) *Baby Face*; No. 6525, 13in (33cm) *Butter Ball*; No. 1823, 19in (48.3cm) *Suzie Sunshine*; No. 8124, 14in (35.6cm) *Baby Button Nose*; and No. 2623, 16in (40.6cm) *Baby Face*. In front are No. 9326, 15in (38.1cm) *Little Luv*, No. 6223B, 11in (27.9cm) *Half Pint*; No. 6224, *Half Pint*; No. 6223 *Half Pint*; and No. 9324, 15in (38.1cm) *Little Luv*. The dolls at the left wear plaid coats and straw hats. The dolls at the top and right wear lace-trimmed multi-colored dresses. *Courtesy of Patricia N. Schoonmaker.*

Baby Classics Collection continued from page 154

2526	*Twinkie*	In infant dress on pillow.
2526B	*Twinkie*	Same as the above as a black doll.
9623	*Sugar Plum*	In organdy dress with pink lace.
9623B	*Sugar Plum*	Same as the above as a black doll.
9624	*Sugar Plum*	In embroidered dress and bonnet.
6123	*Baby Winkie*	In lace-trimmed fleece bunting.
6123B	*Baby Winkie*	Same as the above as a black doll.
6124	*Baby Winkie*	Same as No. 6123 with rooted hair.
6523	*Butter Ball*	In diaper set and blanket.
6523B	*Butter Ball*	Same as the above as a black doll.
6524	*Butter Ball*	In lace-trimmed dress.
6524B	*Butter Ball*	Same as the above as a black doll.
9323	*Little Luv*	In check dress with rickrack trim.
9323B	*Little Luv*	Same as the above as a black doll.
9325	*Little Luv*	In fleece snowsuit and hood.
9423	*Sweetie Pie*	In dimity infant dress.
9423B	*Sweetie Pie*	Same as the above as a black doll.
9424	*Sweetie Pie*	In check dress with rickrack trim.
9424B	*Sweetie Pie*	Same as the above as a black doll.
9425	*Sweetie Pie*	In dimity dress and bonnet.
1323	*Pun'kin*	In long multi-colored dress.
1323B	*Pun'kin*	Same as the above as a black doll.
1324	*Pun'kin*	In plaid pleated dress; straw hat.
1823	*Suzie Sunshine*	In long multi-colored dress.
1823B	*Suzie Sunshine*	Same as the above as a black doll.
2623	*Baby Face*	In long multi-colored dress.
2623B	*Baby Face*	Same as the above as a black doll.
2624	*Baby Face*	In plaid coat, straw hat and dress.
6223	*Half Pint*	In checked dress.
6223B	*Half Pint*	Same as the above as a black doll.
6224	*Half Pint*	In ballerina outfit.

6224B	*Half Pint*	Same as the above as a black doll.
6525	*Butter Ball*	In plaid coat, straw hat and dress.
8124	*Baby Button Nose*	Multi-colored body with matching top.
9324	*Little Luv*	In multi-colored dress.
9326	*Little Luv*	In plaid coat, straw hat and dress.
2123	*Babykin*	In infant gown and blanket.
2124	*Babykin*	In fleece bunting and hood.
2125	*Babykin*	In dimity dress.
2323	*Tiny Tubber*	In diaper set and fleece blanket.
2323B	*Tiny Tubber*	Same as the above as a black doll.
2324	*Tiny Tubber*	In infant dress and bonnet on pillow.
2324B	*Tiny Tubber*	Same as the above as a black doll.
2325	*Tiny Tubber*	In fleece bunting with dimity lining.
2325B	*Tiny Tubber*	Same as the above as a black doll.
2326	*Tiny Tubber*	In dimity dress.
2326B	*Tiny Tubber*	Same as the above as a black doll.
8123	*Baby Button Nose*	In fleece pajamas.
8123B	*Baby Button Nose*	Same as the above as a black doll.
9123	*Lil' Darlin'*	In infant dress with pink lace.
9123B	*Lil' Darlin'*	Same as the above as a black doll.
9124	*Lil' Darlin'*	In white and check dress.
9124B	*Lil' Darlin'*	Same as the above as a black doll.

Pajama Kids Collection

Each doll is dressed in sleep wear with a white top
and red bottom.

1357	*Pun'kin*	2657	*Baby Face*
1357B	*Pun'kin* (black)	6157	*Baby Winkie*
1557	*Chipper*	9157	*Lil' Darlin'*
2357	*Tiny Tubber*		

Crochet Classics Collection

All of the dolls are wearing hand-crocheted outfits.

2379	*Tiny Tubber*	6579B	*Butter Ball* (black)
5679	*Dydee*	9379	*Little Luv*
6279	*Half Pint*	9379B	*Little Luv* (black)
6578	*Butter Ball*	9479	*Sweetie Pie*
6579	*Butter Ball*	9479B	*Sweetie Pie*

Travel Time Collection

Each doll has extra clothing, a layette and accessories.
Twinkie and *Baby Winkie* are in a wicker hamper;
Butter Ball is in a suitcase.

2509	*Twinkie*	6109	*Baby Winkie*	6509	*Butter Ball*

1079   Carriage blanket and organdy pillow (doll not included).

5700	*Dy Dee Educational Doll*	20in (50.8cm)
5700B	*Dy Dee Educational Doll* (black)	20in (50.8cm)

1975 Catalog

The basic dolls are the same as 1974, with the following additions:

Doll	Description	Size
Floppy	Vinyl head; cloth body girl. Rooted hair; sleep eyes.	21in (53.3cm)
Pint Size	Vinyl head; cloth body baby. Molded hair; sleep eyes.	14in (35.6cm)
Lovums	Vinyl head, arms and legs; cloth body. Baby. Molded hair; sleep eyes; cry voice. Also with vinyl head and arms; gingham body.	18in (45.7cm)

18in (45.7cm) *Dy Dee* was not used in 1975; she returned in 1976.

Lovums Collection

This collection is the *Lovums* doll, a "newborn cutie," in different outfits.

8451	Gingham body. Dressed in lace-trimmed gingham dress.
8452	In infant dress.
8452B	Same as the above as a black doll.
8453	In sleeper and fleece blanket.
8453B	Same as the above as a black doll.
8454	In lace-trimmed fleece bunting.
8455	In dimity infant dress and bonnet.
8455B	Same as the above as a black doll.
8456	Same as No. 8455 on a pillow.

Illustration 232. 11in (27.9cm) *Pun'kin* from *Granny's Corner Collection*, No. 1366, 1975. All-vinyl and fully-jointed. Blonde rooted hair; blue sleep eyes with molded lashes. The old-fashioned dress is a cotton paisley print. She has pantaloons and wears a lace-trimmed dust cap. Head marked: "EFFANBEE // 19 © 66."

Granny's Corner Collection

All of the dolls, except the *Pun'kin* boy, are dressed in
an old-fashioned paisley print dress. The *Pun'kin* boy
(No. 1365) is dressed in velveteen pants, a lace-trimmed
shirt and a velveteen cap.

1365	*Pun'kin* (boy)	2566	*Twinkie*
1366	*Pun'kin*	6566	*Butter Ball*
1566	*Chipper*	9366	*Little Luv*
1766	*Miss Chips*	9666	*Sugar Plum*
1866	*Suzie Sunshine*		

Crochet Classics Collection

All of the dolls are dressed in "hand-knit" outfits.

1372	*Pun'kin*	6571	*Butter Ball*
2372	*Tiny Tubber*	6571B	*Butter Ball* (black)
2372B	*Tiny Tubber* (black)	6572	*Butter Ball* (in bunting)
2572	*Twinkie*	9172	*Lil' Darlin'*
2572B	*Twinkie* (black)	9372	*Little Luv*
6272	*Half Pint*	9472	*Sweetie Pie*
6272B	*Half Pint* (black)	9472B	*Sweetie Pie* (black)

Illustration 233. The Bridal Suite Collection from the 1975 Effanbee Doll Corporation catalog. At the top are No. 1583B, 15in (38.1cm) Chipper; No. 1782, 18in (45.7cm) Miss Chips as a bridesmaid in a lace-trimmed pink taffeta dress; and No. 1783, 18in (45.7cm) Miss Chips as a bride in organdy and lace. In front are No. 1582, 15in (38.1cm) Chipper as a bridesmaid that matches Miss Chips; No. 1583, Chipper as a bride; No. 1383, 11in (27.9cm) Pun'kin as a flower girl in a gown that matches that of the bridesmaids; and Pun'kin as the ring boy. Courtesy of Patricia N. Schoonmaker.

Bridal Suite Collection

1382	*Pun'kin*	Ring boy in velveteen pants and taffeta shirt.
1383	*Pun'kin*	Flower girl in taffeta dress.
1582	*Chipper*	In lace-trimmed taffeta dress and hat.
1582B	*Chipper*	Same as the above as a black doll.
1583	*Chipper*	In organdy and lace bridal gown.
1583B	*Chipper*	Same as the above as a black doll.
1782	*Miss Chips*	In lace-trimmed taffeta dress and hat.
1783	*Miss Chips*	In organdy and lace bridal gown.
1783B	*Miss Chips*	Same as the above as a black doll.

Baby Classics Collection

9352	*Little Luv*	In organdy and dimity print dress.
9352B	*Little Luv*	Same as the above as a black doll.
9353	*Little Luv*	In striped dimity dress and bonnet.
9354	*Little Luv*	In batiste dress and bonnet.
9452	*Sweetie Pie*	In organdy and dimity print dress.
9453	*Sweetie Pie*	In striped dimity dress and bonnet.
9453B	*Sweetie Pie*	Same as the above as a black doll.
9454	*Sweetie Pie*	In batiste dress and bonnet.
9652	*Sugar Plum*	In organdy and dimity print dress.
9653	*Sugar Plum*	In striped dimity dress and bonnet.
9654	*Sugar Plum*	In batiste dress and bonnet.
2551	*Twinkie*	In diaper set and fleece blanket.
2551B	*Twinkie*	Same as the above as a black doll.
2552	*Twinkie*	In diaper set and ruffled fleece blanket.
2553	*Twinkie*	In infant dress.
2553B	*Twinkie*	Same as the above as a black doll.
2554	*Twinkie*	In fleece bunting.
2555	*Twinkie*	In infant dress and bonnet; on pillow.
9151	*Lil' Darlin'*	Gingham body. In gingham shortie dress.
9151B	*Lil' Darlin'*	Same as the above as a black doll.
9152	*Lil' Darlin'*	In infant dress.
9152B	*Lil' Darlin'*	Same as the above as a black doll.
9351	*Little Luv*	Gingham body. In white organdy dress.
1351	*Pun'kin*	In long dimity print dress.
1551	*Chipper*	In long dimity print dress.
1551B	*Chipper*	Same as the above as a black doll.
1751	*Miss Chips*	In long dimity print dress.
1851	*Suzie Sunshine*	In long dimity print dress.
1851B	*Suzie Sunshine*	Same as the above as a black doll.
2651	*Baby Face*	In long dimity print dress.
2651B	*Baby Face*	Same as the above as a black doll.
6551	*Butter Ball*	In diaper set and fleece blanket.
6551B	*Butter Ball*	Same as the above as a black doll.

Illustration 234. 9in (22.9cm) *Babykin*, No. 2152, 1975, from the *Baby Classics Collection*. All-vinyl and fully-jointed. Painted hair; blue sleep eyes with molded lashes; open mouth nurser. She wears a diaper, a hooded pink flannel jacket and is in a pink flannel bunting. Head marked: "EFFANBEE" with two indiscernible lines following.

6552	*Butter Ball*	In dimity print dress and bonnet.
6553	*Butter Ball*	In diaper set and ruffled blanket.
2151	*Babykin*	In dimity print infant gown.
2152	*Babykin*	In fleece bunting and hood.
2153	*Babykin*	In dimity print dress.
2351	*Tiny Tubber*	In diaper set and fleece blanket.
2351B	*Tiny Tubber*	Same as the above as a black doll.
2352	*Tiny Tubber*	In dimity print infant dress and bonnet; on a pillow.
2353	*Tiny Tubber*	In fleece bunting.
2354	*Tiny Tubber*	In dimity print dress.
2354B	*Tiny Tubber*	Same as the above as a black doll.
6151	*Baby Winkie*	In fleece bunting.
6151B	*Baby Winkie*	Same as the above as a black doll.
6152	*Baby Winkie*	Same as No. 6151 with rooted hair.
6152B	*Baby Winkie*	Same as No. 6151B with rooted hair.
6251	*Half Pint*	In dimity print dress.
6251B	*Half Pint*	Same as the above as a black doll.
6252	*Half Pint*	In ballerina outfit.

Half Pints Collection

This collection features *Half Pint,* the 11in (27.9cm) toddler in four costumes. All the dolls have velvet shoes with spats.

6253	In embroidered dress with straw hat.
6254	In gingham dress and cap.
6255	In jersey dress and straw hat.
6272	In hand-crocheted jacket and hood with muff; worn over leotards.
6272B	Same as the above as a black doll.

Illustration 236. The *Duck Duck Goose Collection* from the 1975 Effanbee Doll Corporation catalog. At the top are No. 1828, 19in (48.3cm) *Suzie Sunshine;* No. 1328, 11in (27.9cm) *Pun'kin;* No. 2628, 16in (40.6cm) *Baby Face;* and No. 9428 (seated), 18in (45.7cm) *Sweetie Pie.* In front are No. 9328, 15in (38.1cm) *Little Luv;* No. 2628B, *Baby Face;* No. 2528, 17in (43.2cm) *Twinkie;* and No. 6528, 13in (33cm) *Butter Ball.* Each child is dressed in a pique and organdy dress that is embroidered with a picture of a duck, followed by another duck and then a goose. *Courtesy of Patricia N. Schoonmaker.*

Illustration 235. 11in (27.9cm) *Half Pint,* No. 6253, 1975. All-vinyl and fully-jointed. Dark brown rooted hair; black pupilless sleep eyes. She wears a white embroidered dress and straw hat. The ribbons are a cranberry color. *Marjorie Smith Collection.*

Pajama Kids Collection

Each doll is dressed in soft pink sleep wear trimmed in white. *Suzie Sunshine* (No. 1856 and 1856B) carries a teddy bear.

1356	*Pun'kin*	2656	*Baby Face*
1356B	*Pun'kin* (black)	6556	*Butter Ball*
1856	*Suzie Sunshine*	9356	*Little Luv*
1856B	*Suzie Sunshine* (black)	9656B	*Little Luv* (black)
2356	*Tiny Tubber*		

Americana Collection

Each doll is dressed in pink or blue gingham and has a white embroidered apron.

1319	*Pun'kin*	2619	*Baby Face*
1319B	*Pun'kin* (black)	6519	*Butter Ball*
1519	*Chipper*	6519B	*Butter Ball* (black)
1819	*Suzie Sunshine*	9319	*Little Luv*
1819B	*Suzie Sunshine* (black)	9619	*Sugar Plum*
		9619B	*Sugar Plum* (black)

162

Travel Time Collection

Each doll has extra clothing, a layette and accessories. *Tiny Tubber*, *Twinkie* and *Butter Ball* are in a wicker hamper; *Baby Winkie* is in a checked suitcase.

2308	*Tiny Tubber*	6108	*Baby Winkie*
2508	*Twinkie*	6508	*Butter Ball*

Duck Duck Goose Collection

Each doll is dressed in a cotton dress with ducks and geese embroidered on the skirt.

1328	*Pun'kin*	6528	*Butter Ball*
1828	*Suzie Sunshine*	9328	*Little Luv*
2528	*Twinkie*	9328B	*Little Luv* (black)
2628	*Baby Face*	9428	*Sweetie Pie*
2628B	*Baby Face* (black)		

Illustration 237. 16in (40.6cm) Baby Face as a black doll, No. 2628B, 1975. All-vinyl and fully-jointed. Dark brown rooted hair; brown sleep eyes with lashes. Head marked: "EFFANBEE // 19 © 67 // 2600." Patricia Gardner Collection.

Ragamuffins Collection

Each doll has a vinyl head and the entire body is stuffed cloth.

8151	*Baby Button Nose*	In pajamas and cap.
8151B	*Baby Button Nose*	Same as the above as a black doll.
8152	*Baby Button Nose*	In shortie dress.
8152B	*Baby Button Nose*	Same as the above as a black doll.
8153	*Baby Button Nose*	In gingham dress and bonnet.
8153B	*Baby Button Nose*	Same as the above as a black doll.
6351	*Pint Size*	In gingham shortie dress.
6352	*Pint Size*	In lace-trimmed dress and straw hat.
6353	*Pint Size*	In dress and cap with velvet trim.
2751	*Floppy*	In multi-colored print dress with matching body.
2752	*Floppy*	In embroidered dress with gingham trim; gingham hat; gingham body.
2753	*Floppy*	In dress, cap and pantaloons. Natural color body.

5700	*Dy Dee Educational Doll*	20in (50.8cm)
5700B	*Dy Dee Educational Doll* (black)	20in (50.8cm)

163

1976 Catalog

Beginning in 1976 the Effanbee Doll Corporation began to use standard basic dolls for several characters. This was the first time the company did this since the 1940s. The first example of this in vinyl was 11in (27.9cm) *Caroline*, who was used for the *International Collection*, the *Historical Collection*, the *Four Seasons Collection* and the *Regal Heirloom Collection*.

The basic dolls are the same as 1975 with the following addition:

Doll	Description	Size
Caroline	All-vinyl and fully-jointed. (Used as both a girl and a boy.) Rooted hair; sleep eyes with plastic molded lashes.	11in (27.9cm)

The following chart shows which doll was used for various "collections." The numbers are the first two digits in the four digit doll number.

Prefix Number	Doll	(See 1973 and 1975 catalog for description.)
11	*Caroline*	(For example, No. 1109 is *Miss Spain.*)
13	*Pun'kin*	
15	*Chipper*	
17	*Miss Chips*	
18	*Suzie Sunshine*	
21	*Babykin*	
23	*Tiny Tubber*	
25	*Twinkie*	
26	*Baby Face*	
27	*Floppy*	
56	*Dy Dee*	
57	*Dy Dee Educational Doll*	
61	*Baby Winkie*	
62	*Half Pint*	
63	*Pint Size*	
65	*Butter Ball*	
81	*Baby Button Nose*	
84	*Lovums*	
91	*Lil' Darlin'*	
93	*Little Luv*	
94	*Sweetie Pie*	
96	*Sugar Plum*	

Illustration 238. 11in (27.9cm) *Miss Ireland,* No. 1105, 1976. All-vinyl and fully-jointed. Rooted red hair; blue sleep eyes with molded lashes. The dress is bright green. Head marked: "EFFANBEE // 19 © 75 // 1176." *Agnes Smith Collection.*

Illustration 239. 11in (27.9cm) *Paul Revere,* No. 1151 of the *Historical Collection,* 1976. All-vinyl and fully-jointed. Dark brown rooted hair; blue sleep eyes with molded lashes. Head marked: "EFFANBEE // 19 © 75 // 1176." *Marjorie Smith Collection.*

International Collection

1101	*Miss U.S.A.*	1106	*Miss Italy*
1102	*Miss France*	1107	*Miss Poland*
1103	*Miss Germany*	1108	*Miss Scotland*
1104	*Miss Holland*	1109	*Miss Spain*
1105	*Miss Ireland*		

Historical Collection

1151	*Paul Revere*
1152	*Betsy Ross*
1153	*Martha Washington*

Bridal Suite Collection

1185	*Caroline*	Dressed in organdy bridal gown.
1384	*Pun'kin*	Ring boy in velveteen pants; taffeta shirt.
1385	*Pun'kin*	Flower girl in flocked sheer gown.

1584	*Chipper*	Bridesmaid in flocked sheer gown.
1584B	*Chipper*	Same as the above as a black doll.
1585	*Chipper*	Dressed in organdy bridal gown.
1585B	*Chipper*	Same as the above as a black doll.
1784	*Miss Chips*	Bridesmaid in flocked sheer gown.
1785	*Miss Chips*	Dressed in organdy bridal gown.

Granny's Corner Collection

All of the dolls, except the *Pun'kin* boy are dressed in
an old-fashioned paisley print dress. The *Pun'kin* boy
(No. 1365) is dressed in velveteen pants, a lace-trimmed
shirt and a velveteen cap.

1365*	*Pun'kin* (boy)		2723	*Floppy*
1366*	*Pun'kin*		6323	*Pint Size*
1566*	*Chipper*		9366*	*Little Luv*
1766*	*Miss Chips*		9666*	*Sugar Plum*
1866*	*Suzie Sunshine*			

Baby Face Collection

This collection features 16in (40.6cm) *Baby Face*,
a toddler, in three different designs.

2621	In velveteen dress with matching hat; pantaloons.
2622	Wears two-tiered embroidered dress with matching cap.
2623	Wears a floral print dress with a white apron.

Four Seasons Collection

This is a portion of the *Grandes Dames Collection*.
It is 11in (27.9cm) *Caroline* in four seasonal cotumes.

1131	*Spring*	Organdy blouse; long ruffled skirt; straw hat.
1132	*Summer*	Ruffled lace-trimmed organdy dress; matching hat.
1133	*Autumn*	Velveteen coat dress with pleated underskirt; matching bonnet.
1134	*Winter*	Lace dress with velveteen cape and hood; scarf and muff.

Grandes Dames Collection

This collection is six models in fancy gowns and hats.
(See chart on page 164 for the dolls used.)

1531	*Peaches and Cream*	Ruffled organdy dress.
1533	*Southern Belle*	Lace-trimmed gingham dress.
1534	*Ma Chere*	Taffeta dress with knife-pleated ruffles.

*Identical to 1975.

1731	*Victorian Lady*	In velveteen ball gown.
1733	*Mint Julep*	In taffeta dress with tiers of lace.
1734	*Mam'selle*	In velveteen coat over lace-trimmed dress.

Baby Classics Collection

9321	*Little Luv*	In organdy and floral print dress.
9321B	*Little Luv*	Same as the above as a black doll.
9322	*Little Luv*	In organdy dress with lace trim.
9421	*Sweetie Pie*	In organdy and floral print dress.
9421B	*Sweetie Pie*	Same as the above as a black doll.
9422	*Sweetie Pie*	In organdy dress with lace trim.
9621	*Sugar Plum*	In organdy and floral print dress.
9621B	*Sugar Plum*	Same as the above as a black doll.
9622	*Sugar Plum*	In organdy dress with lace trim.
2521	*Twinkie*	In diaper set with fleece blanket.
2521B	*Twinkie*	Same as the above as a black doll.
2522	*Twinkie*	In diaper set with fleece blanket.
2523	*Twinkie*	In infant dress with lace trim.
2523B	*Twinkie*	Same as the above as a black doll.
2524	*Twinkie*	In organdy infant dress on pillow.
6121	*Baby Winkie*	In lace-trimmed fleece bunting.
6121B	*Baby Winkie*	Same as the above as a black doll.
6122	*Baby Winkie*	In lace-trimmed fleece bunting.
9121	*Lil' Darlin'*	In infant dress with lace trim.
9121B	*Lil' Darlin'*	Same as the above as a black doll.
1321	*Pun'kin*	In long flocked floral dress.
1521	*Chipper*	In long flocked floral dress.
1521B	*Chipper*	Same as the above as a black doll.
1721	*Miss Chips*	In long flocked floral dress.
1821	*Suzie Sunshine*	In long flocked floral dress.
1821B	*Suzie Sunshine*	Same as the above as a black doll.
6521	*Butter Ball*	In diaper set with fleece blanket.
6521B	*Butter Ball*	Same as the above as a black doll.
6522	*Butter Ball*	In diaper set with ruffled fleece blanket.
6523	*Butter Ball*	In flocked floral dress and bonnet on pillow.
2121	*Babykin*	In floral print gown and fleece blanket.
2122	*Babykin*	In fleece bunting and hood.
2123	*Babykin*	In floral print dress.
2321	*Tiny Tubber*	In diaper set and fleece blanket.
2321B	*Tiny Tubber*	Same as the above as a black doll.
2322	*Tiny Tubber*	In floral print dress and bonnet on pillow.
2322B	*Tiny Tubber*	Same as the above as a black doll.
2323	*Tiny Tubber*	In lace-trimmed fleece bunting.
2323B	*Tiny Tubber*	Same as the above as a black doll.
2324	*Tiny Tubber*	In floral print dress.
2324B	*Tiny Tubber*	Same as the above as a black doll.

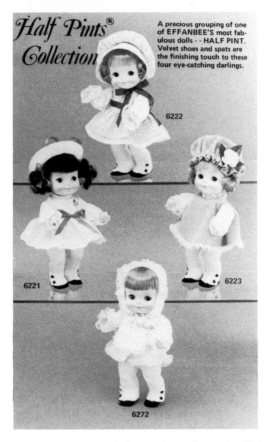

Illustration 240. Part of the *Baby Classics Collection* from the 1976 Effanbee Doll Corporation catalog. On the top are No. 2324B, 11in (27.9cm) *Tiny Tubber*; No. 2323, *Tiny Tubber*; and No. 2324 *Tiny Tubber*. In the center are No. 2322, *Tiny Tubber* and No. 2321, *Tiny Tubber*. On the bottom are No. 2121, 9in (22.9cm) *Babykin*, No. 2123 *Babykin* with rooted hair; and No. 2122, *Babykin*. *Courtesy of Al Kirchof*.

Illustration 241. *Half Pints Collection* from the 1976 Effanbee Doll Corporation catalog. 11in (27.9cm) *Half Pint* dressed in old-fashioned costumes, Nos. 6222, 6221, 6223 and 6272. *Courtesy of Al Kirchof*.

Half Pints Collection

11in (27.9cm) *Half Pint* toddler in four costumes. Each girl wears velvet shoes with spats.

6221	In embroidered dress with straw hat.
6222	In gingham dress and bonnet.
6223	In velveteen dress with matching cap.
6272	In hand-crocheted jacket, hood and muff; leotards.
6272B	Same as the above as a black doll.

Lovums Collection

18in (45.7cm) *Lovums* with molded hair in five costume styles.

8421	In infant dress with lace trim.
8421B	Same as the above as a black doll.
8422	In lace-trimmed fleece bunting.
8423	In dimity infant dress and bonnet.
8424	Same as the above on a pillow.

Crochet Classics Collection

All of the dolls are presented in "hand-knit" outfits.

1372*	Pun'kin		6571*	Butter Ball
2372*	Tiny Tubber		6572*	Butter Ball (in bunting)
2372B*	Tiny Tubber (black)		6572B	Same as the above as black doll.
5672	Dy Dee		9372*	Little Luv
5672B*	Dy Dee (black)		9372B	Little Luv (black)
6272*	Half Pint		9472*	Sweetie Pie
6272B*	Half Pint (black)		9472B*	Sweetie Pie (black)

Prairie Nights Collection

Each doll is dressed in an old-fashioned nightgown and
   sleeping cap.

1358	Pun'kin		2358	Tiny Tubber
1358B	Pun'kin (black)		6558	Butter Ball
1558	Chipper		6558B	Butter Ball (black)
1858	Suzie Sunshine			

Pajama Kids Collection

Each doll is dressed in soft pink sleep wear trimmed in
   white. Suzie Sunshine (No. 1856 and 1856B) and Dy Dee
   (No. 5656 and 5656B) all carry a teddy bear.

1356*	Pun'kin		1856B*	Suzie Sunshine (black)
1356B*	Pun'kin (black)		5656	Dy Dee
1856*	Suzie Sunshine		5656B	Dy Dee (black)

Americana '76 Collection

Each doll is dressed in pink or blue gingham checked
   aprons over a white dress and has a matching bonnet,
   except for Butter Ball (No. 6576) who wears a dress and cap.

1376	Pun'kin		1867B	Suzie Sunshine (black)
1376B	Pun'kin (black)		6576	Butter Ball
1576	Chipper		9376	Little Luv
1576B	Chipper (black)		9676	Sugar Plum
1876	Suzie Sunshine			

Spirit of '76 Collection

A boy and a girl dressed in "Revolutionary" outfits.

1313	Pun'kin (boy)		1314	Pun'kin (girl)

*Identical to 1975.

Illustration 242. The *Americana '76 Collection.* Each doll is dressed in a "colonial" costume. In the top row are No. 1576B, 15in (38.1cm) *Chipper;* No. 9376, 15in (38.1cm) *Little Luv;* No. 1876, 19in (48.3cm) *Suzie Sunshine;* and 1876B *Suzie Sunshine. Seated at the right, center,* is No. 9676, 20in (50.8cm) *Sugar Plum.* In front are No. 1576, 15in (38.1cm) *Chipper,* No. 6576, 13in (33cm) *Butter Ball;* No. 1376, 11in (27.9cm) *Pun'kin;* No. 1314, *Pun'kin;* and No. 1313, *Pun'kin. Courtesy of Al Kirchof.*

Illustration 243. The *Ragamuffins Collection* from the 1976 Effanbee Doll Corporation catalog. This set of dolls had vinyl heads with rooted hair and sleep eyes with lashes. The bodies were soft filling covered with a material that matched the costume. At the top are No. 2723, 21in (53.3cm) *Floppy;* No. 6321, 14in (35.6cm) *Pint Size;* No. 2722, *Floppy;* and No. 6323, *Pint Size.* In front are No. 8121, 14in (35.6cm) *Baby Button Nose;* No. 6322, 14in (35.6cm) *Pint Size;* No. 8121B *Baby Button Nose;* and No. 2721, 21in (53.3cm) *Floppy. Courtesy of Al Kirchof.*

Travel Time Collection

Each doll has extra clothing, a layette and accessories
and is fitted into a wicker hamper.

2399	*Tiny Tubber*	6599	*Butter Ball*
2599	*Twinkie*		

Ragamuffins Collection

Each *Ragamuffin* has a vinyl head and the entire body
is stuffed cloth.

8121	*Baby Button Nose*	In gingham dress and bonnet with matching body.
8121B	*Baby Button Nose*	Same as the above as a black doll.
6321	*Pint Size*	In gingham dress with matching body.
6322	*Pint Size*	In white dress and straw hat; red body with white polka dots.
6323	*Pint Size*	In white dress and cap with print body.
2721	*Floppy*	In dress, cap and pantaloons. Natural color body.
2722	*Floppy*	In dress with gingham trim; matching hat, pantaloons; matching gingham body.
2723	*Floppy*	In dress, cap and pantaloons. The print body matches the dress.

Regal Heirloom Collection

1148	*The Crown Princess*	In lace bridal gown with ruffles.
1548	*The Baroness*	In lace-trimmed velveteen dress.
1747	*The Duchess*	In lace-trimmed velveteen dress.
1748	*Her Royal Highness*	In lace bridal gown with ruffles.
2548	*The Princess*	In lace-trimmed infant gown with lace-trimmed velveteen pillow.
9448	*The Countess*	In lace-trimmed velveteen coat with matching bonnet. Dress underneath.

5700	*Dy Dee Educational Doll*	20in (50.8cm)
5700B	*Dy Dee Educational Doll* (black)	20in (50.8cm)

LEFT: Illustration 244. Here is evidence that collectors cannot trust all the listings in a doll catalog: 21in (53.3cm) *Floppy*, No. 2723, 1976. This vinyl head is the *Suzie Sunshine* mold, unlike the *Floppy* heads shown in the 1976 catalog, which were the heads of *Baby Face*, as they had also been in 1975. In 1977 the Effanbee catalog showed *Floppy* using the *Suzie Sunshine* mold. All of this was no doubt an example of the company utilizing existing doll component parts. The head shown here is marked: "EFFANBEE // ©." *Patricia Gardner Collection.*

RIGHT: Illustration 245. 21in (53.3cm) *Floppy* of 1976, using the *Suzie Sunshine* head. Note the freckles on the cheeks. The *Floppy/Suzie Sunshine* also came without freckles and with hair of various colors. *Patricia Gardner Collection.*

1977 Catalog

Discontinued dolls:

9in (22.9cm)	*Babykin*
20in (50.8cm)	*Dy Dee Educational Doll*
13in (33cm)	*Lil' Darlin'*

New for 1977:

Doll	Description	Size
Little Lovums Prefix No. 83	Vinyl head, arms and legs; cloth body. Molded hair or rooted hair; sleep eyes; cry voice. Baby.	15in (38.1cm)

Number prefix change:

Floppy	Prefix changed from 27 to 19.

International Collection

1101 to 1109 Same as 1976.

1110	*Miss Black America*
1111	*Miss Sweden*
1112	*Miss Switzerland*

Historical Collection

1152 and 1153 Same as 1976.   No. 1151 *Paul Revere* discontinued.

1154	*Davy Crockett*	1156	*Pavlova*
1155	*Florence Nightingale*	1157	*Pocahontas*

(See Chart on Page 190 showing changes in *Historical Collection*.)

Storybook Collection

1175	*Alice in Wonderland*	1178	*Little Red Riding Hood*
1176	*Cinderella*	1179	*Mary, Mary*
1177	*Little Bo Peep*	1180	*Snow White*

Illustration 246. 11in (27.9cm) *Miss Germany,* No. 1103, 1977. All-vinyl and fully-jointed. Blonde rooted hair; blue sleep eyes with molded lashes. Head marked: "EFFANBEE // 19 © 75 // 1176." Note: In 1976 this doll had different colored clothing and a different apron. The basic color here is red; the bodice is black. *Marjorie Smith Collection.*

172

ABOVE: Illustration 247. 11in (27.9cm) Betsy Ross, No. 1152, 1977. All-vinyl and fully-jointed. Blonde rooted hair; blue sleep eyes with molded lashes. Head marked: "EFFANBEE // 19 © 75 // 1176." Note: In 1976 Betsy Ross had a dress fabric of a different pattern. Marjorie Smith Collection.

ABOVE RIGHT: Illustration 248. 11in (27.9cm) Pavlova, No. 1156, 1977. All-vinyl and fully-jointed. Dark brown rooted hair; blue sleep eyes with molded lashes. Head marked: "EFFANBEE // 19 © 75 // 1176." Marjorie Smith Collection.

RIGHT: Illustration 249. 11in (27.9cm) Alice in Wonderland, No. 1175, 1977. All-vinyl and fully-jointed. Blonde rooted hair; blue sleep eyes with molded lashes. Head marked, as are all of the Storybook Collection: "EFFANBEE // 19 © 75 // 1176." Agnes Smith Collection.

Illustration 250. 11in (27.9cm) *Cinderella*, No. 1176, 1977-1978. All-vinyl and fully-jointed. Blonde rooted hair; blue sleep eyes with molded lashes. This gown was used only in 1977; the crown was used after 1978. *Sararose Smith Collection.*

Illustration 251. 11in (27.9cm) *Little Bo Peep*, No. 1177, 1977. All-vinyl and fully-jointed. Blonde rooted hair; blue sleep eyes with molded lashes. *Agnes Smith Collection.*

Illustration 253. 15in (38.1cm) *Bridesmaid* from the *Bridal Suite Collection* (*Chipper*). All-vinyl and fully-jointed. Blonde rooted hair; blue sleep eyes with lashes. Head marked: "EFFANBEE." White embroidered organdy dress over a blue slip; blue ribbon in hair; pink rose in right hand. *Sararose Smith Collection.*

Illustration 252. 11in (27.9cm) *Snow White*, No. 1180, 1977. All-vinyl and fully-jointed. Dark brown rooted hair; blue sleep eyes with molded lashes.

Bridal Suite Collection

1187	*Caroline*	Embroidered white organdy bridal gown.
1187B	*Caroline*	Same as the above as a black doll.
1386	*Ring Boy*	Velveteen pants and lace-trimmed shirt; ring on pillow.
1387	*Flower Girl*	White taffeta dress and bonnet.
1586	*Bridesmaid*	White organdy dress over blue slip.
1587	*Bride*	Embroidered white organdy bridal gown.
1587B	*Bride*	Same as the above as a black doll.
1787	*Bride*	Embroidered white organdy bridal gown.

Yesterdays Collection

Each doll is dressed in an old-fashioned stripe and print costume trimmed with white and black.

1377	*Boy*	2578	*Twinkie*
1378	*Pun'kin*	6378	*Pint Size*
1578	*Chipper*	9378	*Little Luv*
1578B	*Chipper* (black)	9378B	*Little Luv* (black)
1778	*Miss Chips*	9478	*Sweetie Pie*
1878	*Suzie Sunshine*	9678	*Sugar Plum*
1978	*Floppy*		

Illustration 254. 11in (27.9cm) Ring Boy, No. 1386 from the 1977 Bridal Suite Collection. All-vinyl and fully-jointed. Red rooted hair; blue sleep eyes. Head marked: "EFFANBEE// 19 © 66." White velveeten pants; blue shirt. Marjorie Smith Collection.

Illustration 255. 11in (27.9cm) Flower Girl from the 1977 Bridal Suite Collection, No. 1387 (Pun'kin). All-vinyl and fully-jointed. Red rooted hair; blue sleep eyes with lashes. She is wearing a lace-trimmed white taffeta dress with a matching bonnet. Marjorie Smith Collection.

Illustration 256. Yesterdays Collection from the 1977 Effanbee Doll Corporation catalog. The costumes are a multi-colored print trimmed with white and black. The three dolls at the top are No. 1578, 15in (38.1cm) Chipper; No. 9478, 18in (45.7cm) Sweetie Pie; and No. 1978, 21in (53.3cm) Floppy. Beginning far left they are No. 1878, 19in (48.3cm) Suzie Sunshine; No. 9678, 20in (50.8cm) Sugar Plum; No. 1778, 18in (45.7cm) Miss Chips; No. 9378, 15in (38.1cm) Little Luv. In front are No. 2578, 17in (43.2cm) Twinkie; No. 6378, 14in (35.6cm) Pint Size; No. 1378, 11in (27.9cm) Pun'kin; and No. 1377, 11in (27.9cm) Boy (Pun'kin). Courtesy of Al Kirchof.

Illustration 257. A Touch of Velvet Collection from the 1977 Effanbee Doll Corporation catalog. Each doll wears a burgundy velveteen dress and a white apron. Top row: No. 1544, 15in (38.1cm) Chipper; No. 9644, 20in (50:8cm) Sugar Plum; and No. 1844, 19in (48.3cm) Suzie Sunshine. Front row: No. 1844B, Suzie Sunshine; No. 9444, 18in (45.7cm) Sweetie Pie; No. 8344, 15in (38.1cm) Little Lovums; and No. 1344, 11in (27.9cm) Pun'kin. Courtesy of Al Kirchof.

Baby Classics Collection

2325	*Tiny Tubber*	Fioral print dress and bonnet.
2326	*Tiny Tubber*	Fleece bunting with floral print lining.
2327	*Tiny Tubber*	Floral print dress.
2327B	*Tiny Tubber*	Same as the above as a black doll.
2525	*Twinkie*	Diaper set with fleece blanket.
2525B	*Twinkie*	Same as the above as a black doll.
2526	*Twinkie*	Infant dress with lace trim.
2526B	*Twinkie*	Same as the above as a black doll.
6125	*Baby Winkie*	In fleece bunting.
6125B	*Baby Winkie*	Same as the above as a black doll.
6126	*Baby Winkie*	Fleece bunting with floral print lining.
6126B	*Baby Winkie*	Same as the above as a black doll.
6525	*Butter Ball*	Diaper set with fleece blanket.
6525B	*Butter Ball*	Same as the above as a black doll.
8425	*Lovums*	Infant dress with lace trim.

A Touch of Velvet Collection

Each doll wears a burgundy velveteen dress and a white
embroidered apron.

1344	*Pun'kin*		1844B	*Suzie Sunshine* (black)
1544	*Chipper*		8344	*Little Lovums*
1544B	*Chipper* (black)		9444	*Sweetie Pie*
1844	*Suzie Sunshine*		9644	*Sugar Plum*

Grandes Dames Collection

(Refer to Chart on page 164 for the dolls used.)

1535	*Madame Du Barry*	Blue taffeta dress; organdy overskirt.
1536	*Violetta*	Fur-trimmed velveteen coat dress; hat.
1537	*Lady Ashley*	Velveteen and taffeta pleated dress; straw hat.
1537B	*Lady Ashley*	Same as the above as a black doll.
1538	*Coquette*	Ruffled and lace dress; velveteen overskirt; pocketbook.
1731	*Victorian Lady*	Velveteen ball gown; lace-trimmed hat.
1734	*Mam'selle*	Velveteen coat and hat; lace-trimmed dress.
1735	*Champagne Lady*	Beige lace-trimmed organdy dress; bonnet.
1735B	*Champagne Lady*	Same as the above as a black doll.
1736	*Fluerette*	Floral print cotton dress and hat.

Four Seasons® Collection

1976's smash success is sure to be a resounding winner again this year. From the sweet fragrance of Spring to the blustery cold of winter, these four breath-taking beauties are a must for all doll lovers.

1131 — 11" SPRING — lace-trimmed organdy blouse, taffeta skirt with embroidery, ruffle. Straw hat with veil and flowers, pocketbook. Pantaloons and pumps.

1133 — 11" AUTUMN — velveteen dress with lace-ruffled insert. Matching bonnet, pocketbook. Pantaloons and pumps.

*1132 — 11" SUMMER — ruffled lace-trimmed organdy dress with slip. Matching hat with flower, basket of flowers. Pantaloons and pumps.

1134 — 11" WINTER — lace and braid-trimmed dress with braided velveteen cape and matching hood. Scarf and muff. Pantaloons and pumps.

Illustration 258. The *Four Seasons Collection* from the 1977 Effanbee Doll Corporation catalog. This group uses the same basic doll that is used for the *International Collection* and others. At the top are No. 1131, *Spring* and No. 1132, *Summer.* At the bottom are No. 1133, *Autumn* and No. 1134, *Winter. Courtesy of Al Kirchof.*

Four Seasons Collection

Same as 1976 with one addition:

1132B   *Summer* (black doll)   Ruffled lace-trimmed organdy dress; matching hat.

Baby Face Collection

16in (40.6cm) *Baby Face* in three different costume designs.

2625   Two-tiered lace-trimmed dress and cap.

2626   Floral print dress; white apron; matching hat.

2627   Velveteen dress with lace-trimmed slip; straw hat.

Blue Heaven Collection

The collection is *Little Lovums, Lovums* and *Sugar Plum* in white organdy dresses over pale blue batiste slips.

8382	*Little Lovums*	8482	*Lovums*
8481	*Lovums*	9682	*Sugar Plum*

Illustration 259. Country Bumpkin Collection from the 1977 Effanbee Doll Corporation catalog. Each doll wears a "country" print accented with blue. At the top are No. 1368, 11in (27.9cm) *Pun'kin;* No. 1367, 11in (27.9cm) *Boy (Pun'kin);* and No. 9468B, 18in (45.7cm) *Sweetie Pie.* In the center row are No. 9468, *Sweetie Pie;* No. 1868, 19in (48.3cm) *Suzie Sunshine;* and No. 1768, 18in (45.7cm) *Miss Chips.* At the bottom are No. 6568, 13in (33cm) *Butterball;* No. 1768B, 18in (45.7cm) *Miss Chips;* and No. 6368, 14in (35.6cm) *Pint Size. Courtesy of Al Kirchof.*

Crochet Classics Collection

Each doll wears a "hand-knit" costume in pastel colors.

2361	*Tiny Tubber*	6562	*Butter Ball* (in bunting)
2362	*Tiny Tubber* (in bunting)	6562B	*Butter Ball* (black doll in bunting)
2362B	*Tiny Tubber* (black doll in bunting)	8362	*Little Lovums*
5662	*Dy Dee*	8362B	*Little Lovums* (black)
6162	*Baby Winkie*	9462	*Sweetie Pie*
6561	*Butter Ball*	9462B	*Sweetie Pie* (black)

Country Bumpkin Collection

Each doll wears a pale print outfit with blue trim or
accessories. *Pint Size* (No. 6368) has an all-cloth body.

1367	*Boy*	6368	*Pint Size*
1368	*Pun'kin*	6568	*Butter Ball*
1768	*Miss Chips*	9468	*Sweetie Pie*
1768B	*Miss Chips* (black)	9468B	*Sweetie Pie* (black)
1868	*Suzie Sunshine*		

Sweet Dreams Collection

1364	*Pun'kin*	Floral print nightgown and cap.
1364B	*Pun'kin*	Same as the above as a black doll.
1564	*Chipper*	Floral print nightgown and cap.
1864	*Suzie Sunshine*	Floral print peignoir and cap.
1864B	*Suzie Sunshine*	Same as the above as a black doll.
5664	*Dy Dee*	Floral print sleeper; has teddy bear.
5664B	*Dy Dee*	Same as the above as a black doll.
6564	*Butter Ball*	Diaper set and floral print fleece blanket.
8164	*Baby Button Nose* (Vinyl arms and legs)	Floral print sleeper.
8164B	*Baby Button Nose* (Vinyl arms and legs)	Same as the above as a black doll.
8364	*Little Lovums*	Floral print infant dress.
8364B	*Little Lovums*	Same as the above as a black doll.

Vanilla Fudge Collection

Each doll is dressed in a brown checked gingham dress
with ecru apron trimmed with lace and brown piping.

1317	*Pun'kin*	6517	*Butter Ball*
1317B	*Pun'kin* (black)	9317	*Little Luv*
1817	*Suzie Sunshine*	9617	*Sugar Plum*
1917	*Floppy*	9617B	*Sugar Plum* (black)

Half Pints Collection

11in (27.9cm) *Half Pint* in three costumes. Each toddler
wears velvet shoes with spats.

6225   White embroidered dress with velveteen bow; matching cap.

6226   Floral print dress with apron and matching hat.

6227   Velveteen dress with lace-trimmed slip; straw hat.

Travel Time Collection

Each doll comes with extra clothing and accessories.
Miss Holland and *Tiny Tubber* are in a trunk; *Twinkie*
and *Butter Ball* are in wicker hampers.

| 1197 | *Miss Holland* | 2599 | *Twinkie* |
| 2397 | *Tiny Tubber* | 6599 | *Butter Ball* |

Regal Heirloom Collection

1146	*The Crown Princess*	Lace bridal gown with ruffles.
1546	*The Baroness*	Lace-trimmed velveteen dress with lace-ruffled insert; velveteen cap.
1745	*The Duchess*	Lace-trimmed velveteen dress with lace-ruffled insert; velveteen cap.
1745B	*The Duchess*	Same as the above as a black doll.
1746	*Her Royal Highness*	Lace bridal gown; petticoat with rows of ruffles.
1846	*The Queen Mother*	Velveteen dress and hat. Baby (11in [27.9cm] *Tiny Tubber*) is in lace-trimmed christening dress.
8346	*The Princess*	Organdy infant gown and cap; on pillow.
9446	*The Countess*	Embroidered dress with lace trim.

The Passing Parade

1551	*Colonial Lady*	Calico print dress with overskirt; cap.
1552	*Frontier Woman*	Gray cotton dress and shawl; bonnet.
1553	*Civil War Lady*	White organdy dress with rows of lace; picture hat.
1554	*Gibson Girl*	Navy blue skirt and jacket; ruffled blouse; straw hat.
1555	*Flapper*	Velveteen coat dress with fur collar; velveteen cloche hat; fur muff.
1556	*The 70s Woman*	Three-tiered chiffon evening gown and scarf.

Illustration 260. The 1977 *Travel Time Collection* from the Effanbee Doll Corporation catalog. At the top left is No. 1197, 11in (27.9cm) *Miss Holland*. The babies are, from left to right: No. 2397, 11in (27.9cm) *Tiny Tubber*; No. 6599, 13in (33cm) *Butter Ball*; and No. 2599, 17in (43.2cm) *Twinkie*. *Courtesy of Al Kirchof.*

Travel Time® Collection

All aboard — and off we go to make-believe babyland. . .Take your EFFANBEE beauty on a trip with her complete ensemble to wear for all occasions. Whether it be boat, plane or car, this little traveler will surely make a hit!

1197

6599

2599

2397

18

®ALL TRADE NAMES
REGISTERED EFFANBEE 1977

EACH ITEM LISTED BELOW COMES WITH LAYETTE AND ACCESSORIES AS ILLUSTRATED.

1197 — International Doll Layette and Trunk — 11" MISS HOLLAND dressed in her national costume.
2397 — TINY TUBBER Layette and Trunk — 11" doll dressed in diaper set with shell-edge fleece blanket.
2599 — TWINKIE Layette and wicker basket — 17" Doll dressed in long embroidered dress with bonnet. On pillow.
6599 — BUTTER BALL Layette and wicker basket — 13" doll dressed in long embroidered dress with bonnet. On pillow.

Illustration 261. The *Regal Heirloom Collection* from the 1977 Effanbee Doll Corporation catalog. The dolls in the top row are No. 1745, 18in (45.7cm) *The Duchess (Miss Chips)*; No. 1746, 18in (45.7cm) *Her Royal Highness (Miss Chips)*; and No. 1846 18in (45.7cm) *The Queen Mother (Suzie Sunshine)* with 11in (27.9cm) *Baby (Tiny Tubber)*. In the bottom row are No. 9446, 18in (45.7cm) *The Countess (Sweetie Pie)*; No. 1546, 15in (38.1cm) *The Baroness (Miss Chips)*; No. 1146, 11in (27.9cm) *The Crown Princess*; and No. 8346, 17in (43.2cm) *The Princess (Little Lovums)*. *Courtesy of Al Kirchof.*

The Passing Parade®

1552

1551

1553

1554

1555

1556

Illustration 262. The *Passing Parade* from the 1977 Effanbee Doll Corporation catalog. This collection, a "salute to the American woman," is six ladies in costumes that reflect different time periods. In the top row are No. 1553, *Civil War Lady*; No. 1552, *Frontier Woman*; and No. 1551, *Colonial Lady*. In the front row are No. 1554, *Gibson Girl*; No. 1555, *Flapper*; and No. 1556, *The 70s Woman*. Each doll is 15in (38.1cm) and is the *Miss Chips* doll. *Courtesy of Al Kirchof.*

181

1978 Catalog

Discontinued dolls:
21in (53.3cm) *Floppy*
16in (40.6cm) *Baby Face*
14in (35.6cm) *Pint Size*
15in (38.1cm) *Little Luv*

New for 1978:

Doll	Description	Size
adult doll (*Currier and Ives*, etc.) Prefix No. 12	All-vinyl and fully-jointed.* Rooted hair; sleep eyes with plastic lashes.	11in (27.9cm)
lady doll (*Passing Parade; Grandes Dames*) Prefix No. 15	All-vinyl and fully-jointed.* Rooted hair; sleep eyes.	15in (38.1cm)
L'il (or *Li'l*) *Suzie Sunshine* Prefix No. 16	All-vinyl and fully-jointed girl.* Rooted hair; sleep eyes; freckles across bridge of nose.	16in (40.6cm)
lady doll (*Grandes Dames*) Prefix No. 17	All-vinyl and fully-jointed.* Rooted hair; sleep eyes.	18in (45.7cm)

*Soft vinyl head and arms; rigid vinyl torso and legs.

Note: The prefix 15 was used for both *Chipper* and the 15in (38.1cm) lady doll.

The prefix 17 was used for both *Miss Chips* and the 18in (45.7cm) lady doll.

International Collection

Nos. 1101 to 1112, same as in 1977.

New for 1978:

1113   *Miss Canada*   1114   *Miss China*   1115   *Miss Russia*

Historical Collection

No. 1153 *Martha Washington* discontinued.

New for 1978:

1158   *Cleopatra*

(See Chart on Page 190 showing changes in *Historical Collection*.)

Illustration 263. 11in (27.9cm) *Miss Russia*, No. 1115, 1978. All-vinyl and fully-jointed. Dark brown rooted hair; blue sleep eyes. Head marked: "EFFANBEE // 19 © 75 // 1176." *Agnes Smith Collection*.

Illustration 264. The *Historical Collection,* 1978 Effanbee Doll Corporation catalog. Each doll is 11in (27.9cm) tall. In the top row are *Davy Crockett,* No. 1154; *Florence Nightingale,* No. 1155; and *Cleopatra,* No. 1158. In the front row are *Betsy Ross,* No. 1152; *Pavlova,* No. 1156; and *Pocahontas,* No. 1157.

Storybook Collection

No. 1175 to 1180 same as 1977.

New for 1978:

1181	*Robin Hood*
1182	*Maid Marian*
1183	*Tinkerbell*

Bridal Suite Collection

1289	*Bride*	Embroidered white organdy bridal gown.
1289B	*Bride*	Same as the above as a black doll.
1388	*Ring Boy*	Velveteen pants and jacket; lace trimmed shirt; ring on pillow.
1389	*Flower Girl*	Beige embroidered skirt; velveteen bodice; matching bonnet.
1588	*Bridesmaid*	Beige embroidered skirt; velveteen bodice; matching bonnet.
1589	*Bride*	Embroidered white organdy bridal gown.
1589B	*Bride*	Same as the above as a black doll.
1789	*Bride*	Embroidered white organdy bridal gown.
1789B	*Bride*	Same as the above as a black doll.

Memories Collection

Each doll, except *Boy* (No. 1315) is dressed in a "memories print" and white organdy dress, trimmed with velveteen. The *Boy* wears velveteen pants, a print shirt and a velveteen cap.

1315	*Boy*		6216	*Half Pint*
1316	*Pun'kin*		6516	*Butter Ball*
1516	*Chipper*		8316	*Little Lovums*
1616	*L'il Suzie Sunshine*		9416	*Sweetie Pie*
1716	*Miss Chips*		9616	*Sugar Plum*
1816	*Suzie Sunshine*			

Baby Classics Collection

2326	*Tiny Tubber*	In fleece bunting with floral print lining.
2327	*Tiny Tubber*	In floral print dress.
2327B	*Tiny Tubber*	Same as the above as a black doll.
2328	*Tiny Tubber*	In infant dress in fleece blanket with floral print trim.
2525	*Twinkie*	In diaper set and fleece blanket.
2525B	*Twinkie*	Same as the above as a black doll.
2526	*Twinkie*	In infant gown with lace trim.
2526B	*Twinkie*	Same as the above as a black doll.
6125	*Baby Winkie*	In lace-trimmed fleece bunting.

Illustration 265. 11in (27.9cm) *Cleopatra*, No. 1158, 1978. All-vinyl and fully-jointed. Long black rooted hair; blue sleep eyes with lashes; heavy eye makeup. Head marked: "EFFANBEE // 19 © 75 // 1176." Note: In 1979 this same doll was *Miss Ancient Egypt*, No. 1116. (See *Illustration 277*.)

Storybook Collection

Illustration 266. The *Storybook Collection*, 1978 Effanbee Doll Corporation catalog. In the top row are *Mary Mary*, No. 1179; *Cinderella*, No. 1176; *Little Bo Peep*, No. 1177; and *Tinkerbell*, No. 1183. In the front row, beginning at far left, are *Robin Hood*, No. 1181; *Maid Marian*, No. 1182; *Little Red Riding Hood*, No. 1178; *Alice in Wonderland*, No. 1175; and *Snow White*, No. 1180.

Illustration 267. 11in (27.9cm) *Little Red Riding Hood*, No. 1178, 1978. All-vinyl and fully-jointed. Blonde rooted hair; blue sleep eyes. Head marked: "EFFANBEE // 19 © 75 // 1176." *Agnes Smith Collection.* Note: The basket in the doll's right hand is different than it was in 1977.

Illustration 268. 11in (27.9cm) *Boy Skater*, No. 1251, and *Girl Skater*, No. 1252, from the *Currier and Ives Collection*, 1978. All-vinyl and fully-jointed. Rooted blonde hair; blue sleep eyes. Head marked: "EFFANBEE // 19 © 75 // 1276." *Agnes Smith Collection.*

Baby Classics Collection continued from page 184.

6125B	Baby Winkie	Same as the above as a black doll.
6126	Baby Winkie	In fleece bunting with floral print lining.
6126B	Baby Winkie	Same as the above as a black doll.
6525	Butter Ball	In diaper set and fleece blanket.
6525B	Butter Ball	Same as the above as a black doll.
8425	Lovums	In infant gown with lace trim.

Currier and Ives Collection

The dolls are inspired by the 19th century Currier and Ives lithographs.

1251	Boy Skater	Velveteen trousers, jacket and hat; muffler. Carries ice skates.
1252	Girl Skater	Pleated taffeta skirt; velveteen jacket, cape and bonnet. Carries ice skates.
1253	Life in the Country	Print dress; velveteen hat.
1254	Wayside Inn	Ruffled taffeta skirt with velveteen bodice; velveteen overskirt; matching bonnet.
1255	A Night on the Hudson	Ruffled taffeta dress with taffeta overskirt; marabou-trimmed bonnet.
1256	Central Park	Taffeta walking dress with matching bonnet.

Grandes Dames Collection

1535	Madame Du Barry	Same as in 1977.
1540	Lady Grey	Taffeta dress with velveteen overskirt and bodice; matching bonnet.
1735	Champagne Lady	Same as in 1977.
1737	Nicole	Embroidered dress with velveteen overskirt; Matching hat with marabou feather.
1538	Coquette	Same as in 1977.
1539	Downing Square	Pleated velveteen dress with lace-trimmed hem and bodice; marabou collar; pocketbook.
1539B	Downing Square	Same as the above as a black doll.
1736	Fleurette	Same as in 1977.
1738	Blue Danube	Woven floral taffeta dress with matching coat. Straw hat with marabou feather.

Four Seasons Collection

1231	Spring	Organdy blouse; taffeta skirt; straw hat.
1232	Summer	Organdy dress; matching hat with flower; basket of flowers.
1233	Autumn	Velveteen dress with matching bonnet; purse.
1234	Winter	Velveteen cape and hood over white dress.

Travel Time Collection

Each doll comes with extra costumes and accessories.
Caroline, Chipper and Tiny Tubber are in trunks;
Twinkie and Butter Ball are in wicker hampers.

1299	Caroline	2599	Twinkie
1599	Chipper	6599	Butter Ball
2399	Tiny Tubber		

Crochet Classics Collection

All of the babies wear hand-crocheted outfits.

2373	*Tiny Tubber*		6574	*Butter Ball* (in bunting)
2373B	*Tiny Tubber* (black)		6574B	*Butter Ball* (black doll in bunting)
2374	*Tiny Tubber* (in bunting)		8374	*Little Lovums*
5674	*Dy Dee*		9474	*Sweetie Pie*
6174	*Baby Winkie*		9474B	*Sweetie Pie* (black)
6573	*Butter Ball*			

Regal Heirloom Collection

1246	*Crown Princess*	Lace bridal gown with rows of ruffled lace.
1345	*Prince*	Lace-trimmed velveteen outfit with matching cape and hat.
1346	*Princess*	Lace-trimmed velveteen dress with matching bonnet.
1745	*The Duchess*	Same as in 1977.
1746	*Her Royal Highness*	Same as in 1977.
1846	*The Queen Mother*	Same as in 1977.
9446	*The Countess*	Same as in 1977.

Sweet Dreams Collection

1365	*Pun'kin*	Floral print sleeping gown and bonnet.
1365B	*Pun'kin*	Same as the above as a black doll.
1665	*Li'l Suzie Sunshine*	Floral print sleeping gown and bonnet.
5665	*Dy Dee*	Floral print sleeper; with teddy bear.
5665B	*Dy Dee*	Same as the above as a black doll.
6565	*Butter Ball*	Floral print diaper and blanket set.
8165	*Baby Button Nose*	Floral print sleeper.
8165B	*Baby Button Nose*	Same as the above as a black doll.
8365	*Little Lovums*	Floral print infant dress.

A Touch of Velvet Collection

Each doll wears a burgundy velveteen dress and a white embroidered apron.

1344*	*Pun'kin*		1844B*	*Suzie Sunshine* (black)
1344B	*Pun'kin* (black)		9444*	*Sweetie Pie*
1544*	*Chipper*		9444B	*Sweetie Pie* (black)
1544B*	*Chipper* (black)		9644*	*Sugar Plum*
1644	*Li'l Suzie Sunshine*			
1844*	*Suzie Sunshine*			

*Same as 1977.

Blue Heaven Collection

Each doll is dressed in white organdy dresses over pale
blue batiste slips.

1382	Pun'kin	8482*	Lovums
1682	Li'l Suzie Sunshine	9481	Sweetie Pie
6582	Butter Ball	9682*	Sugar Plum
8382*	Little Lovums		

*Same as in 1977.

Illustration 270. 11in (27.9cm) *Life in the Country* from the *Currier and Ives Collection*, No. 1253, 1978. All-vinyl and fully-jointed. Blonde rooted hair; blue sleep eyes. Head marked: "EFFANBEE // 19 © 75 // 1276." *Sararose Smith Collection.*

Illustration 269. 11in (27.9cm) *Boy Skater* from the *Currier and Ives Collection*, No. 1251, 1978.

Illustration 271. 18in (45.7cm) *Nicole* from the *Grandes Dames Collection*, No. 1737, 1978. All-vinyl and fully-jointed. Blonde rooted hair; blue sleep eyes. The doll wears an embroidered dress with a velveteen overskirt caught at the sides with roses. The hat matches the dress and has a veil over the face. Head marked: "EFFANBEE // 19 © 78 // 1178." *Patricia Gardner Collection.*

Illustration 272. 15in (38.1cm) *Little Lovums*, No. 8374, from the *Crochet Classics Collection*, 1978. Vinyl head, arms and legs; cloth body with cryer voice. Molded hair; blue sleep eyes with lashes. Dressed in a lace and embroidery-trimmed white dress and a pink crocheted sweater, cap and booties. *Emily and Ruth Jones Collection.*

Illustration 273. The *Regal Heirloom Collection* from the 1978 Effanbee Doll Corporation catalog. The dolls in the top row are No. 1745, 18in (45.7cm) *The Duchess (Miss Chips)*; No. 1746, 18in (45.7cm) *Her Royal Highness (Miss Chips)*; and No. 1846, 18in (45.7cm) *The Queen Mother (Suzie Sunshine)* with 11in (27.9cm) *Baby (Tiny Tubber)*. In the front row are No. 1246, 11in (27.9cm) *Crown Princess (Caroline)*; No. 1345, 11in (27.9cm) *Prince (Pun'kin)*; No. 1346, 11in (27.9cm) *Princess (Pun'kin)*; and No. 9446, 18in (45.7cm) *The Countess (Sweetie Pie)*. Compare this group with the *Regal Heirloom Collection* from 1977, *Illustration 261.*

189

The Passing Parade

This is the doll used for the *Grandes Dames* and *The Passing Parade*. She is 15in (38.1cm). In 1977 *Chipper* was used for this collection.

1501	*Colonial Lady*	Calico print dress with overskirt; cap.*
1502	*Frontier Woman*	Gray cotton dress and shawl; bonnet.*
1503	*Civil War Lady*	White organdy dress with rows of lace; picture hat.*
1504	*Gay Nineties*	Fringe-trimmed velveteen skirt with bustle; velveteen jacket; matching bonnet.
1505	*The Hourglass Look*	Velveteen walking coat with fur trim; fur cape; fur-trimmed bonnet.
1506	*Gibson Girl*	Navy blue skirt and jacket; ruffled blouse; straw hat.*
1507	*Flapper*	Velveteen coat dress with fur collar; velveteen cloche hat; fur muff.*
1508	*The 70s Woman*	Chiffon blouse; velveteen skirt.

Illustration 274. 15in (38.1cm) *The 70s Woman,* No. 1508, from *The Passing Parade,* 1978. All-vinyl and fully-jointed. Dark brown rooted hair; blue sleep eyes with lashes. Head marked: "EFFANBEE // 19 © 78 // 1578." She wears a black velveteen skirt with a matching bow in the hair and a white chiffon blouse. *Patricia Gardner Collection.*

*This is the same costume as in 1977, when it was worn by *Chipper.*

Innocence Collection

The babies (*Twinkie, Little Lovums* and *Sweetie Pie*) are outfitted in embroidered batiste dresses and booties. The ladies (*Caroline, Chipper* and *Miss Chips*) wear tiered batiste gowns with embroidered overskirts and straw hats. The toddlers (*Half Pint, Li'l Suzie Sunshine* and *Suzie Sunshine*) wear short batiste dresses and straw hats.

1221	*Caroline*	1821B	*Suzie Sunshine* (black)
1221B	*Caroline* (black)	2521	*Twinkie*
1521	*Chipper*	6221	*Half Pint*
1621	*L'il Suzie Sunshine*	8321	*Little Lovums*
1721	*Miss Chips*	9421	*Sweetie Pie*
1821	*Suzie Sunshine*	9421B	*Sweetie Pie* (black)

Historical Collection

Stock No.	Doll	1976	1977	1978
1151	*Paul Revere*	*		
1152	*Betsy Ross*	*	* 1	*
1153	*Martha Washington*	*	*	
1154	*Davy Crockett*		*	*
1155	*Florence Nightingale*		*	*
1156	*Pavlova*		*	*
1157	*Pocahontas*		*	*2
1158	*Cleopatra*			*

[1]Print pattern in dress changed.

[2]Trim on skirt changed.

Illustration 276. 15in (38.1cm) *Gay Nineties*, No. 1504, from *The Passing Parade*, 1978. All-vinyl and fully-jointed. Blonde rooted hair; blue sleep eyes. Head marked: "EFFANBEE // 19 © 78 // 1578." The doll is dressed in a fringe-trimmed velveteen skirt with a bustle, a lace-trimmed velveteen jacket and a matching bonnet. She carries a velveteen purse in her right hand. *Patricia Gardner Collection*.

Illustration 275. 15in (38.1cm) *Flapper*, No. 1507, from *The Passing Parade*, 1978. All-vinyl and fully-jointed. Dark brown rooted hair; blue sleep eyes. Head marked: "EFFANBEE // 19 © 78 // 1578." The costume is a velveteen coat dress and hat in red. The collar and the muff are gray "fur." *Patricia Gardner Collection*.

1979 Catalog

New for 1979:

Doll	Description	Size
Faith Wick Originals Prefix No. 70	All-vinyl and fully-jointed boy and girl in two styles. Rooted hair; sleep eyes with lashes.	16in (40.6cm)
Buttercup *Prefix No. 93*	Vinyl head, arms and legs; filled cotton body. Rooted hair; sleep eyes with lashes; cry voice.	15in (38.1cm)

Note: This is not the same *Buttercup* that was used in 1973 only.
The 1973 *Buttercup* was 13in (33cm) and all-vinyl.

Note: The prefix 15 was used for both *Chipper* and the 15in (38.1cm)
lady doll.
The prefix 17 was used for both *Miss Chips* and the 18in (45.7cm)
lady doll.

International Collection

Nos. 1101 to 1115 same as 1978.

New for 1979:

1116	*Miss Ancient Egypt*
1117	*Spain* (boy)
1118	*Miss Mexico*
1119	*Miss India*

Storybook Collection

No. 1175 to 1180 same as 1978.
No. 1181 *Robin Hood*, No. 1182 *Maid Marian*, No. 1183 *Tinkerbell*
discontinued.
New for 1979:

1184	*Goldilocks*
1185	*Pavlova*
1186	*Jack*
1187	*Jill*

Illustration 277. 11in (27.9cm) Miss Ancient Egypt, No. 1116, from the 1979 International Collection. All-vinyl and fully-jointed. Long black rooted hair; blue sleep eyes with molded lashes; heavy eye makeup. This is the same doll as Cleopatra, No. 1158, 1978. Head marked: "EFFANBEE // 19 © 75 // 1176."

Illustration 278. 11in (27.9cm) *Miss Spain, No. 1109, 1979, and Spain,* No. 1117, 1980, from the *International Collection.* All-vinyl and fully-jointed. Dark rooted brown hair; brown sleep eyes. Heads marked: "EFFANBEE // 19 © 75 // 1176." Her costume is red trimmed in black; his is black trimmed in gold. These costumes are good examples of how most doll companies depict dolls in regional costumes. Both the flamenco costume of the girl and the matador outfit of the boy are greatly over-simplified, and lack most of the details of original folk costumes.

Illustration 279. The *Storybook Collection* from the Effanbee Doll Corporation catalog, 1979. In the top row are *Goldilocks,* No. 1184; *Little Bo Peep,* No. 1177; and *Snow White,* No. 1180. In the middle row are *Little Red Riding Hood,* No. 1178; *Pavlova,* No. 1185 (formerly No. 1156 of the *Historical Collection,* 1977 and 1978); and *Mary, Mary,* No. 1179. In the front row are *Jack,* No. 1186; *Jill,* No. 1187; *Cinderella,* No. 1176; and *Alice in Wonderland,* No. 1175.

Illustration 280. 11in (27.9cm) *Mary, Mary,* No. 1179, from the 1979 *Storybook Collection.* All-vinyl and fully-jointed. Blonde rooted hair; blue sleep eyes. Head marked: "EFFANBEE // 19 © 75 // 1176." The dress is green with flowers. In 1978 it was red and instead of a watering can *Mary, Mary* carried a basket. *Agnes Smith Collection.*

Illustration 281. The 1979 *Bridal Suite Collection* from the Effanbee Doll Corporation catalog. In the top row are 15in (38.1cm) *Bridesmaid* with a dark blue bodice and a white organdy skirt over a blue slip, No. 1511; 18in (45.7cm) *Bride,* No. 1712; and 15in (38.1cm) *Bride,* No. 1512. In front are 11in (27.9cm) *Bride,* No. 1212; 11in (27.9cm) *Ring Boy (Pun'kin)* in dark blue velveteen pants with a pale blue shirt, No. 1311; 11in (27.9cm) *Flower Girl (Pun'kin)* with a dark blue bodice and white organdy skirt over a blue slip, No. 1312; and 15in (38.1cm) *Bride* (black *Chipper*), No. 1512.

Illustration 282. 11in (27.9cm) *Pun'kin,* No. 1384, from the *Rainbow Parfait Collection,* 1979. All-vinyl and fully-jointed. Blonde rooted hair; blue sleep eyes. Head marked: "EFFANBEE // 19 © 66." The long gown is pale yellow organdy. *Patricia Gardner Collection.*

Bridal Suite Collection

1212	*Bride*	Embroidered white organdy gown.
1212B	*Bride*	Same as the above as a black doll.
1311	*Ring Boy*	Velveteen pants and lace-trimmed shirt. Ring on a pillow.
1312	*Flower Girl*	Embroidered organdy skirt with velveteen bodice; matching bonnet.
1511	*Bridesmaid*	Embroidered orgnady skirt with velveteen bodice; matching bonnet.
1512	*Bride*	Embroidered white organdy gown.
1512B	*Bride*	Same as the above as a black doll.
1712	*Bride*	Tucked organdy bridal gown; organdy picture hat.

Baby Classics Collection

2322	*Tiny Tubber*	In lace-trimmed fleece bunting.
2322B	*Tiny Tubber*	Same as the above as a black doll.
2323	*Tiny Tubber*	In lace-trimmed floral print dress.
2323B	*Tiny Tubber*	Same as the above as a black doll.
2324	*Tiny Tubber*	In lace-trimmed infant dress.
2324B	*Tiny Tubber*	Same as the above as a black doll.
2523	*Twinkie*	In diaper set and fleece blanket.
2523B	*Twinkie*	Same as the above as a black doll.
2524	*Twinkie*	In infant gown with lace trim.
2524B	*Twinkie*	Same as the above as a black doll.
6123	*Baby Winkie*	In lace-trimmed fleece bunting.
6124	*Baby Winkie*	Same as No. 6123 with rooted hair.
6124B	*Baby Winkie*	Same as No. 6124 as a black doll.
8424	*Lovums*	In infant gown with lace trim.

Currier and Ives Collection

No. 1251 to 1254 same as 1978.

No. 1255 and 1256 discontinued.

New for 1979:

| 1257 | *Castle Garden* | Pleated taffeta dress with velveteen overskirt and bodice; straw picture hat. |
| 1258 | *Plymouth Landing* | Velveteen-trimmed taffeta dress; matching hat. |

Four Seasons Collection

All four designs are the same as in 1978, with one addition:

| 1232B | *Summer* | As a black doll. |

Faith Wick Originals

See also Chapter 4, *Craftsmen's Corner.*

| 7001 | *Boy Party Time* | 7003 | *Boy Anchors Aweigh* |
| 7002 | *Girl Party Time* | 7004 | *Girl Anchors Aweigh* |

Rainbow Parfait Collection

Each doll wears a pastel organdy dress. No. 6584 *Butterball* has a matching pillow.

1384	*Pun'kin*	9684	*Sugar Plum*
1384B	*Pun'kin* (black)	8484	*Lovums*
1684	*Li'l Suzie Sunshine*		
6584	*Butterball*		
9384	*Buttercup*		

Soft'n Sweet Collection

Each doll wears a muted varied-print dress with a velveteen bow.

1318	*Pun'kin*	6218	*Half Pint*
1518	*Chipper*	6518	*Butterball*
1618	*Li'l Suzie Sunshine*	9318	*Buttercup*
1718	*Miss Chips*	9418	*Sweetie Pie*
1818	*Suzie Sunshine*	9618	*Sugar Plum*

Grandes Dames Collection

No. 1539 *Downing Square* is the same as 1978.

1531	*Blue Bayou*	Pleated taffeta dress and velveteen jacket with matching hat.
1532	*Magnolia*	Tiered taffeta dress with matching bonnet.
1532B	*Magnolia*	Same as the above as a black doll.
1731	*Lady Snow*	Floral taffeta walking coat trimmed in fringe and braid; matching hat.
1732	*Cherries Jubilee*	Ruffled print with velveteen overskirt; matching hat and purse.
1533	*Emerald Isle*	Taffeta dress with lace and pleated under-skirt; matching hat with flowers.
1733	*Crystal*	Taffeta coat dress; matching hat.
1737	*Nicole*	Embroidered dress with velveteen overskirt caught at the sides with flowers; matching hat.

Innocence Collection

This collection is the same as it was in 1978 with the following changes:

Nos. 1221B *Caroline*, 1821B *Suzie Sunshine* and 8321 *Little Lovums* are discontinued.

No. 9321 *Buttercup* has been added for 1979.

Illustration 283. Four of the 1979 *Grandes Dames Collection* dolls from the Effanbee Doll Corporation catalog. From top down: 15in (38.1cm) *Emerald Isle*, No. 1533; *Downing Square*, No. 1539; 18in (45.7cm) *Nicole*, No. 1737; and *Crystal*, No. 1733.

Illustration 284. 15in (38.1cm) *Blue Bayou*, No. 1531, from the 1979 *Grandes Dames Collection.* All-vinyl and fully-jointed. Blonde rooted hair; blue sleep eyes. Head marked: "EFFANBEE // 19 © 78 // 1578." She wears a blue pleated taffeta dress with black lace trim and a black velveteen jacket and a matching hat. *Emily and Ruth Jones Collection.*

Illustration 285. 16in (40.6cm) *Li'l Suzie Sunshine,* No. 1655, from the 1979 *Sweet Dreams Collection.* All-vinyl and fully-jointed. Blonde rooted hair; blue sleep eyes; freckles. The doll wears a floral print cotton gown with rows of lace ruffles at the hem and a matching sleeping cap trimmed in lace. *Marjorie Smith Collection.*

Illustration 286. 11in (27.9cm) *Pun'kin,* No. 1374, from the 1979 *Crochet Classics Collection.* All-vinyl and fully-jointed. Blonde rooted hair; blue sleep eyes. Head marked: "EFFANBEE // 19 © 66." *Pun'kin* wears a pale pink hand-crocheted jacket, leggings, cap and shirt. *Agnes Smith Collection.*

Travel Time Collection

Each doll comes with extra costumes and accessories.
Caroline, Chipper and *Tiny Tubber* are in trunks. *Twinkie*
and *Butterball* are in wicker hampers. *Little Lovums* is dressed
in a christening dress and is in a wicker rocker.

1296	*Caroline*		2596	*Twinkie*
1596	*Chipper*		6596	*Butterball*
2396	*Tiny Tubber*		8396	*Little Lovums*

Sweet Dreams Collection

1355	*Pun'kin*	Dressed in long floral print gown.
1355B	*Pun'kin*	Same as the above as a black doll.
1655	*Li'l Suzie Sunshine*	Dressed in long floral print gown.
5655	*Dy Dee*	Dressed in floral print sleeper. Has teddy bear.
5655B	*Dy Dee*	Same as he above as a black doll.
6555	*Butterball*	In floral print diaper and fleece blanket.
6555B	*Butterball*	Same as the above as a black doll.
8155	*Baby Button Nose*	Dressed in floral print sleeper.
8155B	*Baby Button Nose*	Same as the above as a black doll.
8355	*Little Lovums*	In floral print infant dress.
9455	*Sweetie Pie*	In floral print two-piece pajamas.

American Beauty Collection

Each doll wears a velveteen dress with a lined tucked
organdy apron trimmed with a matching velveteen bow.

1348	*Pun'kin*		1848	*Suzie Sunshine*
1548	*Chipper*		9348	*Buttercup*
1548B	*Chipper* (black)		9448	*Sweetie Pie*
1648	*Li'l Suzie Sunshine*		9648	*Sugar Plum*

Keepsake Collection

1242	*Antique Bride*	The same as No. 1246 *Crown Princess* of 1978 with a different colored flower.
1742	*Antique Bride*	The same as No. 1746 *Her Royal Highness* of 1978 with a different colored flower.
6241	*Old-Fashioned Boy*	Dressed in velveteen knicker suit with matching hat.
6242	*Old-Fashioned Girl*	In lace-trimmed embroidered dress with matching bonnet. Velveteen ribbon trim.
9442	*Old-Fashioned Baby*	Same as No. 9446 *The Countess* of 1978.

Note: In 1978 the similar dolls were in the *Regal Heirloom*
Collection.

Gigi

In 1979 the collection *Through the Years with Gigi— 1830-1910* was introduced. It was repeated in 1980. The Effanbee Doll Corporation advertised the dolls as a "must for collectors." The first three dolls show *Gigi* as a young girl and use the mold from the *International Collection*, which is marked on the head: "EFFANBEE // 19 © 75 // 1176." The three dolls of *Gigi* as a lady use the *Caroline* mold doll, which is marked on the head: "EFFANBEE // 19 © 75 // 1276." Each model of *Gigi* has a distinct name for the year that it represents. Each doll is all-vinyl and fully-jointed. The first five models have dark brown hair; the last doll— *Grand-Mère*—has gray hair. They all have blue sleep eyes.

Illustration 287. 1838—*Papa's Pet*, No. 1161. *Gigi* wears a lace-trimmed party dress and pantaloons. *Sararose Smith Collection.*

Illustration 288. 1842—*School Girl*, No. 1162. The costume is a dark blue sailor dress and a white straw hat.

Illustration 289. 1846—*Ingenue*, No. 1163. Pale blue batiste dress with embroidery and lace trim; pantaloons. *Sararose Smith Collection.*

200

Illustration 290. 1851—Femme Fatale, No. 1264. The gown is pink taffeta trimmed with ruffles and bows. *Sararose Smith Collection.*

Illustration 291. 1865—Mama, No. 1265. The costume is a lace dress and a straw bonnet with a veil. *Sararose Smith Collection.*

Illustration 292. 1895—Grand-Mère, No. 1266. The dress is lace-trimmed velveteen. The matching hat has a veil. *Sararose Smith Collection.*

Crochet Classics Collection

Each doll wears a hand-crocheted outfit. The models are the
same as 1978 except for the following additions:

1374	*Pun'kin*	
1674	*Li'l Suzie Sunshine*	

The Passing Parade

1561	*Colonial Lady*	Same as No. 1501 in 1978.
1562	*Frontier Woman*	Wears gingham dress with apron; fringe-trimmed shawl; matching bonnet.
1565	*The Hour Glass Look*	Velveteen skirt and jacket; blouse with tucked jabot; matching hat.
1566	*Gibson Girl*	Braid-trimmed skirt; lace-trimmed blouse; straw hat.
1563	*Civil War Lady*	Same as No. 1503 in 1978.
1564	*Gay Nineties*	Fringe-trimmed velveteen skirt; lace trimmed velveteen jacket; lace jabot; matching bonnet.
1567	*Flapper*	Same as No. 1507 in 1978 with the addition of a belt with a buckle.
1568	*The 70s Woman*	Net ruffled gown over a taffeta slip.

Through the Years with Gigi 1830-1900

The collection represents six stages in the life of a French woman.

1161	*Papa's Pet — 1838*	Batiste party dress and pantaloons.
1162	*School Girl — 1842*	Pleated sailor dress; straw hat.
1163	*Ingenue — 1846*	Batiste dress with embroidery trim and ruffled lace hem.
1264	*Femme Fatale — 1851*	Lace-trimmed taffeta dress with rows of ruffles; flowers in hair.
1265	*Mama — 1865*	Lace dress with pleated hem; straw hat.
1266	*Grand-Mère — 1895*	Lace-trimmed velveteen dress; matching hat.

1980-1983

The Effanbee Doll Corporation was "ready for the 80s" by the late 1970s. The Effanbee Limited Edition Doll Club, begun in 1974 with the announcement of the *Limited Edition Precious Baby*, was continuing each year with a new doll for collectors. The *Craftsmen's Corner*, which featured dolls by well-known doll designers, was initiated in 1979 with the introduction of Faith Wick's *Anchors Aweigh* boy and girl and *Party Time* boy and girl. This concept continued with the release of Astry Campbell's *Baby Lisa* in 1980, more dolls by Faith Wick, Joyce Stafford's *Orange Blossom* in 1982, and Jan Hagara's admission to the distinguished group in 1983. In 1980 *The Legend Series* began with the *W.C. Fields Centennial Doll*, one of Effanbee's most exciting innovations ever.

The above dolls are all of special interest to collectors. There were too many new doll models from the short period of 1980 to 1983 to cite all of the ones of collector appeal, but the author feels that, besides the above-mentioned dolls, others of special merit are *Hattie Holiday* in 1981, the *Bobbsey Twins* in 1982 and *Huckleberry Finn* in 1983.

Effanbee Dolls continues to address the market of play dolls with new designs, which in the future will immeasurably elevate their worth as desirable collectibles. Play dolls are, after all, the basis upon which all doll collecting is founded.

1980 Catalog

Discontinued Dolls:

    18in (45.7cm) *Suzie Sunshine*

New for 1980:

Doll	Description	Size
Baby Lisa Prefix No. 10	All-vinyl and fully-jointed baby. Molded hair; painted eyes.	11in (27.9cm)
W.C. Fields Centennial *Doll* Prefix No. 19	All-vinyl and fully-jointed. Molded hair; painted eyes.	15in (38.1cm)
Day by Day Collection *child* Prefix No. 14	All-vinyl and fully-jointed girl. Rooted hair; sleep eyes; freckles across bridge of nose.	11in (27.9cm)
Floppy Prefix No. 27	Vinyl *Suzie Sunshine* head; all-cloth body.	20in (50.8cm)

Note: The prefix 15 was used for both *Chipper* and the 15in (38.1cm) lady doll.

             The prefix 17 was used for both *Miss Chips* and the 18in (45.7cm) lady doll.

International Collection

Nos. 1101 to 1119 same as 1979, with two discontinued models:

1110   *Miss Black America*   1116   *Miss Ancient Egypt*

New for 1980:

1120   *Miss Brazil*
1121   *Greece (soldier)*
1122   *Miss Israel*

Storybook Collection:

Nos. 1175 to 1187 same as 1979, with the following discontinued:

1185   *Pavlova*

New for 1980:

1188   *Mother Hubbard*
1189   *Prince Charming*
1190   *Sleeping Beauty*
1191   *Heidi*

Illustration 293. 11in (27.9cm) *Miss Brazil of the International Collection,* No. 1120, 1980. All-vinyl and fully-jointed. Head marked: "EFFANBEE // 19©75 // 1176." *Marjorie Smith Collection.*

204

Illustration 294. 11in (27.9cm) *Greece (soldier)* from the *International Collection,* No. 1121, 1980. All-vinyl and fully-jointed. Dark brown rooted hair; blue sleep eyes with lashes; painted moustache. Head marked: "EFFANBEE // 19©75 // 1176." *Marjorie Smith Collection.*

Bridal Suite Collection

1514	*Bridesmaid*		1515B	*Bride* (black)
1515	*Bride*		1715	*Bride*

Note: These models are the "lady dolls."

Cream Puff Collection

The babies in this collection are dressed in pastel colors.

2585	*Twinkie* (with pillow)		9385	*Buttercup*
6585	*Butterball*		9485	*Sweetie Pie*
8185	*Baby Button Nose*		9685	*Sugar Plum*
8485	*Lovums*			

Currier and Ives Collection

Nos. 1251, 1252, 1257 and 1258 same as 1979.
New for 1980:

1259	*Crystal Palace*		1260	*Charleston Harbor*

Heart to Heart Collection

Each doll is dressed in traditional outfits. The fabric
    pattern is hearts and flowers with the Effanbee "signature"
    in the background.

1351	*Pun'kin*		8151	*Baby Button Nose*
1351B	*Pun'kin* (black)		8151B	*Baby Button Nose* (black)
1651	*Li'l Suzie Sunshine*		8451	*Lovums*
2351	*Tiny Tubber*		9351	*Buttercup*
2351B	*Tiny Tubber* (black)		9451	*Sweetie Pie*
2352	*Tiny Tubber* (in dress)		9651	*Sugar Plum*
2352B	*Tiny Tubber* (black, in dress)			
2353	*Tiny Tubber* (in blanket)			
2353B	*Tiny Tubber* (black, in blanket)			
2551	*Twinkie*			
2551B	*Twinkie* (black)			
6151	*Baby Winkie*			
6151B	*Baby Winkie* (black)			

Four Seasons Collection

All five models are the same as in 1979.

Crochet Classics Collection

Each doll wears a hand-crocheted outfit.

1374	Pun'kin	6573	Butterball
2373	Tiny Tubber	6574	Butterball (in blanket)
2373B	Tiny Tubber (black)	6574B	Butterball (black in blanket)
2374	Tiny Tubber (in blanket)	8374	Little Lovums
5674	Dy Dee	9474	Sweetie Pie
6174	Baby Winkie	9474B	Sweetie Pie (black)

Cotton Candy Collection

Each doll wears a pink check gingham dress and a white apron with embroidery trim, except No. 6225 Half Pint Boy, who has white pants.

1526	Chipper	6526	Butterball
1526B	Chipper (black)	9326	Buttercup
1626	Li'l Suzie Sunshine	9426	Sweetie Pie
2726	Floppy	9426B	Sweetie Pie (black)
6225	Half Pint Boy	9626	Sugar Plum
6226	Half Pint Girl		

Illustration 295. 11in (27.9cm) *Goldilocks* from the *Storybook Collection,* No. 1184, 1980. All-vinyl and fully-jointed. Blonde rooted hair; blue sleep eyes. The bodice of the dress and the style of the hair are both different than for the same doll in 1979. Head marked: "EFFANBEE// 19©75// 1176." *Agnes Smith Collection.*

Illustration 296. The *Cotton Candy Collection* from the 1980 Effanbee Doll Corporation catalog. The dolls in the top row are 20in (50.8cm) *Sugar Plum,* No. 9626; 11in (27.9cm) *Half Pint Boy,* No. 6225; 11in (27.9cm) *Half Pint Girl,* No. 6226; 15in (38.1cm) *Chipper,* No. 1526; and 20in (50.8cm) *Floppy,* No. 2726. In the bottom row are 16in (40.6cm) *Li'l Suzie Sunshine,* No. 1626; 18in (45.7cm) *Sweetie Pie,* No. 9426; 13in (33cm) *Butterball,* No. 6526; 15in (38.1cm) *Chipper* (black doll), No. 1526B; and 15in (38.1cm) *Buttercup,* No. 9326. Each doll is dressed in pink check gingham. The girls have white aprons; the boy has white pants; *Butterball* has booties.

11

Grandes Dames Collection

This collection is lady dolls in elegant costumes.

1571	*Jezebel*	1771	*Coco*
1572	*Ruby*	1772	*Carnegie Hall*
1572B	*Ruby* (black)	1773	*La Vie En Rose*
1573	*Magnolia*	1774	*Night at the Opera*
1574	*Hyde Park*		

Note: *Magnolia* was No. 1532 in 1979. The 1980 doll is identical.

Petite Filles Collection

Each little girl is dressed in elaborate costumes like their
    "big sisters," the *Grandes Dames.*

The dolls used are *Half Pint* (Prefix 62) and *Li'l Suzie Sunshine*
    (Prefix 16).

1631	*Lili*	6231	*Babette*
1632	*Gabrielle*	6232	*Madeleine*
1633	*Monique*	6233	*Mimi*
1634	*Giselle*	6234	*Brigitte*

Illustration 297. Four of the dolls from the 1980 *Grandes Dames Collection* from the Effanbee Doll Corporation catalog. From left to right: 15in (38.1cm) *Ruby*, No. 1572; 18in (45.7cm) *Coco*, No. 1771; 18in (45.7cm) *Carnegie Hall*, No. 1772; and 15in (38.1cm) *Jezebel*, No. 1571.

207

Faith Wick Originals

See also Chapter 4, *Craftsmen's Corner*

No. 7001—7004 same as 1979

New models for 1980, using same doll:

7005	*Clown—Boy*
7006	*Clown—Girl*

Baby Lisa by Astri

See also Chapter 4, *Craftsmen's Corner*

1011	*Baby Lisa*	Wrapped in a blanket.
1012	*Baby Lisa*	Wears dress and bonnet and lies on a pillow.
1013	*Baby Lisa*	Lies in a wicker hamper and has a layette.

Keepsake Collection

The following three dolls were also in this collection in 1979:

1242	*Antique Bride*
1742	*Antique Bride (Miss Chips)**
9442	*Old Fashioned Baby (Sweetie Pie)*

Through the Years with Gigi

All six dolls are identical with the models in 1979.

Travel Time Collection

Each doll comes with extra costumes and accessories.
   Caroline, *Li'l Suzie Sunshine* and *Tiny Tubber* are in trunks.
   The *Tiny Tubber Twins* and *Twinkie* are in wicker hampers.
   Baby Winkie is in a wicker cradle. *Little Lovums* is in a
   wicker bed.

1297	*Caroline*		2597	*Twinkie*
1697	*Li'l Suzie Sunshine*		6197	*Baby Winkie*
2396	*Tiny Tubber**		8397	*Little Lovums*
2397	*Tiny Tubber Twins*			

Sweet Dreams Collection

The babies in sleep wear is a similar concept to that of
   1979, except that each costume is a "hearts and flowers"
   pattern with the Effanbee "signature" in the background.

5655	*Dy Dee* with teddy bear		8155	*Baby Button Nose*
5655B	Same as the above as a black doll.		8155B	*Baby Button Nose* (black)
			8355	*Little Lovums*
6155	*Baby Winkie*		9455	*Sweetie Pie*
6555	*Butterball*		9455B	*Sweetie Pie* (black)
6555B	*Butterball* (black)			

*Same as 1979.   208

Rhapsody in Blue Collection

Each doll is dressed in dark blue and white dresses that
are trimmed with wide lace.

1340	Pun'kin	9340	Buttercup
1540	Chipper	9440	Sweetie Pie
1640	L'il Suzie Sunshine	9640	Sugar Plum
1740	Miss Chips		

Day by Day Collection

Each 11in (27.9cm) little girl is dressed in a costume
that is appropriate for each day of the week.

1401	Monday	1405	Friday
1402	Tuesday	1406	Saturday
1403	Wednesday	1407	Sunday
1404	Thursday		

W.C. Fields Centennial Doll
See Chapter 3, *The Legend Series.*

Illustration 298. 18in (45.7cm) *La Vie En Rose* from the 1980 *Grandes Dames Collection*, No. 1773. All-vinyl and fully-jointed. Dark brown rooted hair; blue sleep eyes with lashes. Head marked: "EFFANBEE // 19©80 // 1780." The gown is taffeta with a flower pattern. The bow in the veiled hat matches the dress. *Patricia Gardner Collection.*

Illustration 299. 18in (45.7cm) *La Vie En Rose*, 1980. *Patricia Gardner Collection.*

1981 Catalog

Discontinued Dolls:

W. C. Fields Centennial Doll
11in (27.9cm) *Caroline*, also used for *Currier and Ives*, etc.

New for 1981:

Doll	Description	Size

John Wayne
    Prefix No. 19
	All-vinyl and fully-jointed.
	    Molded hair; painted eyes.
		17in (43.2cm)

Pierrot*
    Prefix No. 22
	All-vinyl and fully-jointed.
	    Black painted head; sleep eyes.
		11in (27.9cm)

Girl/Boy *(Pride of South)*
    Prefix No. 33
	All-vinyl and fully-jointed.
	    Rooted hair; sleep eyes.
		13in (33cm)

Girl *(Four Seasons)*
    Prefix No. 35
	All-vinyl and fully-jointed.
	    Rooted hair; sleep eyes.
		15in (38.1cm)

Girl *(Petite Filles)*
    Prefix No. 36
	All-vinyl and fully-jointed.
	    Rooted hair; big sleep eyes
	    with heavy painted lashes.
		16in (40.6cm)

Pierrot*
    Prefix No. 45
	Vinyl head, arms and legs; soft body.
	    Black painted head; sleep eyes.
		15in (38.1cm)

Cookie
    Prefix No. 46
	All-vinyl and fully-jointed.
	    Molded hair; sleep eyes.
		16in (40.6cm)

Pierrot*
    Prefix No. 47
	Vinyl head, arms and legs; soft body.
	    Black painted head; sleep eyes.
		18in (45.7cm)

Pierrot*
    Prefix No. 55
	All-vinyl and fully-jointed.
	    Black painted head; sleep eyes.
		15in (38.1cm)

Girl *(Huggables)*
    Prefix No. 63
	Vinyl head with rooted hair and
	    sleep eyes. Stuffed cloth body.
		14in (35.6cm)

Witch (Faith Wick)
    Prefix No. 71
	Vinyl head with rooted hair and
	    painted eyes. Stuffed cloth body.
		18in (45.7cm)

Pierrot*
    Prefix No. 77
	All-vinyl and fully-jointed.
	    Black painted head; sleep eyes.
		18in (45.7cm)

Baby *(Petite Filles)*
    Prefix No. 95
	Vinyl head, arms and legs. Soft
	    body. Rooted hair; sleep eyes;
	    cry voice.
		18in (45.7cm)

*These dolls are the standard molds without rooted hair.

Note: The prefix 15 was still used for both *Chipper* and the 15in (38.1cm) lady doll. The prefix 17 was still used for both *Miss Chips* and the 18in (45.7cm) lady doll.

International Collection

Same as 1980 with the following discontinued:

1117   *Spain* (boy)   1121   *Greece (soldier)*

Illustration 300. 11in (27.9cm) *Jill* and *Jack* from the *Storybook Collection*, Nos. 1187 and 1186, 1981. All-vinyl and fully-jointed. Reddish-blonde rooted hair; blue sleep eyes. Heads marked: "EFFANBEE // 17© 75 // 1176." In catalog illustrations *Jack* never had a vest like this; *Jill* had a different braid trim on her apron in 1979 and 1980. *Agnes Smith Collection.*

New for 1981:

1123   *Miss Czechoslovakia*

1124   *Miss Denmark*

1125   *Miss Norway*

Storybook Collection

Same as 1980 with the following new for 1981:

1192	*Pinocchio*	1195	*Gretel*
1193	*Mother Goose*	1196	*Mary Had a Little Lamb*
1194	*Hansel*		

Illustration 301. 11in (27.9cm) *Pinocchio* from the *Storybook Collection* of 1981, No. 1192. All-vinyl and fully-jointed. This is the same head mold as all other *Storybook* dolls except that the mold was expanded for the longer nose, which is painted bright red. (This is *not* the Walt Disney Pinocchio.) The clothing and shoes are felt.

Les Enfants Collection

This collection is babies in pastel dresses.

2587	*Twinkie*	8487	*Lovums*
6587	*Butterball*	9387	*Buttercup*
8187	*Baby Button Nose*	9487	*Sweetie Pie*
8387	*Little Lovums*	9687	*Sugar Plum*

Pride of the South Collection

This collection is five ladies in gowns and one gentleman
in a three-piece suit.

3331	*Riverboat Gambler*	3334	*Savannah*
3332	*Natchez*	3335	*New Orleans*
3333	*Mobile*	3336	*Charleston*

Illustration 302. 11in (27.9cm) *Mother Goose* from the *Storybook Collection* of 1981, No. 1193. All-vinyl and fully-jointed. Blonde rooted hair; blue sleep eyes. *Marjorie Smith Collection.*

Illustration 303. 11in (27.9cm) *Gretel* and *Hansel* from the 1981 *Storybook Collection,* Nos. 1195 and 1194. All-vinyl and fully-jointed. Yellow rooted hair; blue sleep eyes. *Marjorie Smith Collection.*

Return with us to the days of yesteryear in the "Old South". This collection of six 13" dolls evokes memories of elegant plantations, majestic riverboats and the smell of fragrant magnolias. Each one is elegantly attired for an afternoon of socializing and mint julips . . . But watch out for the Riverboat Gambler!

Illustration 304. Pride of the South Collection from the 1981 Effanbee Doll Corporation catalog. Each doll is 13in (33cm) tall. In the top row: *Mobile*, No. 3333; *Charleston*, No. 3336; and *Natchez*, No. 3332. In front are *Riverboat Gambler*, No. 3331; *New Orleans*, No. 3335; and *Savannah*, No. 3334.

Illustration 305. 13in (33cm) *Riverboat Gambler* from the 1981 *Pride of the South Collection*, No. 3331. All-vinyl and fully-jointed. Dark brown rooted hair; blue sleep eyes. Head marked: "EFFANBEE // 3381 // 19©81."

213

Crochet Classics Collection

The dolls in hand-crocheted outfits are the same as 1980,
with the following changes:

Discontinued:

2374	Tiny Tubber (with blanket)	8374	Little Lovums

New for 1981:

2375	Tiny Tubber (with pillow)	6174B	Baby Winkie (black doll with pillow.)
4674	Cookie		
		9374	Buttercup

Over the Rainbow Collection

Each doll wears an outfit of pastel gingham and white,
trimmed with gingham bows.

1328	Pun'kin	6228	Half Pint Girl
1328B	Pun'kin (black)	6528	Butterball
1528	Chipper	9328	Buttercup
1528B	Chipper (black)	9428	Sweetie Pie
1728	Miss Chips	9428B	Sweetie Pie (black)
2728	Floppy	9628	Sugar Plum
6227	Half Pint Boy		

Illustration 306. 16in (40.6cm) Genevieve of the Petite Filles Collection of 1981, No. 3642. All-vinyl and fully-jointed. Dark brown rooted hair; brown sleep eyes with heavy painted lashes. Head marked: "EFFANBEE // 3681 // 19©81." Patricia Gardner Collection.

Grandes Dames Collection

The lady dolls in elegant gowns for 1981 are:

1156	Francoise	1558	Gramercy Park
1157	Lady Ascot	1559	Shauna
1158	Peaches and Cream	1756	Daphne
1158B	Peaches and Cream (black)	1757	Opal
1159	Saratoga	1758	Topaz
1556	Chantilly	1759	Turquoise
1557	Covent Garden		

Petite Filles Collection

This collection is vinyl dolls with faces that look
like that of antique porcelain dolls. The Prefix No. 95
is the 18in (45.7cm) baby; the Prefix No. 36 is the 16in
(40.6cm) girl. Each pair of dolls is dressed in matching
dresses.

3641	Denise	3643	Marianne
9541	Bébé Denise	9543	Bébé Marianne
3642	Genevieve	3644	Nanette
9542	Bébé Genevieve	9544	Bébé Nanette

Illustration 307. Part of the *Petite Filles Collection* from the 1981 Effanbee Doll Corporation catalog. From left to right: 16in (40.6cm) *Denise*, No. 3641; 18in (45.7cm) *Bèbè Denise*, No. 9541; 16in (40.6cm) *Marianne*, No. 3643; and 18in (45.7cm) *Bèbè Marianne*, No. 9543.

Illustration 308. 16in (40.6cm) *Nanette* of the 1981 *Petite Filles Collection*, No. 3644. All-vinyl and fully-jointed. Blonde rooted hair; blue sleep eyes with heavy painted lashes. Head marked: "EFFANBEE // 3681 // 19©81." *Patricia Gardner Collection.*

Heart to Heart Collection

These dolls are dressed in the "hearts and flowers pattern
with the Effanbee signature" in the background.

1359	*Pun'kin*	2359B	*Tiny Tubber* (black with pillow)
1359B	*Pun'kin* (black)	2559	*Twinkie*
2357	*Tiny Tubber* (with blanket)	2559B	*Twinkie* (black)
		6159	*Baby Winkie*
2357B	*Tiny Tubber* (black)	6159B	*Baby Winkie* (black)
2358	*Tiny Tubber*	8159	*Baby Button Nose*
2358B	*Tiny Tubber*	8459	*Lovums*
2359	*Tiny Tubber* (with pillow)	9359	*Buttercup*
		9459	*Sweetie Pie*
		9659	*Sugar Plum*

Four Seasons Collection

A new 1981 girl in four seasonal costume changes.

3531	*Spring*	3533	*Autumn*
3532	*Summer*	3534	*Winter*

*Illustrataion 309. 16in (40.6cm) Hattie Holiday, No. 1663
Halloween, 1981. All-vinyl and fully-jointed. Blonde rooted
hair; blue sleep eyes. This is the same doll as Li'l Suzie
Sunshine and she is marked on the head: "EFFANBEE //
19©72 // 1672. Patricia Gardner Collection.*

Day By Day Collection

All seven models are the same as in 1980.

Bridal Suite Collection

1525	*Bride*	3324	*Bridesmaid*
1525B	*Bride* (black)	3325	*Bridesmaid*
1725	*Antique Bride**		

Faith Wick Originals

See also Chapter 4, *Craftsmen's Corner.*

7005	*Clown—Boy;*	7006 *Clown—Girl. Same as 1980.*

New for 1981:

7015	*Peddler*
7110	*Wicket Witch*
7111	*Hearth Witch*

Baby Lisa by Astri

See also Chapter 4, *Craftsmen's Corner.*

1010	*Baby Lisa* in bonnet with blanket.

1012 and 1013 *Baby Lisa* same as 1980.

*Same as *Antique Bride*, No. 1742 in 1979 and 1980.

Illustration 310. 15in (38.1cm) *Autumn* of the *Four Seasons Collection* of 1981, No. 3533. All-vinyl and fully-jointed. Blonde rooted hair; blue sleep eyes; freckles across nose. Head marked: "EFFANBEE // 19©81 // 1431." *Patricia Gardner Collection.*

Huggables Collection

Three 14in (35.6cm) vinyl head, soft body storybook characters.

6375	Alice in Wonderland
6377	Little Bo-Peep
6378	Little Red Riding Hood

Sweet Dreams Collection

Nine models are identical to those of 1980, with one
addition:

| 6255 | Half Pint |

Send in the Clowns Collection

Five different sizes of *Pierrot* all dressed in a white
costume with red trim.

2245	11in (27.9cm)	4745	18in (45.7cm) (soft body)
4545	15in (38.1cm) (soft body)	7745	18in (45.7cm)
5545	15in (38.1cm)		

Travel Time Collection

This collection is the same as 1980, except that *Caroline*
in the trunk, No. 1140, wears a sailor outfit and is sub-
stituted for *Caroline*, No. 1297 of 1980. The Prefix No. 11
also shows that *Caroline* now used the 11in (27.9cm) doll of the
International Collection.

Hi! I'm Hattie Holiday

This collection is *Li'l Suzie Sunshine* dressed in four
seasonal costumes.

| 1661 | Easter (dress) | 1663 | Halloween (gypsy with mask) |
| 1662 | July 4th (majorette) | 1664 | Christmas (in red coat and hat) |

Note: The *Hattie Holiday* outfits were also sold separately.

John Wayne

See Chapter 3, *The Legend Series.*

Illustration 311. 14in (35.6cm) *Alice in Wonderland* from the *Huggables
Collection*, No. 6375, 1981. Vinyl head with blonde rooted hair and black
side-glancing pupilless eyes. The body is stuffed cloth and is jointed at the
arms and legs. *Patricia Gardner Collection.*

1982 Catalog

Discontinued Dolls:

1981 John Wayne

16in (40.6cm) girl (*Petite Filles*)

16in (40.6cm) *Cookie*

18in (45.7cm) *Pierrot* with soft body.

18in (45.7cm) baby (*Petite Filles*)

New for 1982:

Doll	Description	Size
Bobbsey Twins Prefix No. 12	All-vinyl and fully-jointed. *Flossie* has rooted hair and sleep eyes. *Freddie* has molded hair and sleep eyes.	11in (27.9cm)
Mae West Prefix No. 19	All-vinyl and fully-jointed. Rooted hair; painted eyes.	18in (45.7cm)
John Wayne (1982) Prefix No. 29	All-vinyl and fully-jointed. Molded hair; sleep eyes.	18in (45.7cm)
Old Fashioned Nast *Santa* Prefix No. 72	Vinyl head and hands; stuffed cloth body. Molded hair and painted eyes.	18in (45.7cm)
Orange Blossom Prefix No. 75	All-vinyl and fully-jointed. Rooted hair; painted eyes.	13in (33cm)
Girl (*Age of Elegance*) Prefix No. 78	All-vinyl and fully-jointed. Rooted hair; sleep eyes with heavy painted lashes.	18in (45.7cm)

Note: The prefix No. 15 was still used for both *Chipper* and the 15in (38.1cm) lady doll. The prefix No. 17 was still used for both *Miss Chips* and the 18in (45.7cm) lady doll.

International Collection

Same as 1981 with the following additions:

1126   *Miss Argentina*

1127   *Miss Austria*

1128   *Turkey*

Storybook Collection

Same as 1981 with the following additions:

1172	*Hans Brinker*	1198	*Mary Poppins*
1173	*Sugar Plum Fairy*	1199	*Rapunzel*
1197	*Peter Pan*		

Illustration 312. 11in (27.9cm) *Sugar Plum Fairy*, No. 1173, from the 1982 *Storybook Collection*. All-vinyl and fully-jointed. Blonde rooted hair; blue sleep eyes. Head marked: "EFFANBEE // 19©75 // 1176." *Patricia Gardner Collection.*

Illustration 313. 11in (27.9cm) *Mary Poppins*, No. 1198, from the *Storybook Collection*, 1982. All-vinyl and fully-jointed. Black rooted hair; blue sleep eyes. The coat and hat are dark blue; the scarf is yellow. *Patricia Gardner Collection.*

Illustration 314. The *Absolutely Abigail Collection*, 1982. Each character is 13in (33cm) tall. From left to right the dolls are: *Cousin Jeremy*, No. 3310; *Recital Time*, No. 3312; *Sunday Best*, No. 3311; *Strolling in the Park*, No. 3313; and *Afternoon Tea*, No. 3314. Each girl must be *Abigail*, as the catalog literature describes *Jeremy* as "*Abigail's* best friend." *Photograph courtesy of the Effanbee Doll Corporation.*

Huggables Collection

Same as 1981 with one addition:

6376   *Pinocchio*

Absolutely Abigail Collection

The set is four girls and a boy from the 19th century.
　　Each doll is 13in (33cm).

3310	*Cousin Jeremy*	3313	*Strolling in the Park*
3311	*Sunday Best*	3314	*Afternoon Tea*
3312	*Recital Time*		

Crochet Classics Collection

This set is nine different babies in hand-crocheted
　　costumes.

2373	*Tiny Tubber*	9374*	*Buttercup*
2373B	*Tiny Tubber* (black)	9474*	*Sweetie Pie*
6174*	*Baby Winkie*	9474B*	*Sweetie Pie* (black)
6573*	*Butterball* (rooted hair)		
6574*	*Butterball* (molded hair)		
6574B*	*Butterball* (molded hair, black doll)		

Hi! I'm Hattie Holiday

All four dolls and the four costumes which could also be ordered
　　separately are identical to 1981.

Sweet Dreams Collection

This collection is babies dressed for bed in the
　　"hearts and flowers pattern with the Effanbee
　　signature."

5655*	*Dy Dee*	8155B*	*Baby Button Nose* (black)
5655B*	*Dy Dee* (black)	8355	*Little Lovums*
6555*	*Butterball*	9455*	*Sweetie Pie*
6555B*	*Butterball* (black)	9455B*	*Sweetie Pie* (black)
8155*	*Baby Button Nose*		

Pride of the South Collection

This set is five lady dolls dressed as Southern belles.
　　They are identical to the dolls of 1981, except that
　　the *Riverboat Gambler* (No. 3331) was discontinued.

---

*Identical to 1981.

Heaven Sent Collection

The collection is six babies attired in sheer pastel
dotted swiss dresses with smocked bodices.

6588	*Butterball*	9388	*Buttercup*
8188	*Baby Button Nose*	9688	*Sugar Plum*
8388	*Little Lovums*		
8488	*Lovums*		

Grandes Dames Collection

The lady dolls in fancy gowns for 1982 are:

1151	*Elizabeth*	1551	*Guinevere*
1152	*Amanda*	1552	*Olivia*
1152B	*Amanda* (black)	1553	*Hester*
1153	*Katherine*	1554	*Claudette*
1154	*Robyn*		

Heart to Heart Collection

The babies are dressed in the "hearts and flowers pattern
with the Effanbee signature" in the background.

1359*	*Pun'kin*	2559*	*Twinkie*
1359B*	*Pun'kin* (black)	2559B*	*Twinkie* (black)
2357	*Tiny Tubber* (bunting)	6159*	*Baby Winkie*
2357B	*Tiny Tubber* (black doll in bunting)	6159B*	*Baby Winkie* (black)
2358	*Tiny Tubber* (in dress)	8459	*Lovums*
		9359	*Buttercup*
2358B	*Tiny Tubber* (black doll in dress)	9459	*Sweetie Pie*

Parade of the Wooden Soldiers

Three different models dressed as soldiers in red and white.

1149	11in (27.9cm) *Soldier*
1549	15in (38.1cm) *Soldier*
1749	18in (45.7cm) *Soldier*

Four Seasons Collection

All four models are identical to 1981.

Day by Day Collection

All seven models are the same as in 1980 and 1981.

---

*Identical to 1981.

The effect is breathtaking. . . .Our array of
eight stunning ladies is dressed in a manner
which reflects "European" couture combined with Effanbee's special "touch" of
originality, workmanship and hand sewn
details.

1552 — 15"
OLIVIA

1554 — 15"
CLAUDETTE

1551 — 15"
GUINEVERE

1553 — 15"
HESTER

1151 — 11" ELIZABETH

1154 — 11" ROBYN

1153 — 11" KATHERINE

*1152 — 11" AMANDA

*Black dolls available in this style.
Add "B" after number.

Page 15

Illustration 315. The 1982 *Grandes Dames Collection* from the Effanbee
Doll Corporation catalog. The dolls in the top row are all 15in (38.1cm) and
they are *Guinevere*, No. 1551; *Olivia*, No. 1552; *Claudette*, No. 1554; and
Hester, No. 1553. The dolls in the front row are all 11in (27.9cm) and they
are *Elizabeth*, No. 1151; *Robyn*, No. 1154; *Katherine*, No. 1153; and
Amanda, No. 1152.

Parade of the Wooden
Soldiers™

Hear the strains of the music
beginning to play?. . .It's
not your imagination. Effanbee
has brought to life this charming bit of nostalgia with their
own smartly uniformed soldiers. So join the parade by
picking your favorite collectible.

1749 — 18" SOLDIER

1549 — SOLDIER

1149 — 11" SOLDIER

Illustration 316. Parade of the Wooden Soldiers from the 1982 Effanbee
Doll Corporation catalog. From left to right, the stock numbers for each
Soldier are: 15in (38.1cm), No. 1549; 18in (45.7cm), No. 1749; and 11in
(27.9cm), No. 1149.

Illustration 317. The *Four Seasons Collection* from the 1982 Effanbee Doll Corporation catalog. Each doll is 15in (38.1cm). At the top are No. 3531, *Spring* and No. 3532, *Summer*. At the bottom are No. 3533, *Autumn* and No. 3534, *Winter*.

Illustration 318. The *Age of Elegance Collection* from the 1982 Effanbee Doll Corporation catalog. Each doll is 18in (45.7cm) tall. The dolls are *Westminster Cathedral*, No. 7854; *Buckingham Palace*, No. 7851; *Versailles*, No. 7852; and *Victoria Station*, No. 7853.

The Age of Elegance Collection

The collection is four models dressed in lavish costumes
of the 19th century. The dolls' faces resemble bisque in design.

7851	*Buckingham Palace*	7853	*Victoria Station*
7852	*Versailles*	7854	*Westminster Cathedral*

Send in the Clowns Collection

The *Pierrot* dolls are the same as in 1981, except that
No. 4745, the 18in (45.7cm) with the soft body, was discontinued.

The Legend Series

1982	*Mae West*	2981	*John Wayne*

See Chapter 3, *Legend Series.*

Enchanted Garden Collection

The collection is 10 different dolls dressed in a flowered print.

1329	*Pun'kin*	2729	*Floppy*
1329B	*Pun'kin* (black)	6529	*Butterball*
1529	*Chipper*	9429	*Sweetie Pie*
1529B	*Chipper* (black)	9429B	*Sweetie Pie* (black)
2529	*Twinkie*	9629	*Sugar Plum*

Illustration 319. Send in the Clowns Collection, 1982. Each Pierrot is, from left to right: 11in (27.9cm), No. 2245; 18in (45.7cm), No. 7745; 15in (38.1cm) with a soft body, No. 4545; and 15in (38.1cm) with a jointed vinyl body, No. 5545. Dolls and sign borrowed from the Effanbee Doll Corporation.

225

Craftsmen's Corner

1012	*Baby Lisa*	Same as in 1980 and 1981.
1013	*Baby Lisa*	Same as in 1980 and 1981.
7501	*Orange Blossom*	
7110	*Wicket Witch*	Same as in 1981.
7111	*Hearth Witch*	Same as in 1981.
7006	*Clown—Girl*	Same as in 1980 and 1981.
7007	*Billy Bum*	
7015	*Peddler*	Same as in 1981.
7201	*Old Fashioned Nast Santa*	

Travel Time Collection

2398	*Tiny Tubber*	In trunk with layette.
2598	*Twinkie*	In wicker hamper with layette.
6197	*Baby Winkie*	Wears jacket, bonnet and diaper. Comes in a wicker cradle with a pillow.

Illustration 320. The *Enchanted Garden Collection* from the 1982 Effanbee Doll Corporation catalog. The dolls' names and the stock numbers are printed with each doll.

Bridal Suite Collection

| 1522 | *Bride (Chipper)* | 3321 | *Bridesmaid* |
| 1522B | *Bride (Black Chipper)* | 3322 | *Bride* |

Just Friends Collection

This set is six different models of *Half Pint* dressed in folk costumes.

6201	*Dutch Treat—Boy*	6204	*Swiss Yodeler—Girl*
6202	*Dutch Treat—Girl*	6205	*Alpine Hikers—Boy*
6203	*Swiss Yodeler—Boy*	6206	*Alpine Hikers—Girl*

Illustration 321. Just Friends Collection, 1982. Each doll is 11in (27.9cm) Half Pint. All-vinyl and fully-jointed. Rooted hair; black side-glancing pupilless eyes. The two top-most dolls are Alpine Hikers Girl, No. 6206, and Boy, No. 6205. From the far left they are Swiss Yodeler Boy, No. 6203 and in front, Swiss Yodeler Girl, No. 6204; Dutch Treat Boy, No. 6201; and Dutch Treat Girl, No. 6202. Photograph courtesy of the Effanbee Doll Corporation.

Bobbsey Twins

This is *Freddie* and *Flossie*, based on the books that
are copyrighted by the Stratemeyer Syndicate. The dolls
each come dressed in a basic outfit and there are four
additional boxed outfits for each doll.

1201   *Freddie*   1212   *Flossie*

Costumes:

1221   *Winter Wonderland* for *Freddie*
1222   *Winter Wonderland* for *Flossie*
1223   *At the Seashore* for *Freddie*
1224   *At the Seashore* for *Flossie*
1225   *Out West* for *Freddie*
1226   *Out West* for *Flossie*
1227   *Go A' Sailing* for *Freddie*
1228   *Go A' Sailing* for *Flossie*

Illustration 322. The Bobbsey Twins, 1982. Each doll is 11in (27.9cm) and
is all-vinyl and fully-jointed. *Flossie*, No. 1202, has blonde rooted hair and
blue sleep eyes. *Freddie*, No. 1201, has molded hair and blue sleep eyes.
The heads are marked: "F & B // THE BOBBSEY TWINS® // © 1982 //
STRATEMEYER SYN." *Photograph courtesy of the Effanbee Doll
Corporation.* "The Bobbsey Twins" is a registered trademark and is
copyrighted by the Stratemeyer Syndicate. The dolls are based on
copyrighted characters from the children's books.

Illustration 323. Freddie, showing his "Bobbsey Twins" wrist tag. "The
Bobbsey Twins" is a registered trademark and is copyrighted by the
Stratemeyer Syndicate.

Illustration 324. *Freddie* and *Flossie* modeling the extra boxed outfits that were sold for each doll. At the top are Nos. 1225 and 1226, "Out West," and Nos. 1227 and 1228, "Go A' Sailing." At the bottom are Nos. 1223 and 1224, "At the Seashore," and Nos. 1221 and 1222, "Winter Wonderland." *Photograph courtesy of the Effanbee Doll Corporation.* "The Bobbsey Twins" is a registered trademark and is copyrighted by the Stratemeyer Syndicate.

Illustration 325. *Flossie's* packaged outfit "At the Seashore," No. 1224. "The Bobbsey Twins" is a registered trademark and is copyrighted by the Stratemeyer Syndicate.

Illustration 326. *Freddie's* boxed outfit "Out West," No. 1225. "The Bobbsey Twins" is a registered trademark and is copyrighted by the Stratemeyer Syndicate.

1983 Catalog

Discontinued Dolls:

> *Mae West*
> *1982 John Wayne*
> 27in (68.6cm) *Floppy (Suzie Sunshine* head)
> 17in (43.2cm) *Miss Chips*

New for 1983:

Doll	Description	Size
lady doll (used for *Women of the Ages*) Prefix No. 13	All-vinyl and fully-jointed. Rooted hair; sleep eyes.	13in (33cm)
Suzie Sunshine (reintroduction of doll discontinued in 1980) Prefix No. 18	All-vinyl and fully-jointed. Rooted hair; sleep eyes.	18in (45.7cm)
Groucho Marx Prefix No. 19	All-vinyl and fully-jointed. Painted hair; painted eyes.	17in (43.2cm)
Cristina Prefix No. 74	All-vinyl and fully-jointed. Rooted hair; painted eyes.	15in (38.1cm)
Mark Twain Prefix No. 76	All-vinyl and fully-jointed. Painted hair; painted eyes.	16in (40.6cm)
Huckleberry Finn Prefix No. 76	All-vinyl and fully-jointed. Painted hair; painted eyes.	13½in (34.3cm)
George Washington Prefix No. 79	All-vinyl and fully-jointed. Painted hair; painted eyes.	16in (40.6cm)
Abraham Lincoln Prefix No. 79	All-vinyl and fully-jointed. Painted hair and beard; painted eyes.	18in (45.7cm)
Mama's Baby Prefix No. 99	Soft vinyl head, arms and legs; cloth body; painted hair; sleep eyes.	25in (63.5cm)

Changes:

Lisa Grows Up Prefix No. 10	This is the same head as *Baby Lisa*. All-vinyl and fully-jointed toddler.	11in (27.9cm)
Lotus Blossom Prefix No. 75	Called *Orange Blossom* in 1982.	

International Collection

Same as 1982 with the following additions:

1110	*Miss Hungary*
1116	*Miss Romania*
1117	*Miss Greece*

Storybook Collection

Discontinued:

1198   *Mary Poppins*

New for 1983:

1171   *Little Miss Muffett*
1174   *Pollyanna*
1181   *Rebecca of Sunnybrook Farm*
1182   *Captain Kidd*
1183   *Musketeer*
1185   *Tinkerbell*

Send in the Clowns Collection

All four models are the same as 1982.

Granny's Corner Collection

In this collection Effanbee "favorites" are all dressed
    in old-fashioned cotton outfits.

1382	*Pun'kin*	2682	*Baby Face*
1382B	*Pun'kin* (black)	6382	*Pint Size*
1582	*Chipper*	6582	*Butterball*
1582B	*Chipper* (black)	9382	*Buttercup*
1681	*Boy (Li'l Suzie Sunshine)*	9482	*Sweetie Pie*
1682	*L'il Suzie Sunshine*	9682	*Sugar Plum*

Just Friends Collection

The set is six different models of *Half Pint* in
    folk costumes.

6201	*Dutch Treat* (boy)*	6204	*Swiss Yodeler* (girl)*
6202	*Dutch Treat* (girl)*	6207	*Fortune Cookie* (boy)
6203	*Swiss Yodeler* (boy)*	6208	*Fortune Cookie* (girl)

Bridal Suite Collection

| 1524 | *Bride* | 3323 | *Bridesmaid* |
| 1524B | *Bride* (black) | 3324 | *Bride* |

The Presidents

| 7901 | *George Washington* | 7902 | *Abraham Lincoln* |

---

*Same as in 1982.

231

Illustration 328. The first two dolls from the series *Great Moments in Literature*, 1983. At the left is 13½in (34.3cm) *Huckleberry Finn*, No. 7632; at the right is 16in (40.6cm) *Mark Twain*, No. 7631. Both dolls are all-vinyl and fully-jointed with painted hair and eyes. *Photograph courtesy of the Effanbee Doll Corporation.*

Pride of the South Collection

Five lady dolls are dressed as Southern belles.

3333	Mobile*	3338	Richmond
3336	Charleston*	3339	Dallas
3337	Atlanta		

The Legend Series

1983	Groucho Marx

Great Moments in Literature

7631	Mark Twain	7632	Huckleberry Finn

Travel Time Collection

2398	Tiny Tubber*	2598	Twinkie*

*Same as in 1982.

Grandes Dames Collection

The lady dolls for 1983 dressed in elegant gowns are:

1155	*Lorraine*	1555	*Coco*
1156	*Vicki*	1556	*Allison*
1157	*Priscilla*	1557	*Stephanie*
1158	*Suzanne*	1558	*Diane*
1158B	*Suzanne* (black)		

Heart to Heart Collection

All of the babies in this collection are dressed in sleep wear in the "Effanbee signature pattern."

2354	*Tiny Tubber* (in bunting)	6555	*Butterball*
		6555B	*Butterball* (black)
2354B	*Tiny Tubber* (black in bunting)	8155	*Baby Button Nose*
		8155B	*Baby Button Nose* (black)
2355	*Tiny Tubber*	8355	*Little Lovums*
2355B	*Tiny Tubber* (black)	8455	*Lovums*
2555	*Twinkie*	9455	*Sweetie Pie*
5655	*Dydee*	9455B	*Sweetie Pie* (black)
5655B	*Dydee* (black)		
6155	*Baby Winkie*		
6155B	*Baby Winkie* (black)		

Four Seasons Collection

All four models are the same as in 1978-1982.

Bobbsey Twins

1231	*1920's Freddie*	1242	*1930's Flossie*
1232	*1920's Flossie*	1251	*1940's Freddie*
1241	*1930's Freddie*	1252	*1940's Flossie*

The Age of Elegance Collection

This collection is four models dressed in lavish costumes of the 19th century. The dolls' faces resemble bisque in design.

7850	*Roma*	7854	*Westminster Cathedral**
7852	*Versailles**	7856	*Gay Paree*

Crochet Classics Collection

The set is nine different babies in hand-crocheted costumes.

2376	*Tiny Tubber*	6576	*Butterball* (sprayed hair)
2376B	*Tiny Tubber* (black)	9376	*Buttercup*
6176	*Baby Winkie*	9476	*Sweetie Pie*
6575	*Butterball*	9476B	*Sweetie Pie* (black)
6575B	*Butterball* (black)		

*Same as in 1982.

Illustration 329. From the *Absolutely Abigail Collection*, 1983. 13in (33cm) *Sunday Best*, No. 3311. All-vinyl and fully-jointed with rooted hair and sleep eyes. Doll borrowed from the Effanbee Doll Corporation.

OPPOSITE PAGE: *Illustration 332* . 18in (45.7cm) *Suzie Sunshine* wearing a pinafore, No. 1862, 1983. All-vinyl and fully-jointed with rooted hair and sleep eyes. Doll borrowed from the Effanbee Doll Corporation.

Illustration 330. 13½in (34.3cm) *Huckleberry Finn,* 1983. Doll borrowed from the Effanbee Doll Corporation.

Illustration 331. The 11in (27.9cm) toddlers from the *One World Collection,* 1983. The dolls are all-vinyl and fully-jointed with rooted hair and sleep eyes. From left to right they are: *Kim,* No. 1414; *Jane,* No. 1410; *Sissy,* No. 1412. Dolls borrowed from the Effanbee Doll Corporation.

234

Suzie Sunshine Collection

18in (45.7cm) *Suzie Sunshine* in three costumes:

1861   Wears an embroidered gown.
1862   Wears a long gown and pinafore.
1863   Wears a print gown.

Madame Butterfly Collection

Three different lady dolls are dressed in "colorful
kimonos" and are painted with "traditional makeup" of
the Orient.

1140   11in (27.9cm)
1540   15in (38.1cm)
1740   18in (43.2cm)

Sheer Delight Collection

The collection is eight babies dressed in "pastel frosted
gowns and bonnets."

2589	*Twinkie*	8489	*Lovums*
6589	*Butterball*	9389	*Buttercup*
8189	*Baby Button Nose*	9489	*Sweetie Pie*
8389	*Little Lovums*	9689	*Sugarplum*

One World Collection

The three dolls in this set are the girl doll used
for the *Day by Day Collection* in 1980, 1981 and 1982.

1410   11in (27.9cm) *Jane*, a white child
1412   11in (27.9cm) *Sissy*, a black child
1414   11in (27.9cm) *Kim*, an oriental child

Women of the Ages Collection

This set consists of four 13in (33cm) lady dolls dressed
to represent:

3371	*Martha Washington*	3379	*Queen Elizabeth*
3372	*Betsy Ross*		
3373	*Florence Nightingale*		

Absolutely Abigail Collection

The collection is four girls and a boy from the 19th century.

3310	*Cousin Jeremy**	3314	*Afternoon Tea**
3311	*Sunday Best**	3315	*Garden Party*
3312	*Recital Time**		

*Same as in 1982.

Craftsmen's Corner

1012	*Baby Lisa*	Same as in 1980, 1981 and 1982.
1013	*Baby Lisa*	Same as in 1980, 1981 and 1982.
1051	*Astri's Lisa Grows Up*	Dressed in pajamas.
1053	*Astri's Lisa Grows Up*	Dressed in knit dress.
1055	*Astri's Lisa Grows Up*	Dressed in a sailor dress.
1057	*Astri's Lisa Grows Up*	Wears a knit sweater and hat.
1059	*Astri's Lisa Grows Up*	In a trunk with extra costumes.
7511	*Little Tiger*	
7512	*Lotus Blossom*	(No. 7501, *Orange Blossom* in 1982.)
7108	*Scarecrow*	
7201	*Old Fashioned Nast Santa*	Same as in 1982.
7006	*Clown-Girl*	Same as in 1980, 1981 and 1982.
7483	*Cristina*	

Mama's Baby

This is a floppy and cuddly baby who is "supersoft."

9950	Dressed in a romper outfit.
9952	Wears a dress.
9954	In a christening outfit with a pillow.
9956	Wears a hat and coat.

Illustration 333. 25in (63.5cm) *Mama's Baby,* 1983. Vinyl head, arms and legs; cloth body; painted hair. This photograph (*Courtesy of the Effanbee Doll Corporation*) was used in the 1983 catalog. It shows the but the production line was to have sleep eyes.

1984 Catalog

International Collection

Same as 1983 with the following additions:

1121	*Miss Thailand*	11in (28cm)
1129	*Miss Peru*	11in (28cm)
1130	*Miss Tahiti*	11in (28cm)
1131	*Holland Boy*	11in (28cm)

Storybook Collection

Same as 1983 with the following additions:

1162	*Pierrot Clown*	11in (28cm)
1163	*Thumbelina*	11in (28cm)
1164	*Little Girl with a Curl*	11in (28cm)
1165	*Robin Hood*	11in (28cm)
1166	*Maid Marian*	11in (28cm)
1167	*The Little Mermaid*	11in (28cm)
1168	*Geni*	11in (28cm)
1169	*Wicked Witch*	11in (28cm)
1170	*Poor Cinderella*	11in (28cm)

Illustration 334. The 11in (28cm) *Lisa* was inspired by the works of Astry Campbell. (Clockwise) No. 1057 *Sweater*, No. 1053 *Dress*, No. 1059 *Lisa with Trunk*, No. 1055 *Sailor*, No. 1051 *Pajamas*.

Craftsman's Corner

Same as 1983 listing with the following:
Discontinued Dolls:
1012 *Baby Lisa*
1013 *Baby Lisa*
7201 *Old Fashioned Nast Santa*
7006 *Clown-Girl*
7511 *Little Tiger*
7512 *Lotus Blossom*

New for 1984:
7351 Contessa
7361 *Flower Girl of Brittany*
7484 *Laurel*   15in (38cm)

The Presidents

Same as 1983 with the following addition:

7903	*Theodore Roosevelt*	17in (43cm)

Dance Ballerina Dance

1141	*Red Shoes*	11in (28cm)
1141B	*Red Shoes* (black)	11in (28cm)
1541	*The Nutcracker*	15in (38cm)
3341	*Swan Lake*	13in (33cm)

The Age of Elegance Collection

7855	*Brussels*	18in (46cm)
7857	*Budapest*	18in (46cm)
7858	*Marseilles*	18in (46cm)
7859	*Old Vienna*	18in (46cm)

Grandes Dames Collection

1146	*Nancy*	11in (28cm)
1147	*Jacqueline*	11in (28cm)
1148	*Erika*	11in (28cm)
1148B	*Erika* (black)	11in (28cm)
1149	*Sherry*	11in (28cm)
1149B	*Sherry* (black)	11in (28cm)
1546	*Grace*	15in (38cm)
1547	*Ingrid*	15in (38cm)
1548	*Amelia*	15in (38cm)
1548B	*Amelia* (black)	15in (38cm)
1549	*Sophia*	15in (38cm)

Crochet Classics Collection

2378	*Tiny Tubber*	11in (28cm)
2378B	*Tiny Tubber* (black)	11in (28cm)
6178	*Baby Winkie*	12in (31cm)
6577	*Butterball* (brown hair)	13in (33cm)
6578	*Butterball*	13in (33cm)
6578B	*Butterball* (black)	13in (33cm)
8378	*Little Lovums*	15in (38cm)
9478	*Sweetie Pie*	18in (46cm)
9478B	*Sweetie Pie* (black)	18in (46cm)

Great Moments in Literature

Same as 1983 with the following addition:

| 7633 | *Becky Thatcher* | 11in (28cm) |

Great Moments in History

| 7641 | *Winston Churchill* | 16¹/₂in (42cm) |

Heart to Heart Collection

Same as 1983 listing with the following discontinued:
2355B *Tiny Tubber* (black)
9455B *Sweetie Pie* (black)

Travel Time Collection

Same as 1983 with the following discontinued:
2398 *Tiny Tubber*

addition:

| 1198 | *Caroline* | 11in (28cm) |

Madame Butterfly Collection

Same as 1983 listing.

Pride of the South Collection

3342	*Charlottesville*	13in (33cm)
3343	*Birmingham*	13in (33cm)
3344	*San Antonio*	13in (33cm)
3345	*Raleigh*	13in (33cm)
3346	*Memphis*	13in (33cm)

Baby's First Collection

9511	*Birthday*	19in (48cm)
9512	*Christmas*	19in (48cm)
9513	*Blessing*	19in (48cm)

Bridal Suite Collection

1526	*Bride*	15in (38cm)
1526B	*Bride* (black)	15in (38cm)
3325	*Bridesmaid*	13in (33cm)
3326	*Bride*	13in (33cm)

Women of the Ages Collection

Same as 1983 with the following addition:

| 3374 | *Lillian Russell* | 13in (33cm) |

each character

7903
Theodore Roc
"Speak Softl
Carry A Big S
1901–19

Illustration 335. 17in (43cm) *Theodore Roosevelt* was the 1984 addition to *The Presidents Series. Teddy* is suited up in the campaign uniform of the "Rough Riders" complete with the "USV" insignia pinned on his collar.

Here Come the Clowns Collection

1150	*Clarence Clown*	11in (28cm)
1550	*Homer Clown*	15in (38cm)
1750	*Jethro Clown*	18in (46cm)
6350	*Elmer Clown*	14in (36cm)

Four Seasons Collection

6231	*Spring*	11in (28cm)
6232	*Summer*	11in (28cm)
6233	*Autumn*	11in (28cm)
6234	*Winter*	11in (28cm)
9231	*Spring*	15in (38cm)
9232	*Summer*	15in (38cm)
9233	*Autumn*	15in (38cm)
9234	*Winter*	15in (38cm)

One World Collection

Same as 1983 listing.

Sweet Things Collection

2581	*Twinkie*	17in (43cm)
2581	*Twinkie* (black)	
6581	*Butterball* (with pillow)	13in (33cm)
8181	*Baby Button Nose* (with pillow)	14in (36cm)
8181B	*Baby Button Nose* (black)	14in (36cm)
8381	*Little Lovums*	15in (38cm)
8481	*Lovums*	18in (46cm)
9381	*Buttercup*	15in (38cm)
9481	*Sweetie Pie*	18in (46cm)
9681	*Sugar Plum*	20in (51cm)

Les Girls Collection

1511	*Chipper* (striped dress)	15in (38cm)
1512	*Chipper* (red dress)	15in (38cm)
1513	*Chipper* (white dress)	15in (38cm)
1864	*Suzie Sunshine* (blue dress)	18in (46cm)
1865	*Suzie Sunshine* (red dress)	18in (46cm)
1866	*Suzie Sunshine* (pink dress)	18in (46cm)

Mama's Li'l Darlin' Collection

8211	*Li'l Darlin'* (romper)	18in (46cm)
8212	*Li'l Darlin'* (stripe dress)	18in (46cm)
8213	*Li'l Darlin'* (blue dress)	18in (46cm)
8214	*Li'l Darlin'* (yellow dress)	18in (46cm)

Mama's Baby Collection

9951	*Mama's Baby* (romper)	25in (64cm)
9953	*Mama's Baby* (pink dress)	25in (64cm)
9957	*Mama's Baby* (white dress)	25in (64cm)
9955	*Mama's Baby* (blue dress)	25in (64cm)

Great Moments in Music

| 7661 | *Louis "Satchmo" Armstrong* | 15¹/₂in (39cm) |

Legend Series

| 1984 | *Judy Garland as Dorothy* | 14¹/₂in (37cm) |

Illustration 336. 14¹/₂in (37cm) Legend Series, Judy Garland as Dorothy in the Wizard of Oz wears a blue and white gingham dress and the famous glittering ruby red slippers.

1985 Catalog

International Collection

Same as 1984 with the following additions:

1132	*Canadian Mountie*	11in (28cm)
1133	*Portugal*	11in (28cm)
1134	*Wales*	11in (28cm)
1135	*England* (Coldstream Guard)	11in (28cm)

Storybook Collection

Same as 1984 with the following additions:

1154	*Santa Claus*	11in (28cm)
1155	*Mrs. Santa Claus*	11in (28cm)
1156	*Dorothy*	11in (28cm)
1157	*Tin Man*	11in (28cm)
1158	*Straw Man*	11in (28cm)
1159	*Cowardly Lion*	11in (28cm)
1160	*Old Woman in the Shoe*	11in (28cm)
1161	*The Little Milk Maid*	11in (28cm)

Great Moments in Sports

| 7651 | *Babe Ruth* | 15$\frac{1}{2}$in (39cm) |

Legend Series

| 1985 | *Lucille Ball* | 16$\frac{1}{2}$in (42cm) |

Here Come the Clowns Collection

Same as 1984 listings.

Sunday Best Collection

1415	*Sam* (black)	11in (28cm)
1416	*Sissy* (black)	11in (28cm)
2615	*Sara* (black)	16in (41cm)
5616	*Sally* (black)	18in (46cm)

Bridal Suite Collection

1027	*Ring Bearer*	11in (28cm)
1028	*Flower Girl*	11in (28cm)
1527	*Bridesmaid*	15in (38cm)
1528	*Bride*	15in (38cm)
2928	*Bride*	18in (46cm)

Heart to Heart Collection

Same as 1984 listing.

International Brides Collection

3310	*United States*	13in (33cm)
3311	*Denmark*	13in (33cm)
3312	*Hungary*	13in (33cm)
3313	*Norway*	13in (33cm)

Travel Time Collection

| 1198 | *Caroline* | 11in (28cm) |
| 5798 | *DyDee* | 18in (46cm) |

The Age of Elegance Collection

7860	*Geneva*	18in (46cm)
7861	*Dublin*	18in (46cm)
7862	*London*	18in (46cm)
7863	*Florence*	18in (46cm)

This brand new series is dedicated to who have achieved so much and s and standard for millions of pr amateur athletes.

Effanbee plans to bring to life th who were and are inspirational sporting world and WILL PRO FOR ONE YEAR ONLY.

Effanbee salutes the Swat" — the "Babe".

We've captured Babe in a 15½" collectible almost see him hitt homerun into the star Stadium!

TO BE MADE FOR 1985

BABE RUTH 7651

Illustration 337. The 15$\frac{1}{2}$in (39cm) *Babe Ruth* appeared as the first in the 1985 *Great Moments in Sports Series.*

Mama's Li'l Darlin' Collection
Same as 1984 listing.

Mama's Baby Collection
Same as 1984 listing.

Walt Disney Character Doll Collection

1590	*Prince Charming*	
3390	*Cinderella*	
3391	*Poor Cinderella*	
3392	*Mary Poppins*	

Four Seasons Collection

7701	*Spring*	17in (43cm)
7702	*Summer*	17in (43cm)
7703	*Autumn*	17in (43cm)
7704	*Winter*	17in (43cm)

Dance Ballerina Dance
Same as 1984 listing.

The Masquerade Ball Collection

1142	*Judith*	11in (28cm)
1143	*Lana*	11in (28cm)
1144	*Lillian*	11in (28cm)
1145	*Debra*	11in (28cm)

Grandes Dames Collection

1542	*Amy*	15in (38cm)
1543	*Barbara*	15in (38cm)
1544	*Jean*	15in (38cm)
1545	*Erin*	15in (38cm)

Pride of the South Collection

3347	*Houston*	13in (33cm)
3348	*Columbia*	13in (33cm)
3349	*Jacksonville*	13in (33cm)
3350	*Nashville*	13in (33cm)
3351	*Louisville*	13in (33cm)

Illustration 338. Dolls appearing in the *Walt Disney Character Doll Collection* are (clockwise) No. 3392 *Mary Poppins*, No. 1590 *Prince Charming*, No. 3390 *Cinderella*, No. 3391 *Poor Cinderella*.

Jan Hagara's Collectible Dolls

7484	*Laurel*	15in (38cm)
7485	*Lesley*	15in (38cm)
7486	*Larry*	17in (43cm)

Great Moments in Literature

Same as 1984 listing.

Pretty as a Picture Collection

1311	*Little Lovums*	15in (38cm)
1811	*Suzie Sunshine*	18in (46cm)
2311	*Tiny Tubber*	11in (28cm)
3511	*Elizabeth*	15in (38cm)
6111	*Baby Winkie* (with pillow)	12in (31cm)
6511	*Butterball* (with pillow)	13in (33cm)
8311	*Little Lovums*	15in (38cm)
9111	*Babykin*	14in (36cm)
9411	*Sweetie Pie*	18in (46cm)

Great Moments in History

| 7641 | *Winston Churchill* | 16½in (42cm) |
| 7642 | *Eleanor Roosevelt* | 14½in (37cm) |

Once Upon a Time

8125	*Pat-A-Cake*
9125	*Tooth Fairy*
9225	*Humpty Dumpty*

Cream Puff Collection

5782	*Dydee*	15in (38cm)
6582	*Butterball*	13in (33cm)
8182	*Baby Button Nose* (with pillow)	14in (36cm)
8382	*Little Lovums*	15in (38cm)
8482	*Lovums*	18in (46cm)
9382	*Buttercup*	15in (38cm)
9482	*Sweetie Pie*	18in (46cm)
9682	*Sugar Plum*	20in (51cm)

Jan Hagara's Love-ables Collection

7521	*Bobby*
7522	*Beth*
7523	*Belinda*

Great Moments in Music

Same as 1984 listing.

Baby's First Collection

Same as 1984 listing.

Through the Years Collection

1401	*Frontier*	12in (31cm)
1402	*Civil War*	12in (31cm)
1403	*Turn of the Century*	12in (31cm)
1404	*Today*	12in (31cm)

The Presidents

| 7903 | *Theodore Roosevelt* | 17in (43cm) |
| 7904 | *Franklin Delano Roosevelt* | 17in (43cm) |

Little Old New York Collection

7301	*Park Avenue*	17in (43cm)
7302	*Central Park*	17in (43cm)
7303	*Madison Park*	17in (43cm)
7304	*Fifth Avenue*	17in (43cm)

Illustration 339. (Left to right) The 18in (46cm) No. 7862 *London* and No. 7861 *Dublin* were both produced for 1985 only in limited editions of 4,000 pieces each.

243

1986 Catalog

International Collection

Same as 1985 listing with the following additions:

1136	*Finland*	11in (28cm)
1137	*Puerto Rico*	11in (28cm)
1138	*Korea*	11in (28cm)
1139	*Japan*	11in (28cm)

Storybook Collection

Same as 1985 listing with the following additions:

1151	*Snow Man*	11in (28cm)
1152	*Snow Queen*	11in (28cm)
1153	*Old King Cole*	11in (28cm)
1172	*Good Witch*	11in (28cm)
1182	*Old MacDonald*	11in (28cm)
1183	*Queen of Hearts*	11in (28cm)

Great Moments in Television

7670	*Jackie Gleason* as *Ralph Kramden*	16½in (42cm)
7671	*Art Carney* as *Ed Norton*	16½in (42cm)

Here Come the Clowns Collection

Same as 1985 listing.

Illustration 340. The 14in (36cm) *Patsy 86* was available in two versions. No. 4101 (left) was dressed in a blue and white gingham dress with a blue hair bow. No. 4102 (right) was dressed in a pink dress with matching bonnet and teddy. Both dolls have light brown molded hair, sparkling blue painted eyes and the famous Patsy pink "pouting" mouth.

Little Women Collection

3421	*Beth*	13in (33cm)
3422	*Jo*	13in (33cm)
3423	*Amy*	13in (33cm)
3424	*Meg*	13in (33cm)

Fantasyland Collection

4811	*Alice in Wonderland*	19in (48cm)
4812	*Little Red Riding Hood*	19in (48cm)
4813	*Little Bo-Peep*	19in (48cm)

Travel Time Collection

Same as 1985 listing.

Victorian Miniatures

1146	*Cornwall*	11in (28cm)
1147	*Salisbury*	11in (28cm)
1148	*Dover*	11in (28cm)
1148B	*Dover* (black)	11in (28cm)
1149	*Coventry*	11in (28cm)

Heart to Heart Collection

Same as 1985 listing.

Four Seasons Collection

Same as 1985 listing.

Jan Hagara's Collectible Dolls

7485	*Lesley*	15in (38cm)
7486	*Larry*	17in (43cm)
7487	*Molly*	11in (28cm)
7488	*Mary Ann*	15in (38cm)

Pretty as a Picture Collection

Same as 1985 listing.

Grandes Dames Collection

1546	*Alicia*
1546B	*Alicia* (black)
1547	*Fiona*
1548	*Maureen*
1549	*Melanie*

Bridal Suite Collection

1011	*Ring Boy*	11in (28cm)
1012	*Flower Girl*	11in (28cm)
1511	*Bridesmaid*	15in (38cm)
1512	*Bride*	15in (38cm)
1512	*Bride* (black)	15in (38cm)
1592	*Groom*	15in (38cm)
2912	*Bride*	18in (46cm)
3412	*Bride*	13in (33cm)

Lynn Hollyn American Countrytime Collection

2601	*Alyssa*	16in (41cm)
2602	*Tessa*	16in (41cm)
2603	*Megan*	16in (41cm)
2604	*Jenna*	16in (41cm)

Dance Ballerina Dance

1140	*Dancing School*
1540	*Katerina*
2940	*Natasha*
3340	*Nadia*

Gotcha!

1601	*L'il Suzie Sunshine*
5601	*Dydee Baby*
9101	*Babykin*

Age of Innocence Collection

1901	*School Time*	18in (46cm)
1902	*Play Time*	18in (46cm)
1903	*Party Time*	18in (46cm)
1904	*Night Time*	18in (46cm)

Cream Puff Collection

Same as 1985 listing.

The Presidents

| 7905 | *John Fitzgerald Kennedy* | 16in (41cm) |

Jewels Collection

7801	*Sapphire*	17in (43cm)
7802	*Emerald*	17in (43cm)
7803	*Ruby*	17in (43cm)

Cassie Collection

8251	*Cassie* (pink dress)	19in (48cm)
8252	*Cassie* (sailor)	19in (48cm)
8253	*Cassie* (red dress)	19in (48cm)

Illustration 341. No. 7905 John F. Kennedy, 1986 edition to The Presidents Series, was produced as a 16in (41cm) collectible doll.

Little Old New York Collection

1205	*Herald Square*	11in (28cm)
1206	*Union Square*	11in (28cm)
7305	*Broadway*	17in (43cm)
7306	*Gramercy Park*	17in (43cm)
7307	*Murray Hill*	17in (43cm)
7308	*Duffy Square*	17in (43cm)

Legend Series

| 1986 | *Liberace* "Mr. Showmanship" | 18in (46cm) |

Great Moments in Sports

| 7652 | *Muhammad Ali* | 18in (46cm) |

Once a Star...Always a Star...Patsy 86

| 4101 | *Patsy* (blue dress) | 14in (36cm) |
| 4102 | *Patsy* (pink dress) | 14in (36cm) |

1986
LIBERACE
"MR. SHOWMANSHIP"

Illustration 342. 1986 Liberace - "Mr. Show-manship" is the eighth doll in the famous Legend Series. The 18in (46cm) doll has an intricate costume including sparkling rings.

1987 Catalog

Wizard of Oz Collection

1156	*Dorothy*	11in (28cm)
1157	*Tin Man*	11in (28cm)
1158	*Straw Man*	11in (28cm)
1159	*Cowardly Lion*	11in (28cm)
1169	*Wicked Witch*	11in (28cm)
1172	*Good Witch*	11in (28cm)

Fairy Tales Collection

1152	*Snow Queen*	11in (28cm)
1173	*Sugar Plum Fairy*	11in (28cm)
1175	*Alice in Wonderland*	11in (28cm)
1176	*Cinderella*	11in (28cm)
1178	*Little Red Riding Hood*	11in (28cm)
1180	*Snow White*	11in (28cm)

Nursery Rhymes Collection

1177	*Little Bo-Peep*	11in (28cm)
1183	*Queen of Hearts*	11in (28cm)
1186	*Jack*	11in (28cm)
1187	*Jill*	11in (28cm)
1193	*Mother Goose*	11in (28cm)
1196	*Mary Had a Little Lamb*	11in (28cm)

Cinderella

7360		17in (43cm)

Effanbee Favorites

1140	*Ballerina Dancing School*	11in (28cm)
6557	*Butterball Drink & Wet*	12in (31cm)
8157	*Baby Button Nose*	12in (31cm)

Puttin' On the Ritz Collection

1561	*Brigitte* (blue)	15in (38cm)
1562	*Marlene* (tuxedo)	15in (38cm)
1563	*Danielle* (white)	15in (38cm)

Patsy Collection

4103	Sailor Outfit	14in (36cm)
4104	Camel Hair Coat & Hat	14in (36cm)

Prom Night Collection

1751	*Deborah*	18in (46cm)
1752	*Margaret*	18in (46cm)
1753	*Lisa*	18in (46cm)

International Collection

1101	*United States*	11in (28cm)
1102	*France*	11in (28cm)
1103	*Germany*	11in (28cm)
1104	*Holland*	11in (28cm)
1105	*Ireland*	11in (28cm)
1106	*Italy*	11in (28cm)
1107	*Poland*	11in (28cm)
1108	*Scotland*	11in (28cm)
1113	*Phillipines*	11in (28cm)
1115	*Russia*	11in (28cm)
1128	*Vietnam*	11in (28cm)
1139	*Japan*	11in (28cm)

Remembrance Dolls

2101	*January*	11in (28cm)
2102	*February*	11in (28cm)
2103	*March*	11in (28cm)
2104	*April*	11in (28cm)
2105	*May*	11in (28cm)
2106	*June*	11in (28cm)
2107	*July*	11in (28cm)
2108	*August*	11in (28cm)
2109	*September*	11in (28cm)
2110	*October*	11in (28cm)
2111	*November*	11in (28cm)
2112	*December*	11in (28cm)

Illustration 343. Patsy '87 features one of the most popular Effanbee dolls in two new outfits. Both dolls stand 14in (36cm) and are limited to an edition of 7,500 pieces. (Left) Camel Coat and Hat *Patsy.* (Right) Sailor Outfit *Patsy.*

Little Old New York Collection

1207	William	11in (28cm)
1208	Priscilla	11in (28cm)
7309	Amanda	17in (43cm)
7310	Sutton Place	17in (43cm)
7311	East End Avenue	17in (43cm)

The Presidents

| 7906 | Dwight D. Eisenhower | 16in (41cm) |

Legend Series

| 1987 | James Cagney | 16in (41cm) |

Limited Edition Doll Club Collection

| Baby Grumpy (vinyl) | 16in (41cm) |
| Baby Grumpy (porcelain) | 14in (36cm) |

Illustration 344 The 16in (41cm) *Dwight D. Eisenhower* is the 1987 addition to *The Presidents Series*.

Illustration 345. 17in (43cm) *Cinderella* wears a breathtaking white gown of tulle over shimmering satin. Pearls adorn the billowing skirt, accent her choker and are entwined in a head piece of beautiful blue flowers.

1988 Catalog

Li'l Innocents

FB2811 *Cindy*	9in (23cm)
FB2812 *Michelle*	9in (23cm)
FB2814 *Christina*	9in (23cm)
FB2815 *Mary Sue*	9in (23cm)
FB2816 *Maryanne*	9in (23cm)
FB2913 *Sandy*	9in (23cm)

Rembrance Dolls of the Month

Same as 1987 listing.

Broadway Footlights Collection

FB1321 *Cosette*   13in (33cm)

Story Book Collection

Same as 1987 listing with the following addition:
FB2903 *Humpty Dumpty*   9in (23cm)

Puttin' on the Ritz

Same as 1987 listing.

Cinderella

Same as 1987 listing.

Joyous Occasions

FB4955 *Namesake Baby*	19in (48cm)
FB8255 *Joyous Ballerina*	
FB8705 *Joyous Bride*	17in (43cm)
FB9785 *Namesake Baby*	17in (43cm)

Baby to Love Ensemble

FB4458 *Baby to Love*	14in (36cm)
FB4958	19in (48cm)
FB6557 *Butterball to Love*	12in (31cm)
FB8157 *Baby Button Nose to Love*	12in (31cm)

Eugenia Dukas Collection

FB9831 *Lady Gabrielle*	18in (46cm)
FB9832 *Lady Anqelique*	18in (46cm)
FB9833 *Lady Gabrielle*	18in (46cm)
FB9835 *Lady Jacqueline*	18in (46cm)

Illustration 346. These two 14in (36cm) bisque porcelain dolls are limited to an edition of 750 pieces. (Left) No. FB9311 *Patsy Girl* and (right) No. FB9312 *Patsy Boy.*

Wizard of Oz Collection

Same as 1987 listing with the following additions:

FB1171 *Wizard of Oz*	11in (28cm)
FB2914 *Munchkin Girl*	9in (23cm)
FB2915 *Munchkin Boy*	9in (23cm)

Patsy Collection

FB4103 Sailor Outfit	14in (36cm)
FB4104 Camel Hair Coat	14in (36cm)
FB9311 *Patsy Girl*	14in (36cm)
FB9312 *Patsy Boy*	14in (36cm)

On the Prairie Collection

FB2161 *Joan*	11in (28cm)
FB2833 *Li'l Judy*	9in (23cm)
FB2835 *Li'l John John*	9in (23cm)
FB8806 *Bessie*	18in (46cm)

Little Old New York

FB1207 *William*	11in (28cm)
FB1208 *Priscilla*	11in (28cm)
FB7309 *Amanda*	17in (43cm)
FB7311 *East End Avenue*	17in (43cm)

Christmas Eve Together

FB2308 *Mother*	11in (28cm)
Patsy Ann	9in (23cm)

The Way We Were

FB2191 *Teresa*	11in (28cm)
FB2831 *Jennifer*	9in (23cm)
FB4491 *Madeline*	14in (36cm)

The Presidents

FB1620 *Harry S. Truman*	16in (41cm)
FB7906 *Dwight D. Eisenhower*	16in (41cm)

The Legend Series

Same as 1987 listing.

Plush Animals

FB6016 *My Piggy to Love*	10in (25cm)
FB6122 *Sitting Tabby*	11in (28cm)
FB6131 *Panda*	11in (28cm)
FB6132 *Ribbon Bear*	10in (25cm)
FB6133 *Koala*	11in (28cm)
FB6225 *Angora*	12in (31cm)
FB6411 *Franklin T. Bear*	14in (36cm)
FB6415 *Champagne*	11in (28cm)
FB6417 *Hug and Hold Puppy*	14in (36cm)
FB6423 *Grey Cat*	14½in (37cm)
FB6624 *High Pile Angora*	16in (41cm)
FB6721 *Lying Tabby*	17in (43cm)
FB6941 *My Bear to Love*	11in (28cm)

Illustration 347. The Little Old New York Collection. (Left to right) No. FB7311 17in (43cm) *East End Avenue*, No. FB1208 11in (28cm) *Priscilla*, No. FB7309 17in (43cm) *Amanda*, No. FB1207 11in (28cm) *William*.

1989 Catalog

Li'l Innocents International

FB2871 *Germany*	9in (23cm)
FB2872 *Holland*	9in (23cm)
FB2873 *Ireland*	9in (23cm)
FB2874 *Italy*	9in (23cm)
FB2875 *Russia*	9in (23cm)
FB2876 *U.S.A.*	9in (23cm)
FB2877 *Japan*	9in (23cm)

Li'l Innocents

Same as 1988 listing with the following additions:

FB2841 *Becky* (Bride)	9in (23cm)
FB2842 *Colleen* (Bride)	9in (23cm)
FB2844 *Beverly*	9in (23cm)
FB2845 *Maria*	9in (23cm)
FB2846 *Wendy*	9in (23cm)
FB2847 *Amy* (Communion)	9in (23cm)

Li'l Innocents Clothing

FB3805 Bed
FB3810 6pc. Assortment
FB3811 Winter Dress
FB3812 Country Dress
FB3813 White Party Dress
FB3814 Apricot Dress
FB3815 Red Dress
FB3816 Blue Dress

Little Girls

FB2241 *Heather*	21in (53cm)
FB2242 *Melissa*	21in (53cm)
FB2243 *Christine*	21in (53cm)
FB2244 *Michelle*	21in (53cm)

Christmas Eve Together

FB2309 *Mother*	13in (33cm)
Patsy Ann	9in (23cm)

Currier and Ives

2310 *Tracey*	13in (33cm)
2311 *Scott*	9in (23cm)
2312 *Beth*	9in (23cm)

Story Book Collection

Same as 1988 listing with the following additions:

FB1141 *Rapunzel*	9in (23cm)
FB1142 *Goldilocks*	9in (23cm)
FB1143 *Sleeping Beauty*	9in (23cm)

Wizard of Oz Collection

Same as 1988 listing with the following addition:

FB1155 *Auntie Em*	9in (23cm)

Remembrance Dolls of the Month

Same as 1988 listing.

FB1321
Cosette

Illustration 348. 13in (33cm) vinyl *Cosette* with long wavy nylon hair and hand-painted eyes.

My Little Baby

FB4263 *Butterball* on pillow	12in (31cm)
FB4459 *Baby to Love*	14in (36cm)
FB4462 *Baby to Love* (w/hair)	14in (36cm)
FB4465 *Baby to Love*	14in (36cm)
FB4710 My Little Baby Collection, 6 piece assortment	
FB4711 *Amy*	7in (18cm)
FB4712 *Barbara*	7in (18cm)
FB4713 *Lisa*	7in (18cm)
FB4960 *Baby to Love*	19in (48cm)
FB6556 *Butterball*	12in (31cm)
FB6558 *Butterball to Love*	12in (31cm)
FB8157 *Baby Button Nose* (sleeper)	12in (31cm)
FB8158 *Baby Button Nose* (jumper)	12in (31cm)

The Way We Were

Same as 1988 listing.

Little Old New York

Same as 1988 listing.

On the Prairie Collection

Same as 1988 listing.

FB2309
Mother and Patsy Ann

Illustration 349. Effanbee captured the warmth and love of the Christmas season with this mother and daughter duo. *Mother*, standing 13in (33cm) tall wears her holiday finery and *Patsy Ann*, 9in (23cm), wears a short dress and tights.

Joyous Occasions

FB1140 *Ballerina*	11in (28cm)
FB1910 *"First Date,"* Nicole	13in (33cm)
FB2157 *Ice Skater*	11$\frac{1}{2}$in (29cm)
FB2356 *Sweet Sixteen*	13in (33cm)
FB4451 *Birthday Baby*	14in (36cm)
FB4956 *Namesake Baby*	19in (48cm)
FB8255 *Joyous Ballerina*	11$\frac{1}{2}$in (29cm)
FB8705 *Joyous Bride*	17in (43cm)
FB9786 *Namesake Baby*	17in (43cm)

Eugenia Dukas Collection

FB9831 *Lady Gabrielle*	18in (46cm)
FB9832 *Lady Angelique*	18in (46cm)
FB9833 *Lady Nichole*	18in (46cm)
FB9836 *Lady Stephanie*	18in (46cm)

Cinderella

FB7360 *Cinderella*	17in (43cm)

Puttin' on the Ritz

FB1561 *Brigitte*	15in (38cm)
FB1562 *Marlene*	15in (38cm)
FB1563 *Danielle*	15in (38cm)

Patsy

FB4103 *Patsy* w/sailor outfit	14in (36cm)
FB4104 *Patsy* w/ camel hair coat	14in (36cm)

Broadway Footlights Collection

Same as 1988 listing.

The Legend Series

FB1988 *Humphrey Bogart*	15in (38cm)

Presidents Collection

Same as 1988 listing with the following addition:

FB1630 *Thomas Jefferson*	16in (41cm)

Effanbee's Soft Friends

Same as 1988 listing with the following discontinued:

FB6417 *Hug & Hold Puppy*
FB6624 *High Pile Angora*

Additions:

FB6131 *Panda*	11in (28cm)
FB6132 *Ribbon Bear*	10in (25cm)
FB6133 *Koala*	11in (28cm)

Illustration 350. 17in (43cm) *Cinderella* wears a breathtaking white gown of tulle over shimmering satin. Pearls adorn the billowing skirt, accent her choker and are entwined in a head piece of beautiful blue flowers.

FB1630
Thomas Jefferson

Illustration 351. No. FB1630 16in (41cm) *Thomas Jefferson* is the 1989 addition to *The Presidents Series.*

1990 Catalog

Li'l Innocents Four Seasons

FB2817 *Margie* (Spring)   9in (23cm)
FB2818 *Lori* (Summer)   9in (23cm)
FB2819 *Meredith* (Autumn)   9in (23cm)
FB2820 *Diana* (Winter)   9in (23cm)

Li'l Innocents

Same as 1989 listing with the following additions:
FB2821 *Audrey*   9in (23cm)
FB2823 *Joy*   9in (23cm)
FB2824 *Elizabeth*   9in (23cm)

Li'l Innocents International

Same as 1989 listing.

Li'l Innocents Clothing

Same as 1989 listing with the following additions:
FB3817 Tennis Outfit
FB3818 Exercise Outfit
FB3819 Ski Outfit
FB3820 Raincoat Outfit

Wizard of Oz Collection

Same as 1989 listing with the following addition:
FB1154 Toto Dog   3³/₄in (10cm)

FB1131 Buckwheat

FB1335 Petey

FB1336 Alfalfa

FB1031 Spanky

©1989 King World Merchandising, Inc.

Illustration 352. (Left to right) *The Little Rascals Collection.* No. FB1131 11¹/₂in (29cm) *Buckwheat,* No. FB1335 4¹/₄in (11in) *Petey,* No. FB1336 11¹/₂in (29cm) *Alfalfa,* No. FB1031 11¹/₂in (29cm) *Spanky.*

254

Story Book Collection

Same as 1989 listing with the following discontinued:
FB2903 *Humpty Dumpty*   9in (23cm)

additions:
FB1150 *Poor Cinderella*	11in (28cm)
FB1181 *Prince Charming*	11in (28cm)
FB1194 *Hansel*	11in (28cm)
FB1195 *Gretel*	11in (28cm)
FB1197 *Pinocchio*	11in (28cm)

Baby to Love Ensemble

Same as 1989 listing with the following discontinued:
FB6556 *My Little Butterball*   12in (31cm)

additions:
FB4675 *Billy*	16in (41cm)
FB4676 *Jill*	16in (41cm)
FB6555 *Baby Butterball*	12in (31cm)
FB6558 *Butterball to Love*	12in (31cm)
FB6560 *Butterball* (black)	12in (31cm)
FB6903 *Monique*	14in (36cm)
FB7402 *Baby Grumpy*	16in (41cm)
FB8100 *My Little Baby in Basket*	7in (18cm)
FB8159 *Baby Button Nose* (hair)	12in (31cm)
FB8160 *Baby Button Nose*	12in (31cm)
FB8162 *Musical Baby Button Nose*	12in (31cm)
FB8163 *Welcome Home Baby*	11in (28cm)
FB8164 *Button Nose* (black)	12in (31cm)

My Little Baby Collection

Same as 1989 listing.

Precious Toddlers

FB2782 *Debbie*	18in (46cm)
FB2783 *Emily*	18in (46cm)
FB2784 *Sarah*	18in (46cm)
FB2787 *Kiki*	18in (46cm)

Joyous Occasions

Same as 1989 listing with the following additions:
FB8256 *New Arrival Vinyl Baby*	19in (48cm)
FB8704 *Bride*	11in (28cm)
FB9787 *New Arrival Porcelain Baby*	17in (43cm)

With Love Doll

FB1145 *Valerie*   11in (28cm)

Cinderella

Same as 1989 listing.

Special Moments Dolls of the Month

FB3300 12 Months Assorted
FB3301 *January*
FB3302 *February*
FB3303 *March*
FB3304 *April*
FB3305 *May*
FB3306 *June*
FB3307 *July*
FB3308 *August*
FB3309 *September*
FB3310 *October*
FB3311 *November*
FB3312 *December*

Eugenia Dukas Collection

FB9837 *Bride* (Renee)	18in (46cm)
FB9838 *Gibson Girl* (Sarabeth)	18in (46cm)
FB9839 *Prima Ballerina* (Natalia)	18in (46cm)

Ladies of Fashion Collection

FB6800 *Roaring Twenties*	18in (46cm)
FB6801 *Turn of the Century*	18in (46cm)
FB6802 *Age of Elegance*	18in (46cm)
FB6803 *The Bride*	18in (46cm)

Little Old New York

The series, same as 1989 listing, was discontinued.

Puttin' On The Ritz

The series, same as 1989 listing, was discontinued.

Thank Heaven For Little Girls

Same as 1989 listing with the following additions:
FB2341 *Jenny*	21in (53cm)
FB2342 *Rachel*	21in (53cm)

French Country Collection

FB6900 *Mama*	11in (28cm)
FB6901 *Lisa*	9in (23cm)
FB6902 *Jonathan*	9in (23cm)
FB6903 *Monique*, French Country Baby	14in (36cm)

Christmas Eve Together

Same as 1989 listing.

Currier and Ives

The series, same as 1989 listing, was discontinued.

FB1625
Andrew Jackson

The Little Rascals

FB1031 *Spanky*	11½in (29cm)
FB1131 *Buckwheat*	11½in (29cm)
FB1335 *Petey*	4¼in (11cm)
FB1336 *Alfalfa*	11½in (29cm)

Presidents Collection

Same as 1989 listing with the following discontinued:
FB7906 *Dwight D. Eisenhower*

addition:
FB1625 *Andrew Jackson*   16in (41cm)

New World Collection

FB1491 *Queen Isabella*
FB1492 *Christopher Columbus*

Effanbee Collector Series

Gordon and *Gilda* by Carol-Lynn Rössel Waugh

FB6425 *Gordon*	15in (38cm)
FB6426 *Gilda*	15in (38cm)
FB6427 *Gordon*	10in (25cm)
FB6428 *Gilda*	10in (25cm)

Effanbee Collector Series

The following series was discontinued:

| FB6429 *Bromley* | 13in (33cm) |
| FB6430 *Bromley* | 11in (28cm) |

Soft Friends

Same as 1989 listing with the following discontinued:
FB6132 *Ribbon Bear*   10in (25cm)

Illustration 353. 16in (41cm) Andrew Jackson is the 1990 addition to The Presidents Series.

Illustration 354. (Left to right) No. FB1491 *Queen Isabella* and No. FB1492 *Christopher Columbus.*

1991 Catalog

The Little Rascals

Same as 1990 listing with the following addition:

FB1337 *Darla*   11½in (29cm)

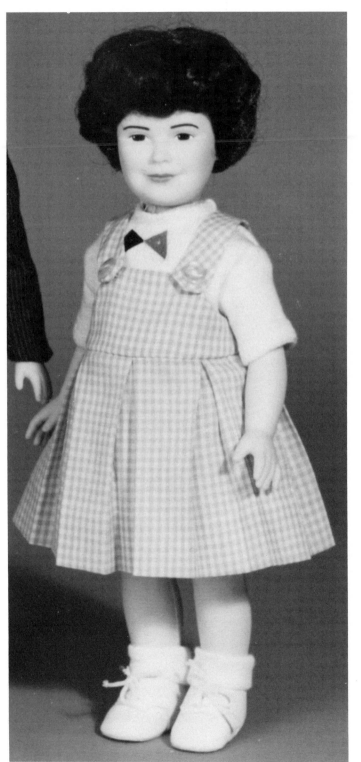

History's Greatest Heroes

FB1951 *General Douglas MacArthur*   16in (41cm)

Here Come the Clowns

FB7200 *Klara*   12in (31cm)
FB7205 *Hermine*   12in (31cm)

Baby to Love

FB8165 *Dydee*   12in (31cm)

Illustration 355. 11in (28cm) *Darla* is the 1991 addition to the *Little Rascals* collection.

1992 Catalog
The Magic Is Back
Irene & Stanley Wahlberg acquire the firm.

Gallery Collection -
International Series

MV109 *Poland*	9in (23cm)
MV111 *Thailand*	9in (23cm)
MV110 *Scotland*	9in (23cm)

Gallery Collection -
Story Book Series

MV101 *Christmas Fairy*	9in (23cm)
MV103 *Little Red Riding Hood*	9in (23cm)
MV104 *Cinderella*	9in (23cm)
MV105 *Snow White*	9in (23cm)

Gallery Collection - Porcelains

MP101 *Patsy*	14in (36cm)
MP102 *Patsy Brother*	14in (36cm)
MP107 *Kathleen*	17in (43cm)
MP110 *Rebecca*	18in (46cm)
MP114 *Benjamin*	14in (36cm)

LITTLE RED RIDING HOOD No. MV103

CINDERELLA No. MV104

SNOW WHITE

CHRISTMAS FAIRY

Illustration 356. The 1992 Gallery Collection includes four 9in (23cm) storybook characters. (Clockwise) No. MV103 *Little Red Riding Hood*, No. MV104 *Cinderella*, No. MV101 *Christmas Fairy*, No. MV105 *Snow White*.

1993 Catalog

Vinyl Collections

Story Book Collection

Same as the 1992 listing with the following addition:
MV108 *Mother Goose*   9in (23cm)

Holidays of the Year

MV122 *Currier & Ives Christmas*	9in (23cm)
MV123 *Valentine's Day*	9in (23cm)
MV124 *Easter*	9in (23cm)
MV125 *Halloween*	9in (23cm)

International Collection

Same as 1992 listing.

Special Moments Collection

MV115 *First Communion*	11¹/₂in (29cm)
MV116 *Prom Night*	11¹/₂in (29cm)
MV117 *Bride*	11¹/₂in (29cm)
MV118 *School Days*	11¹/₂in (29cm)
MV119 *Cheerleader*	11¹/₂in (29cm)
MV120 *First Ballet Recital*	11¹/₂in (29cm)

Lil' Miss Grow-Up

SV148 *Age 1* (Blonde)	12in (31cm)
SV149 *Age 2* (Blonde)	12¹/₂in (32cm)
SV150 *Age 3* (Blonde)	13in (33cm)
SV151 *Age 4* (Blonde)	13¹/₂in (34cm)
SV152 *Age 5* (Blonde)	14in (36cm)
SV153 *Age 1* (Brown)	12in (31cm)
SV154 *Age 2* (Brown)	12¹/₂in (32cm)
SV155 *Age 3* (Brown)	13in (33cm)
SV156 *Age 4* (Brown)	13¹/₂in (34cm)
SV157 *Age 5* (Brown)	14in (36cm)

Bitsy Trunk Set

SV108 *Bitsy Trunk Set*

Fairy Tale Collection

SV117 *Alice in Wonderland*	11¹/₂in (29cm)
SV118 *Queen of Hearts*	11¹/₂2in (29cm)
SV119 *Mad Hatter*	11¹/₂in (29cm)
SV120 *Sherezhade*	11¹/₂in (29cm)
SV121 *Genie*	11¹/₂in (29cm)
SV122 *Aladdin*	11¹/₂in (29cm)
SV123 *Little Miss Muffet*	11¹/₂in (29cm)
SV124 *Little Bo Peep*	11¹/₂in (29cm)
SV125 *Snow White*	11¹/₂in (29cm)
SV126 *Cinderella*	11¹/₂in (29cm)
SV127 *Sleeping Beauty*	11¹/₂in (29cm)
SV128 *Snow Queen*	11¹/₂in (29cm)
SV129 *Princess & the Pea*	11¹/₂in (29cm)
SV130 *Lady Elaine*	11¹/₂in (29cm)
SV131 *Sir Launcelot*	11¹/₂in (29cm)
SV132 *Guinevere*	11¹/₂in (29cm)
SV133 *Clara Nutcracker*	11¹/₂in (29cm)
SV134 *Nutcracker Prince*	11¹/₂in (29cm)
SV135 *Sugar Plum Fairy*	11¹/₂in (29cm)
SV136 *Snow Fairy*	11¹/₂in (29cm)
SV137 *Christmas Fairy*	11¹/₂in (29cm)
SV138 *Currier & Ives Christmas*	11¹/₂in (29cm)
SV139 *Wicked Witch*	12in (31cm)
SV140 *Cowardly Lion*	12in (31cm)
SV141 *Straw Man*	12in (31cm)
SV142 *Tin Man*	12in (31cm)
SV143 *Dorothy*	12in (31cm)

Pocket O'Love

SV145 *Love Pockets* (Red dress)	13in (33cm)
SV146 *Love Pockets* (Green dress)	13in (33cm)
SV147 *Love Pockets* (Black dress)	13in (33cm)

Illustration 357. The 9in (23cm) 1993 International Collection featuring (clockwise) No. MV110 Scotland, No. MV111 Thailand, No. MV109 Poland.

Vinyl Babies

MV126 *Wonder* (Blue dress)
MV127 *Brooke* (Pink dress)
SV158 *Katelyn* (Green dress)
SV159 *Cecily* (Sailor Suit)

Gallery Collections

"Thank Heaven for Little Girls"

MP105 *Ashlea*	16in (41cm)
MP106 *Jessica*	16in (41cm)
MP107 *Kathleen*	16in (41cm)
MP109 *Tiffany*	16in (41cm)

Porcelains

MP101 *Patsy*	14in (36cm)
MP102 *Patsy Brother*	14in (36cm)
MP103 *Felicia*	20in (51cm)
MP104 *Lauren Ann*	21in (53cm)
MP108 *Mary Beth*	17in (43cm)
MP110 *Rebecca*	18in (46cm)
MP111 *Elizabeth*	18in (46cm)
MP112 *Danielle*	22in (56cm)
MP114 *Benjamin*	14in (36cm)
MP115 *Nichole*	12in (31cm)
MP116 *Shelby*	20in (51cm)
MP117 *Bride*	20in (51cm)
MP118 *Lady Alexandra*	22in (56cm)
SP101 *Baby January*	13in (33cm)
SP102 *Bethany*	12$\frac{1}{2}$in (32cm)
SP103 *Sarah*	14in (36cm)
SP104 *Kesia*	16in (41cm)
SP105 *Rachel*	18in (46cm)
SP106 *Allison*	17in (43cm)
SP107 *Mella*	
SP108 *Laura*	

Illustration 358. The 1993 12in (31cm) vinyl *Fairy Tale Collection.* (Clockwise) No. SV139 *Wicked Witch*, No. SV140 *Cowardly Lion*, No. SV143 *Dorothy*, No. SV141 *Straw Man*, No. SV142 *Tin Man.*

1994 Catalog

Wizard of Oz Collection

MV157	*Dorothy*	9in (23cm)
MV158	*Tin Man*	9in (23cm)
MV159	*Cowardly Lion*	9in (23cm)
MV160	*Scarecrow*	9in (23cm)
MV161	*Wicked Witch*	9in (23cm)
MV162	*Glinda*	9in (23cm)

Best Friends Collection

MV134	*Suzie*	9in (23cm)
MV135	*April*	9in (23cm)
MV136	*Sandy*	9in (23cm)
MV137	*Molly*	9in (23cm)
MV179	*Happy Birthday* (Brown)	9in (23cm)
MV179B	*Happy Birthday* (Blonde)	9in (23cm)
MV180	*Stacy*	9in (23cm)

Fairy Tale Collection

MV101	*Xmas Fairy*	9in (23cm)
MV103	*Red Riding Hood*	9in (23cm)
MV104	*Cinderella*	9in (23cm)
MV105	*Snow White*	9in (23cm)
MV106	*Alice in Wonderland*	9in (23cm)
MV142	*Mistress Mary*	9in (23cm)
MV163	*Sleeping Beauty*	9in (23cm)
MV164	*Goldilocks*	9in (23cm)
MV165	*Peter Pan*	9in (23cm)
MV166	*Tinkerbell*	9in (23cm)
MV167	*Wendy*	9in (23cm)
MV168	*Captain Hook*	9in (23cm)
MV183	*Little Mermaid*	9in (23cm)
MV184	*Fairy Godmother*	9in (23cm)
MV185	*Pinocchio*	9in (23cm)
MV186	*Gepetto*	12in (31cm)
MV187	*Blue Fairy*	12in (31cm)
MV188	*Pocahontas*	9in (23cm)

International Collection

MV109	*Poland*	9in (23cm)
MV110	*Scotland*	9in (23cm)
MV111	*Thailand*	9in (23cm)
MV170	*Russia*	9in (23cm)
MV172	*Miss USA*	9in (23cm)
MV173	*Italy*	9in (23cm)
MV174	*Holland*	9in (23cm)
MV175	*Mexico*	9in (23cm)
MV178	*Ireland*	9in (23cm)

Holidays of the Year Collection

Same as 1993 listing with the following additions:

MV138	*Miss Winter*	9in (23cm)
MV139	*Miss Spring*	9in (23cm)
MV140	*Miss Summer*	9in (23cm)
MV141	*Miss Autumn*	9in (23cm)

Special Moments Collection

Same as 1993 listing.

Ladies of Elegance Collection

MV145	*Diana*	12in (31cm)
MV146	*Elizabeth*	12in (31cm)
MV147	*Katherine*	12in (31cm)
MV150	*Jacqueline*	12in (31cm)

Illustration 359. 9in (23cm) *Effanbee's First Annual Vinyl Christmas Doll.*

262

Porcelain Dolls

Same as 1993 listing with the following additions:

MP122 *Victoria*	19in (48cm)
MP123 *Samantha*	15in (38cm)
MP124 *Michelle*	19in (48cm)
MP125 *Corinne*	19in (48cm)
MP126 *Melanie*	18in (46cm)
MP127 *Merrie*	15in (38cm)
MP128 *Kimberly*	15in (38cm)
MP129 *Alice*	16in (41cm)
MP130 *Kristen*	16in (41cm)
MP131 *Heather*	22in (56cm)
MP132 *Beth*	16in (41cm)
MP133 *Patsy*	15in (38cm)
MP134 *Corky*	19in (48cm)
MP135 *Amanda*	14in (36cm)
MP136 *Lady Alexandra* at High Tea	23in (58cm)

Vinyl Babies

Same as 1993 listing with the following additions:

MV189 *Honey Bun* (Sleeper)	14in (36cm)
MV190 *Honey Bun* (Stripe)	14in (36cm)
MV191 *Honey Bun* (White)	14in (36cm)
MV192 *Butterball* (Stripe)	12in (31cm)
MV193 *Butterball* (Gingham)	12in (31cm)
MV194 *Butterball* (Pajamas)	12in (31cm)
MV195 *Butterball* Layette	12in (31cm)
SV158 *Katelyn*	22in (56cm)
SV159 *Cecily*	22in (56cm)

Cuddles by Effanbee

MV196 *Cuddles* (Aqua Dress)
MV197 *Cuddles* (Pink Dress)
MV198 *Cuddles* (Sleeper)
MV199 *Cuddles* (Bunting)
MV200 *Cuddles* (Pajamas)

Pocketful O'Love

Same as 1993 listing.

Little Miss Grow-Up

Same as 1993 listing.

Christmas Doll

MV144 *Vinyl Christmas Dolls*   9in (23cm)

For **1995** and **1996 Effanbee Catalog Listings**, see pages 287–290.

Illustration 360. 9in *Fairy Tale Collection* (Clockwise) No. MV166 *Tinkerbell*, No. MV167 *Wendy*, No. MV165 *Peter Pan*, No. MV168 *Captain Hook*.

II. EFFANBEE'S LIMITED EDITION DOLL CLUB DOLLS*

by Alma Wolfe

In August 1974, the Effanbee Doll Corporation sent a letter to collectors announcing the founding of their exciting, innovative Limited Edition Doll Club. In the two-page letter, collectors were introduced to the "Premiere Selection," *Precious Baby,* and were invited to become charter members of the club. The initial enrollment was limited to 2,880 members. Enthusiastic response has prompted Effanbee to expand the membership. The 1982 Edition, *Princess Diana,* was offered to 4,220 subscribers.

The exciting, different Limited Edition Dolls (with the exception of *Precious Baby*) are all-vinyl and fully-jointed. The dolls are "exclusively sculpted and designed" for the Limited Edition Doll Club. The molds, created for each year's edition, are used only for that year's subscription and will never be used again.

Only a designated number of each edition is manufactured, thus insuring their collectible value in the years to come. The first Limited Edition Doll, *Precious Baby,* is purported to be selling for as much as $400.00. As the years pass, all Effanbee Limited Edition Dolls should take a quantum leap in value.

A yearly mid-winter letter introduces the new selection. The brochure enclosed with the letter shows a color photograph of the doll and gives pertinent information of the doll's genealogy. The price of the doll "is dependent upon the cost factors involved." The subscription form must be returned by a specified date, or else the opportunity to purchase the doll could be forfeited.

The dolls are manufactured with the utmost care; thus, it is usually mid July before the members receive the dolls. Members are advised via postcard as to when the dolls will be shipped. Each doll is accompanied by a numbered certificate of authentication. The certificate attests to the fact that the Effanbee Limited Edition Doll Club label is sewn into the costume and that the doll is distinctively marked on the head and on the back.

Since the introduction of the first edition, a re-issue of a much-loved modern baby doll, there have been reproductions of two of Effanbee's outstanding composition dolls, an original doll designed exclusively for the club, three portrait dolls, and a replica of an "Old Master" painting. These unique dolls from diversified fields are works of art to be treasured today and passed on to future generations as the "Dolls of Yesterday."

---

*Most of this material was printed originally in *Collecting Modern Dolls,* copyright 1981 by Hobby House Press, Inc.

THE LIMITED EDITION DOLL CLUB DOLLS
1975. Precious Baby.

Precious Baby was designed by Bernard Lipfert, doll maker extraordinaire for over half a century, and is one of the last dolls he made for Effanbee. The *Baby* was first introduced in the Effanbee line in 1962 and was available until 1970.

Precious Baby was chosen as the club's "Premiere Edition," Effanbee's "fond farewell" to a doll that will never again be manufactured. The cuddly 25in (63.5cm) baby has a vinyl head, arms and legs, and a soft body and a "voice." She is dressed in a charming white organdy christening dress and bonnet and rests her head on her own taffeta pillow. Around her neck is an Effanbee metal heart with the raised letters, "Effanbee Durable Dolls." Effanbee found a number of these hearts in storage and planned to use them on the Limited Edition Dolls until they ran out.

Illustration 361. 25in (63.5cm) *Precious Baby,* 1975. *Marjorie Smith Collection.*

1976. Patsy '76.

The second Limited Edition Doll was *Patsy '76* — a superlative translation of Effanbee's "best known and most loved doll." The "little over 16in" (40.6cm) tall *Patsy* wears a white organdy party dress, the "Patsy" ribbon around her molded hair and pink velveteen Mary Janes. Her bracelet is a treasured Effanbee Golden Heart, lovingly tied on her right wrist with a pink satin ribbon.

At the height of the composition *Patsy* doll's popularity, a lady, calling herself "Aunt Patsy" traveled across America, visiting *Patsy's* little friends. It was a delightful surprise to the new *Patsy's* owners to see the signature of "Aunt Patsy" on the authentication certificate.

Illustration 335. 16in (40.6cm) *Patsy '76*, 1976, and 14in (35.6cm) *Skippy*, 1979.

Illustration 336. Patsy '76.

Illustration 337. The metal heart bracelet on the left arm of *Patsy '76*. These metal bracelets were on the arms of the composition Effanbee dolls during the 1930s and the 1940s. At that time they were held on with a bead chain rather than a ribbon.

1977. Dewees Cochran.

In 1977, Effanbee contracted with Dewees Cochran, America's foremost doll artist, to reproduce the self-portrait doll Mrs. Cochran had sculpted for a photograph of herself at age eight. The one-of-a-kind prototype was created by the artist in 1964. Mrs. Cochran was ecstatic over the prospect of creating a self-portrait doll for the club. She stated, "Little did I think that after 40 years of doll making something like this would happen."

Mrs. Cochran "immediately set to work to re-create and re-design her own image as a young lady at the 'turn of the century.'" Mrs. Cochran's signature is on the certificate.

The 16¹/₂in (41.9cm) portrait doll is the epitome of perfection with her long blonde hair styled in the "turn of the century" schoolgirl fashion and is dressed in a long-sleeved white organdy party dress enhanced with lace, tucking and black ribbon. The Effanbee Limited Edition Doll, the prototype and the photograph were displayed as part of the Cochran Retrospective Exhibition at the National Institute of American Doll Artist Convention held in Chicago, Illinois, in June 1977.

1978. Crowning Glory.

The club's fourth edition presented in 1978 was a very special doll sculpted and designed by a lady who has been very special to Effanbee since 1947. The consummate craftsmanship of Eugenia Dukas, "Effanbee's chief designer for over 30 years," is more evident in her design of *Crowning Glory* - a doll of beauty with the aura of royalty.

The 16in (40.6cm) doll's delicately molded face with moving blue eyes is framed by her auburn hair elegantly coiffed in a pompadour style. *Crowning Glory's* ball gown of gold floral brocade lamé was inspired by the fashion of the 17th century.

The fabulously fetching *Crowning Glory* is, indeed, a wonderful tribute to her creator, Eugenia Dukas, whose superbly designed dolls have thrilled little girls and collectors for several decades.

Illustration 365. Dewees Cochran. Marjorie Smith Collection.

Illustration 366. 16in (40.6cm) Crowning Glory, 1978. Marjorie Smith Collection.

Illustration 367. 14in (35.6cm) *Skippy*, 1979.

Illustration 368. 15in (38.1cm) *Susan B. Anthony*, 1980. *Marjorie Smith Collection.*

1979. Skippy.

Club members, who had suggested that a *Skippy* doll be re-issued were especially happy to receive the announcement that *Skippy* was the club's fifth anniversary selection.

Effanbee contacted the estate of Percy Crosby, the renowned cartoonist who had created the *Skippy*, comic strip in 1925. Contractual arrangements for Effanbee's new *Skippy* were made with Joan Crosby Tibbetts, daughter of Percy Crosby and president and owner of Skippy, Inc.

Two other ladies helped immensely in the production of the fifth Limited Edition Doll - Sharon Smith of Florence, Oregon, loaned her original composition *Skippy* doll and Helene Quinn of New York, New York, loaned her *Skippy* outfit.

Skippy at 14in (35.6cm) is a captivating rendition of the Crosby comic strip prankster. His jaunty, infectious charm is enhanced by his "best outfit," the always droopy socks and the "devil-may-care manner" in which he wears his infamous hat. On his left coat lapel he "sports a reproduction of the original *Skippy* button."

1980. Susan B. Anthony.

The commerative doll, *Susan B. Anthony*, number six in the series, was not only a tribute to the woman who was a human rights advocate and fought for the right to vote for women, but also a tribute to the American women who had made great strides in their quest for liberation and equality in the decade of the 1970s.

The expressive face of the 15in (38.1cm) *Susan B. Anthony* doll captures the determination and courage of this "Great Lady." Her fixed brown eyes are eloquent. Her costume is stylishly designed of gray moire taffeta. At the center of her lace collar is a delicately painted porcelain brooch. A Susan B. Anthony dollar coin in a souvenir case was included with the doll.

1981. Renoir's A Girl with a Watering Can.

The 1981 selection was phenomenal - a breathtaking replica of Renoir's "A Girl with a Watering Can."

With many economists advising the American public to invest in "collectibles" as a hedge against inflation, Effanbee deemed it most feasible to go to the "World of the Old Masters" and combine two "collectibles" - dolls and art - into their seventh club presentation.

Effanbee produced with precise detail the work of the "Old Master," Pierre Auguste Renoir, the French Impressionistic painter. The 16in (40.6cm) seventh Limited Edition Doll looks as though she just stepped from the painting. She is authentically costumed in a royal blue velveteen dress; she has painted blue eyes and thick, blonde curly hair caught with a red bow at the top of her head. She holds a spray of flowers in her left hand, and in her right hand she holds a watering can.

1982. A Royal Bride - Diana, Princess of Wales.

Lady Diana Spencer was introduced to the public in 1980 as the fiancee of Charles, the Prince of Wales. "Lady Di" became one of the most photographed and written about persons of modern times. On July 29, 1981, millions of viewers all over the world watched the wedding of Lady Diana to the Prince of Wales on television. The Effanbee Limited Edition Doll Club members were offered a "piece of this fantasy."

The doll, *Diana, Princess of Wales*, is 18in (45.7cm) tall and is dressed in an "authentic" copy of her wedding gown. She is all-vinyl and has blue painted eyes and rooted hair, "appropriately styled in the manner Diana has made so popular."

Above: Illustration 369. 18in (45.7cm) *Diana, Princess of Wales,* 1982.

Left: Illustration 370. 16in (40.6cm) Renoir's *A Girl With A Watering Can,* 1981.

1983. Sherlock Holmes.

At this writing it is known that *Sherlock Holmes* from the mystery stories of Sir Arthur Conan Doyle will be the Effanbee Limited Edition Doll Club doll for 1983. The doll is all-vinyl with painted hair and painted eyes and is dressed in the coat and cap that actor Basil Rathbone wore as Holmes in several films during the late 1930s and early 1940s. The face of the doll is a portrait of Rathbone.

Sherlock Holmes is 18in (45.7cm) tall and he is an outstanding rendition of the fictional character that Doyle created for his four *Sherlock Holmes* novels and the 58 short stories that were first published in 1887. This doll, like all others in the Limited Edition Doll Club series, is only available to subscribers to the club and will not be for sale in other outlets, nor will the special mold be used for other Effanbee dolls.

1984. Bubbles.

Bubbles is a faithful reproduction of an original *Bubbles* produced by Effanbee in 1924. The doll is a darling 15in (38cm) vinyl and soft bodied doll. One of the outstanding features of *Bubbles* is her bent arm which allows a finger to go to her mouth. She has moving blue eyes and beautiful sprayed sculptured hair. *Bubbles* is wearing a reproduction of one of her original outfits - a long lawn dress trimmed in lace with an embroidered ruffle. The dress has a lace trimmed yoke with an embroidered motif. Her lawn bonnet is ruffled with matching embroidery. She has a pink slip, flannel diaper and knitted booties.

As a special extra surprise, a cache of the original Effanbee Golden Hearts is affixed around her neck on a chain.

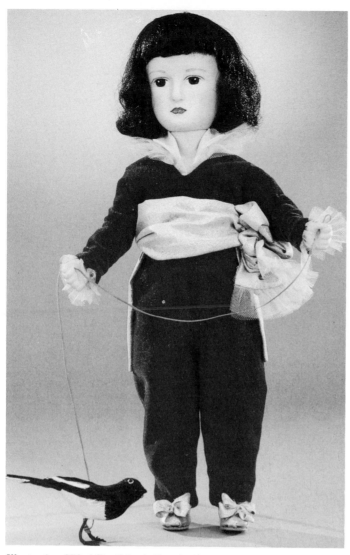

Illustration 373. 14in (36cm) *Goya's "Don Manuel Osorio Manrique de Zuñiga"*, 1985.

Illustration 374. 15in (38cm) *China Head Doll*, 1986.

1985. Don Manuel

As the Club entered its second decade, they presented to their club members the eleventh doll *Goya's "Don Manuel Osorio Manrique de Zuñiga"* modeled after the famous painting. Goya was a well known Spainish artist who painted in rococo and baroque styles. In 1788 Goya was commissioned to paint the four-year-old son of the Count of Altamira, Don Manuel. Goya's portraits reflected his keen powers of observation and insight. He combined happiness and sadness with superbly realistic detail. "Don Manuel" epitomizes this winning style.

Effanbee captured those portrayed emotions in the 14in (36cm) vinyl doll with dark painted eyes and thick, wavy chestnut hair. *Don Manuel* is attired in a bright red velvet suit, beige taffeta shirt and ecru tulle trim at the neck and cuffs. A magpie, a favorite pet of that time, is at the end of a string held in the boy's hand. This doll was limited to an edition of 4,470 pieces.

1986. China Head Doll

The Club's 12th presentation was a re-creation of a magnificent 19th Century *China Head Doll* from the Margaret Woodbury Strong Museum. China head dolls were produced commercially from 1840 to 1920 predominantly in Germany and Denmark. The one piece head and shoulders were made of porcelain and the bodies were either cloth or leather. The facial features and hair were commonly painted on the dolls.

The 15in (38cm) *China Head Doll* re-creation has a stuffed cloth body. Her arms and legs are sewn into the body so that she is multijointed. Her armlets (from the elbow to the fingertips) are made of vinyl as are the head and shoulders. This replica is limited to an edition of 4,470 pieces.

Illustraion 375. 14in (36cm) bisque porcelain *Baby Grumpy* and 16in (41cm) vinyl *Baby Grumpy*, 1987. *Photograph courtesy of the Effanbee Doll Corporation.*

1987/1988. Baby Grumpy.

For 1987 the Effanbee Limited Edition Doll Club chose to re-create one of it's most sought-after original composition dolls - *Baby Grumpy*. This was a truly unique collectible as it was the first time that Effanbee offered a re-creation in both 16in (41cm) vinyl and 14in (36cm) bisque porcelain.

Both dolls feature that sweetly petulant expression which won little girls' hearts early in the century. Porcelain *Baby Grumpy* has jointed limbs, and is entirely painted by hand. Vinyl *Baby Grumpy* has jointed legs and a special high-gloss finish.

Each dressed in the style of the time, the porcelain wears a crisp white-corded playsuit with blue and white striped percale trim, a matching bonnet and diaper. Vinyl *Baby Grumpy* features a powder-pink cotton dress, with lace adorning the yoke, sleeves, and panties. Knit booties and bonnet finish her outfit beautifully.

Units Produced of the Effanbee Limited Edition Dolls

Year	Doll	Produced
1975	*Precious Baby*	872
1976	*Patsy '76*	1200
1977	*Dewees Cochran*	3166
1978	*Crowning Glory*	2200
1979	*Skippy*	3485
1980	*Susan B. Anthony*	3485
1981	*Renoir's A Girl with A Watering Can*	3835
1982	*Princess Diana*	4220
1983	*Sherlock Holmes*	4470
1984	*Bubbles*	4470
1985	*Goya's "Don Manuel"*	4470
1986	*China Head Doll*	4470
1987/88	*Baby Grumpy* (porcelain)	2500
	Baby Grumpy (vinyl)	5000

271

III. THE LEGEND AND GREAT MOMENTS SERIES

In 1980 Effanbee introduced the dolls that comprise *The Legend Series*. Again, Effanbee created a "first" for doll collectors. It is extremely expensive to design and produce a doll. This is the reason why most doll companies use the same component parts for dolls over and over again. A change of wig and costume creates a new character and new designs do not need to be executed and new molds do not need to be made.

The dolls of *The Legend Series* are a unique design for each doll and each doll is only produced for the year. Criticism has been leveled at Effanbee because the dolls of *The Legend Series* seem to be produced in such great quantities. This is unfair, because compared with output of other doll companies, the dolls are indeed a "limited production," and the head molds are not used to make any other doll, nor different versions of the same basic doll. *The Legend Series* dolls are all portrait dolls, as compared with the most celebrity dolls produced in the past, which are a resemblance of the celebrity and are identified by costume, hair color and such. The dolls of *The Legend Series* have heads sculpted in such a realistic manner that they actually look like miniatures of the people who inspired the dolls. Each

doll also has accessories such as hats and walking sticks, and each doll has an authentic costume that is carefully styled and tailored. The dolls are unique in that they are made of contemporary materials (vinyl) and in that everything about them reflects quality.

So far, all of the dolls in the series are "show business legends." They have been *W.C. Fields, 1981 John Wayne, 1982 John Wayne, Mae West, Groucho Marx,* and *George Burns* in 1996. These dolls are among the most expensive dolls that Effanbee produces, but considering that they are only made for one year and that the mold can not be utilized for other dolls, they are well within the range of reasonable, price-wise, for currently produced collectibles. Since Effanbee introduced the concept of the limited edition *Legend* dolls that will only be produced for a single year other doll companies have taken up the same trend. But the Effanbee dolls will remain desirable because they are a series that began with the introduction of *W.C. Fields* in 1980, and the set is continuing.

With the advent of 1984 *The Legend Series* began to expand to a variety of special collection dolls. The Presidents Series brought to life the great leaders of the past

Illustration 376. The first four of *The Legend Series* dolls. From left to right: *W.C. Fields*, 1981 *John Wayne, Mae West* and 1982 *John Wayne.*

272

with a production time of two years. *Great Moments in History Series* included fascinating historical characters produced for two years only. In 1984 the *Great Moments in Music Series* was introduced with the intent to bring to life the personalities, behind the tunes, operas, jazz, jingles, with characters being produced for two years only. In 1985 a new category was added – *Great Memories in Sports*. Most of these series lasted only a matter of a few years and some never had any additional doll added. In 1991 The *Legend and Great Moments Series* were temporarily retired. No new character dolls were issued until the advent of 1996 and *George Burns*.

Illustration 378. 17in (43cm) *John Wayne Commerative Doll*, 1981. All-vinyl and fully-jointed. Light colored painted hair; blue painted eyes. Head and back marked: "WAYNE//ENT//19©81." The attached paper tag called the doll "John Wayne. American Symbol of the West." A portion of the sale of each John Wayne doll was donated to the John Wayne Cancer Research Fund at the University of California at Los Angeles.

Illustration 377. 15-1/2in (39cm) *W.C. Fields Centennial Doll*, 1980. All-vinyl and fully-jointed. Reddish painted hair and blue painted eyes. Head marked: "W.C. FIELDS//EFFANBEE/19©80." Back marked: "W.C. FIELDS//EFFANBEE//©1979//W.C. FIELDS PROD. INC."

Illustration 379. 18in (46cm) *Mae West*, 1982. All-vinyl and fully-jointed. Light blonde rooted hair; blue painted eyes. *Mae* is dressed in a form-fitting black taffeta gown with a matching black hat. The hat is trimmed in marabou feathers that match the gray boa over her shoulders. She carries a walking stick. Head and back marked: "©1982//EST. MAE WEST//effanbee."

273

The Legend Series

Dolls	Series	Year
W.C. Fields	LS	1980
John Wayne	LS	1981
John Wayne	LS	1982
Mae West	LS	1983
Groucho Marx	LS	1983
Judy Garland as Dorothy	LS	1984
Louise Armstrong	GM	1984
Theodore Roosevelt	PS	1984
Winston Churchill	GH	1984
Lucille Ball	LS	1985
Babe Ruth	GS	1985
Eleanor Roosevelt	GH	1985
Franklin Delano Roosevelt	PS	1985
Liberace – "Mr. Showmanship"	LS	1986
Art Carney as Ed Norton	GT	1986
Jackie Gleason as Ralph Kramden	GT	1986
John Fitzgerald Kennedy	PS	1986
Muhammad Ali	GS	1986
James Cagney	LS	1987
Dwight D. Eisenhower	PS	1987
Harry S. Truman	PS	1988
Humphrey Bogart	LS	1989
Thomas Jefferson	PS	1989
Claudette Colbert	LS	1990
Andrew Jackson	PS	1990
Queen Isabella	NW	1990
Christopher Columbus	NW	1990
General Douglas MacArthur	WH	1991
George Burns	LS	1996

LS = Legend Series
GM = Great Moments in Music
PS = Presidents Series
GH = Great Moments in History
GS = Great Moments in Sports
GT = Great Moments in Television
NW = New World Collection
WH = World's Greatest Heroes

Illustration 380. 18in (46cm) *John Wayne*, No. 2981, 1982. All-vinyl and fully-jointed. Painted hair; blue painted eyes. Head marked: "EFFANBEE//©1982//WAYNE ENT." Back marked: 'EFFANBEE//ENT//19©81." This dolls is a "younger version" of *John Wayne* and is dressed in a cavalry outfit. The paper tag call the doll "John Wayne. American Guardian of the West."

Illustration 381. 17in (43cm) *Groucho Marz*, 1983. All-vinyl and fully-jointed. Black painted hair and moustache; painted eyes; wire rimmed glasses. The doll is copyrighted by Groucho Marx Prod. Inc. *Photograph courtesy of the Effanbee Doll Corporation.*

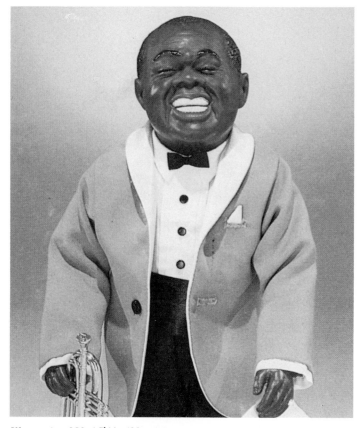

Illustration 382. 15½in (39cm) *Louis Armstrong, 1984. Great Moments in Music Series.*

Illustration 383. 16½in (42cm) *Winston Churchill, 1984. Great Moments in History Series.*

Illustration 384. 17in (43cm) *Franklin Delano Roosevelt, 1985. The Presidents Series.*

Illustration 385. 14½in (37cm) *Eleanor Roosevelt, 1985. Great Moments in History Series.*

Illustration 386. 18in (46cm) *Muhammad Ali "I Am the Greatest"*, 1986.
Great Moments in Sports.

Illustration 387. Both 16½in (41cm) dolls of *Art Carney as Ed Norton* and
Jackie Gleason as Ralph Kramden, 1986. *Great Moments in Television.*

Illustration 388. 16½in (42cm) *Lucille Ball*, 1985. *Legend Series.*

276

Illustration 389. 16in (41cm) *James Cagney, 1987. The Legend Series.*

Illustration 390. 16in (41cm) *Harry S. Truman, 1988. The Presidents Series.*

Illustration 391. 15in (38cm) *Humphrey Bogart, 1989. The Legend Series.*

Illustration 392. 16in (41cm) *General Douglas MacArthur, 1991. The World's Greatest Heroes.*

Illustration 393. 17in (43cm) *George Burns*, 1996. *The Legends Series.*

IV. EFFANBEE'S CRAFTSMEN'S CORNER

Effanbee was the first commercial doll company to recognize the value and the artistry of dolls made by American doll artists and to single out this art form in designs especially produced for collectors. During the late 1930s Effanbee marketed dolls which were designed by Dewees Cochran, the most popular of which are the *America's Children* series of dolls. In 1979 this tradition was revived with the *Craftsmen's Corner* dolls. (They were not called *Craftsmen's Corner* until 1980.)

The first American doll artist to have her work and her designs rendered as vinyl dolls by Effanbee was Faith Wick, in 1979. In 1980 Astry Campbell's *Baby Lisa* was added to the collection. In 1982 Joyce Stafford became the third important American doll artist to have her designs executed by Effanbee. All three of these artists are members of NIADA. NIADA, the National Institute of American Doll Artists, was organized in 1962 with six artists who made original dolls for collectors. NIADA is a prestigious organization whose members must meet their high standards of excellence to be inducted into the organization. In 1983 Jan Hagara, an artist famous for her paintings of children and dolls, became the fourth *Craftsmen's Corner* designer.

All of the *Craftsmen's Corner* dolls can be considered play dolls for children, as they meet with design standards recommended for play dolls and are offered at affordable prices. These dolls are also works of art because of the originality and the artistry of their design and execution.

Faith Wick

Faith Wick, who grew up in Minnesota, has a catalog of dolls that is probably wider in scope than that of any other American doll designer. Among her doll creations are babies, toddlers, ladies and men, portrait dolls, elves, clowns and ugly witches.

Mrs. Wick has a Master's degree in Art, and taught art for several years before she began to design and produce dolls full time. Her catalog of manufactured dolls, which were produced for several different distributors, begins in 1977. Faith developed her interest in sculpture because of an amusement park that she and her husband operated. The park featured figures of various animals in cement. When the Wicks purchased the park these animals required restoration work so Faith began to repair them and make replacement parts where it was required. Before long Faith was making dolls, jewelry, Christmas tree ornaments, figurines and other objects. She also traveled around the country exhibiting her models and meeting with people who came to see her work. At the same time she was offering classes in sculpture to students.

The United Federation of Doll Clubs (UFDC) selected two different Faith Wick designs to present as souvenirs of national conventions. Faith Wick was already renowned for her original porcelain dolls before the first of the UFDC dolls *L'il Apple*, an impish little boy, was given in New York, New York, in 1979. Her portrait doll, *Lindbergh*, was the souvenir in 1981 in St. Louis, Missouri, for the UFDC Convention. By that time Faith Wick was one of the most famous of the NIADA artists.

The first Faith Wick Originals offered by Effanbee were the *Party Time Boy* and *Girl* and the *Anchors Aweigh Boy* and *Girl*, in 1979. These dolls are from a toddler design that has been used for other dolls since, the most recent being the head of the Scarecrow in 1983. This head design also translated well into the face of an old woman for the *Peddler* in 1981. The two witches, offered in 1981 and 1982, are two of her most unique creations. Probably the most loved of the *Faith Wick Originals* in the *Craftsmen's Corner* series is the *Old Fashioned Nast Santa*, released in 1982.

Illustration 394. The Faith Wick Originals from the 1980 Effanbee Doll Corporation catalog. All six dolls are from the same basic mold and each one is 16in (41cm) tall. In the top row, from left to right: No. 7005 *Clown-Boy*, No. 7001 *Party Time-Boy*; and No. 7004 *Anchors Aweigh-Girl.* In the front row, from left to right: No. 7006. *Clown-Girl*; No. 7002 *Party Time-Girl*; and No. 7003 *Anchors Aweigh-Boy*.

Illustration 395. 18in (46cm) *Wicket Witch*, a Faith Wick Original, No. 7110, 1981-1982. Vinyl head with blonde rooted hair and painted features; stuffed cloth body. She is dressed in black. Head marked: "EFFANBEE//FAITH WICK//7110 19 © 81." *Patricia Gardner Collection.*

Illustration 396. Faith Wick's 16in (41cm) *Peddler*, No. 7015, 1981-1982. All-vinyl and fully-jointed. White rooted hair; blue sleep eyes with lashes. The head is marked: "EFFANBEE//© 1979//FAITH WICK." *Patricia Gardner Collection.*

Illustration 397. 18in (46cm) *Old Fashioned Nast Santa* by Faith Wick, No. 7201, 1982-present. Vinyl head and hands; unjointed stuffed cloth body. The head has molded and painted features. It is marked: 'effanbee//7201 © 1982//FAITH WICK."

280

Astry Campbell

Astry Campbell also earned a Master's degree in Fine Arts. Her interest in art developed at an early age. She had majored in art in high school and in college and had studied sculpture procedures with various artists.

The first original doll that Astry Campbell purchased for her collection was one by Dewees Cochran. She met Mrs. Cochran in 1967 in Boston, Massachusetts, at the National UFDC Convention and developed an even keener interest in being elected to NIADA. She was accepted by NIADA in 1968 and from 1971 to 1973 served as President of the organization. In *The American Doll Artist, Volume II* by Helen Bullard (Athena Publishing Company, 1975) it is reported that Astry Campbell designed the NIADA logo, the Institute's brochure, letterhead, certificate and other documents.

Baby Lisa by Astri (Astry Campbell) entered the *Craftsmen's Corner* in 1980. The 11in (27.9cm) baby doll in vinyl was made from Astry's 9in (22.9cm) all-bisque and fully-jointed original of 1971. The doll represents a three-month-old baby. One of the original porcelain models was purchased by the Smithsonian Institution to be used in an exhibition of dolls by American artists. In 1983 *Baby Lisa* was also offered by Effanbee as a toddler, *Baby Lisa Grows Up*, one of the most clever concepts in doll production that has been conceived. *Baby Lisa* and *Astri's Lisa Grows Up* are offered in various costumes and accessories, unlike the other *Craftsmen's Corner* dolls, which have not been.

Illustration 398. 11in (28cm) *Baby Lisa* by Astry Campbell, No. 1012, 1980-present. All-vinyl and fully-jointed with painted hair and eyes. *Agnes Smith Collection.*

Illustration 399. 11in (28cm) *Baby Lisa by Astri* from the 1980 Effanbee Doll Corporation catalog. All-vinyl and fully-jointed. Painted hair and features. At the top is No. 1013, *Baby Lisa* with pillow, layette and wicker backet; at the left she rests on a pillow, No. 1012; at the bottom right is No. 1011 *Baby Lisa* in a blanket.

Joyce Stafford

Joyce Stafford, called "Jo" by her friends, became a member of the Craftsmen's Corner in 1982 with the introduction of the *Orange Blossom*, a Chinese tot.

Jo, like Faith Wick and Astry Campbell, also holds a Master's degree in Art. While she was studying art, Jo learned to sculpt and to make molds, which she later adapted to her doll production. Her first sculpture was a bust of Joan of Arc, for which she earned a prize while in high school.

Joyce Stafford taught kindergarten in Colorado and California for ten years after she graduated from college. In the meantime she had married John Stafford and they had a son in 1958. When her son entered school, Jo quit teaching and returned to her hobbies, which centered around creating original art work. One of her interests was collecting old Indian jewelry. To add to her collection, she began making her own Indian jewelry and took classes at California State University at San Jose to perfect the technique of handcrafting jewelry of American Indian designs.

Dolls were always one of Jo's great passions. Her favorite dolls from her own childhood were Effanbee's *Dy-Dee Baby* and *Baby Bright Eyes*. Besides collecting dolls, Jo also restored antique porcelain dolls. Then she began to experiment with making her own dolls. Another of her many talents was designing and sewing costumes, which she translated to doll making. She combined her many talents and interests and hobbies into doll making on a professional basis.

Over the years Jo Stafford had made cloth dolls as gifts and for her own amusement. Her first "important" porcelain doll was named *Ada Lou* (1966) and it was a portrait of her mother. For her second porcelain doll *Little Ruth*, a portrait of her sister-in-law, she won a blue ribbon at the California State Fair. Six months later she was asked to show her dolls at the Montalvo Gallery in Saratoga, California. Her first two movie star dolls, *W.S. Hart*, a cowboy player from the silent screen, and little *Jackie Coogan*, the adorable waif from the 1920s films, were exhibited in 1966.

In 1969 Joyce Stafford was elected to NIADA. The catalog of her original dolls from the late 1960s included babies and toddlers, adults and portrait dolls. By the early 1970s her original designs also included *Estrellita*, a Mexican girl, and *Sue Ling*, a Korean toddler, as well as other film players, including *Mary Pickford, Sonja Henie, Jeanette MacDonald* and *Nelson Eddy*. She also made doll house dolls, scaled 1in (3cm) to 1ft (31cm), and called them the Primm Family. In 1976 her *Lotta Crabtree* was the UFDC souvenir for the National Convention in San Francisco, California.

Joyce Stafford's *Orange Blossom* by Effanbee was the vinyl rendition of her porcelain original *Poppy*, which was made in a limited edition of 50 dolls in a 12in (31cm) size. *Orange Blossom* was one of the biggest hits of Toy Fair in New York, New York, in 1982. An unofficial poll of collectors conducted in early 1983 by the author found *Orange Blossom* to be the favorite, or best, 1982 commercial doll. (This finding has nothing to do with the fact that the doll was made by Effanbee. See *Orange Blossom* and *Poppy* on page 10.)

Joyce Stafford, in spite of her tremendous talent and imagination, is an unassuming person who prefers to "be left alone to work" rather than to promote her productions. Her work came to the attention of representatives of the Effanbee Doll Corporation at the NIADA exhibit during the United Federation of Doll Clubs National Convention in New York, New York, in 1979.

Jo is delighted to have an important commercial doll company such as Effanbee interested in making dolls from her original designs. She is a doll collector herself, and the older Effanbee dolls are among her favorites. She also collects celebrity dolls and other movie star memorabilia.

Jo says, "I have come full circle since I was a child." The circle is far from completed though. Jo Stafford is still designing and making new dolls; other dolls, both as originals in porcelain and dolls for Effanbee, are in the formation stage.

Joyce Stafford, like many true artists, is not content with what she had done. She says "I am very pleased with the honor of Effanbee making one of my dolls for the commercial market, but I still want to do something very special." She claims. "The only person I really want to please is myself, and I haven't done that yet."

For 1983 Effanbee changed the name of Jo Stafford's *Orange Blossom* to *Lotus Blossom* because Kenner Products had already named a doll of the *Strawberry Shortcake* series *Orange Blossom*, which Effanbee did not realize at the time Jo Stafford's doll was introduced into the *Craftsmen's Corner*. In 1983 *Lotus Blossom* was jointed with *Little Tiger*, a Chinese boy companion.

Illustration 400. Joyce Stafford in her studio at work making costumes for *Poppy. Photograph by John Stafford.*

Jan Hagara

From the time she was a child in Oklahoma, Jan Hagara excelled in drawing. Jan Hagara has been described as a "self-taught artist who learned to paint in all mediums." All true artists are self-taught, but most artists require formal training so they can translate their ideas into the perfection seen in a Jan Hagara original.

Jan's earliest works were landscapes and flower subjects. When she began to paint with watercolors and render paintings of children dressed in old-fashioned clothing she became famous. The expression that Jan Hagara captures in a child's eyes has become her trademark.

Jan's first commercial successes were her paintings of children. Next she began to produce limited edition prints of her paintings so that they would be more affordable for purchasers who wanted her works. In 1979 Mrs. Hagara's porcelain collector's plates were produced by her own company. The first collector's plate was Lisa and the Jumeau Doll, a portrait of a dark haired little girl clutching an antique French doll.

The paintings, prints and other designs of Jan Hagara became especially popular with doll collectors, as her children were so winsome and the dolls in the designs evokes so much nostalgia and sentiment.

The first Jan Hagara doll from Effanbee is *Cristina*, an old-fashioned girl from her original painting. Jan Hagara is a doll collector with an eclectic collection that concentrates on antique bisque and composition dolls. She particularly likes the German all-bisque children. Jan's own children played with Effanbee dolls. Because of her love of dolls she was thrilled when Effanbee approached her about making one of her designs in a three-dimensional form.

Effanbee sculptors made *Cristina* from Jan's original art work. Jan designed the clothing to her own specifications and painted the face of the prototype doll that Effanbee would produce, after she had approved the design.

Jan Hagara said, "Effanbee works hard for collectors. I am very happy with the job that they did on *Cristina*. When people see the doll they want to know if it is bisque because the vinyl from which the doll is made has such a nice look to it."

She further reported, "The Effanbee people were at first horrified by the long curls that I wanted on the doll. They were afraid that the rooted wig would lose its curl, but after testing it under humid conditions were satisfied that my design would work."

In the future Jan Hagara will sculpt the dolls that Effanbee will produce for the *Craftsmen's Corner*. Each of her designs will be limited to a production of two years.

Illustration 401. 15in (38cm) *Cristina* by Jan Hagara, No. 7483, 1983. All-vinyl and fully-jointed. Rooted brown hair; blue painted eyes. The dress is white with a royal blue sash at the waist. Head marked: "effanbee//© 1983//JAN HAGARA." *Courtesy of Suzanne Chordar of The Doll's Nest.*

283

Edna Hibel

Edna Hibel is a world renowned artist whose distinctive style brought her to the forefront of her profession. She began working with Effanbee in 1984. Most recently Ms. Hibel was selected as the 1984 Collectible Artist of the Year by the Academy of Collectible Arts, and she also received a citation from Pope Paul II for her humanitarianism in art.

llustration 402. The 1984 Collectible Dolls of Edna Hibel:(left to right) No. 7361 *Flower Girl of Brittany* and No. 7351 *Contessa.*

HOW EFFANBEE DOLLS ARE MADE

Effanbee dolls are not made by happy little elves who reside at the North Pole with Santa Claus. Before an Effanbee doll reaches a doll collector or a child who will treasure it as a plaything, it goes through a long and complex process from inception to completion.

The merchandising committee, composed of Irene and Stanley Wahlberg and Margiann Flanagan confer with merchants and toy wholesalers gathering their opinions as to what doll collectors are looking for. They also meet and interview many consumers, at doll shows and at special "focus groups". "We feel that it is important to understand what our merchants and consumers want, before we do a new doll line," says Irene. The team then plans the new line, focusing it, and refining the concepts.

The overall 'look' of the Effanbee line is, today, the responsibility of Irene Wahlberg, Effanbee's Vice President of Merchandising, and Margiann Flanagan, the Vice President of Design. Irene grew up in a small town in New Jersey. As a child, she showed artistic talent, and made clothes for her own doll collection. Margiann Flanagan studied design in Montana and worked in the Broadway theater on costume design before joining Effanbee. Together these two talented people head up the Effanbee Merchandising and Design team.

When a new doll head is needed, an artist sculpts the original model. This is then cast in a special wax, and painted the way it would look as a finished doll. After the team approves it, the wax is made into a master mold. All Effanbee waxes and master molds are made in the United States. After approval of the vinyl master "skins", the master molds are sent overseas where production molds and spray masks are made. Effanbee dolls are currently made in China, Taiwan, and Thailand. Stanley Wahlberg says that "these countries provide us with a pool of talented labor who are capable of producing the quality that we demand in our dolls, while keeping them at an affordable price."

While the master molds are being made, Margiann and Irene working 'in house' and with several sample makers, execute the costume concepts and designs. After approval, patterns are made, and the design prototype and patterns are sent overseas for duplication. The team also designs the style of each doll's hair at this stage. After the overseas factories duplicate the design prototypes, the merchandising team makes an extended trip to supervise and approve the new line. At this time, final samples are modified, and fabrics and trims approved. Many changes can take place before the stamp of approval is given, and a doll goes into production.

The actual production process of an Effanbee doll is complicated. Doll parts have to be molded in special machines. Faces are subtly painted by experts who add coloring to lips, blush to cheeks, eyelashes and eyebrows, and other highlights. Nylon hair is rooted in a time consuming process that requires a high degree of skill. A special machine inserts eyes into empty eye sockets. When the doll is painted, assembled, and wigged, it is ready for dressing.

Now the clothing cutters and sewers spring into action. Working from patterns supplied by Effanbee, fab-

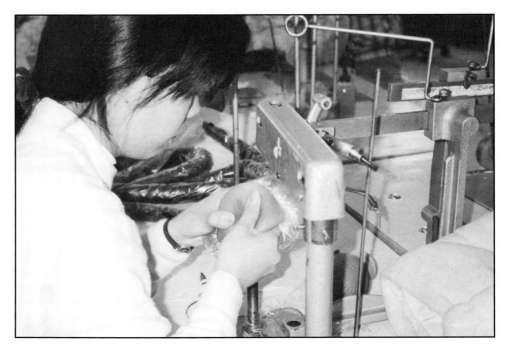

Illustration 403. Nylon hair is rooted in a time consuming process that requires a high degree of skill.

ric is hand cut and sewn. Laces, trims, and ribbons are added, and all costumes are hand finished. After a careful inspection process, the dolls are packed and shipped to the Effanbee headquarter warehouse in New Jersey.

While the workers in the Effanbee production facilities are assembling, dressing, packing, and shipping Effanbee dolls, samples of the dolls from each year's line are displayed in the permanent Effanbee showroom at the Toy Building on 5th Avenue in New York. Here, during Toy Fair in February, customers (wholesale only) can see the new line and place their orders. Catalogs are also sent to thousands of merchants around the country. Effanbee also shows their line at a number of toy and gift wholesale trade shows around the country.

Effanbee dolls are sold in thousands of doll, toy, and gift shops throughout the United States and Canada. Recently, some Effanbee dolls have also become available through cable television shopping networks. An International Division is also being formed, so that children and collectors around the world can enjoy these beautiful dolls.

The Effanbee team spends 24 hours a day breathing life back into this fine doll company. Stanley, Irene, and Margiann feel the same way: "Effanbee has been a wonderful challenge for us" they say. "It is one of the oldest and finest doll companies in America and we are privileged to have the opportunity to bring it back. We are enjoying every minute of it."

Illustration 404. Irene Wahlberg, Vice President of Merchandising (*ABOVE*) and Margiann Flanagan, Vice President of Design (*BELOW*), work as a team developing doll molds, hair styles, and costume designs.

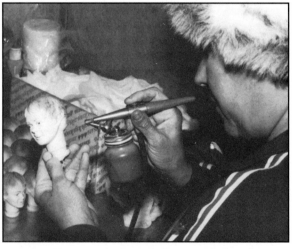

Illustration 405. Faces are subtly painted by experts who add coloring to lips, blush to cheeks, eyelashes and eyebrows, and other highlights.

Illustration 406. Working from patterns supplied by Effanbee, fabric is hand cut and sewn. Laces, trims, and ribbons are added, and all costumes are hand finished.

286

1995 CATALOG LISTING

Story Book Collection
MV204 *Jo*   9in (23cm)
MV205 *Beth*   9in (23cm)
MV206 *Amy*   9in (23cm)
MV207 *Meg*   9in (23cm)
MV208 *Anne With An E*   9in (23cm)
MV209 *Heidi*   9in (23cm)
MV210 *Secret Garden*   9in (23cm)
MV211 *Pollyanna*   9in (23cm)

Wizard of Oz
Same as 1994 listing with the following additions:
MV213 *Boy Munchkin*   9in (23cm)
MV212 *Girl Munchkin*   9in (23cm)

Fairy Tale Favorites
Same as 1994 listing with the following addition:
MV202 *Poor Cinderella*   9in (23cm)
And the following deletions:
MV101 *Xmas Fairy*
MV142 *Mistress Mary* (repositioned into Nursery Rhyme category.)

Nursery Rhymes
MV142 *Mistress Mary*   9in (23cm)
MV214 *Queen of Hearts*   9in (23cm)
MV215 *Mary Had A Little Lamb*   9in (23cm)
MV216 *Miss Muffet*   9in (23cm)
MV217 *Bo Peep*   9in (23cm)
MV218 *Girl With A Curl*   9in (23cm)
MV219 *Jack Horner*   9in (23cm)

International Collection
Same as 1994 listing with the following additions:
MV227 *Japan*   9in (23cm)
MV228 *Brazil*   9in (23cm)
MV229 *Spain*   9in (23cm)
MV230 *France*   9in (23cm)
And the following deletions:
MV109 *Poland*
MV110 *Scotland*
MV111 *Thailand*
MV174 *Holland*

Special Memories
MV179 *Happy Birthday*   9in (23cm)
   MV179B — *Blonde Hair*
   MV179R — *Red Hair*
MV232 *Bride*   9in (23cm)
MV233 *Black Bride*   9in (23cm)
MV234 *First Communion*   9in (23cm)
   MV234B — *Blonde Hair*
   MV234R — *Red Hair*

MV240 *Tooth Fairy*   9in (23cm)
MV241 *Guardian Angel*   9in (23cm)

Holidays of the Year
Same as 1994 listing with the following addition:
MV143 *Thanksgiving*   9in (23cm)
And the following deletion:
MV123 *Valentine's Day*

Ladies of Elegance
Same as 1994 listing.

Illustration 407. 17in (43cm) *Patsy Joan* is molded from the original 1946 Patsy and comes complete with the **Patsy Doll Family Encyclopedia** by Patricia N. Schoonmaker (Hobby House Press, Inc., 1992).

Enchanted Garden

MV221 *Rose*	9in (23cm)
MV222 *Tiger Lily*	9in (23cm)
MV223 *Violet*	9in (23cm)
MV224 *Daisy*	9in (23cm)
MV225 *Morning Glory*	9in (23cm)
MV226 *Poppy*	9in (23cm)

Best Friends Collection

Samantha Trunk Set (Includes doll in a party dress, together with a fabric covered trunk, that includes a clothes rack, hangers, and accessory drawers, plus additional outfits including: pajamas, bathrobe, slippers, play outfit, sneakers, slippers, pillow and teddy bear.)

MV249 *Brown Hair*	9in (23cm)
MV249B *Blonde Hair*	9in (23cm)

Additional Outfits Sold Separately:

MV250 *Denim Outfit*
MV251 *Coat Set*
MV252 *School Dress*
MV253 *Bathing Suit Set*
MV254 *Sailor Play Suit*

Best Friends

MV134 *Suzie*	9in (23cm)
MV135 *April*	9in (23cm)
MV136 *Sandy*	9in (23cm)
MV137 *Molly*	9in (23cm)
MV180 *Stacy*	9in (23cm)

Vinyl Babies Collection

Same as 1994 listing with the following additions:

MV244 *Bunny*	9in (23cm)
MV246 *Kitten*	9in (23cm)
MV255 *Katy*	9in (23cm)
MV256 *Butterball Basket*	
MV257 *Sarah*	12in (31cm)
MV258 *Chrissy*	12in (31cm)
MV259 *Bonnie*	14in (36cm)
MV260 *Kesia*	14in (36cm)
MV262 *Amy*	14in (36cm)
MV197 *Pink*	16in (41cm)
MV261 *Bath Baby*	16in (41cm)

Pocket O' Love

Same as 1994 listing.

Porcelain Collection

MP150 *Cinderella* (LE 2,500)	25in (64cm)

Fairy Princesses

Each doll is numbered and comes with a certificate of authenticity. LE 5,000

MP149 *Athena*	15-1/2in (39cm)
MP158 *Eve*	15-1/2in (39cm)
MP159 *Aurora* (pillow included)	15-1/2in (39cm)
MP132 *Beth* (LE 2,500)	
MP133 *Patsy* (LE 5,000)	
MP135 *Amanda* (w/trunk & 2 add. outfits, LE 5,000)	14in (36cm)
MP136 *Lady Alexandra At High Tea* (LE 2,500)	23in (58cm)
MP138 *Girl With Watering Can* (numbered, certificate of authenticity, and framed print of original work of art)	18in (46cm)
MP139 *Girl With a Hoop* (numbered, certificate of authenticity, and framed print of original work of art)	18in (46cm)
MP143 *Clara* (Nutcraker included)	
MP145 *Sugar Plum Fairy*	
MP147 *Little Bo Peep* (LE 2,500)	17in (43cm)
MP148 *Red Riding Hood* (LE 2,500)	16in (41cm)
MP151 *Alexandra's Wedding* (LE 5,000)	23in (58cm)
MP152 *Laura* (musical, plays "Lara's Theme", LE 2,500)	20in (51cm)
MP153 *Christine From Phantom of the Opera* (musical, plays "All I Ask of You")	20in (51cm)
MP154 *Patsy Baby* (LE 2,500)	
MP155 *Patsy* (LE 5,000)	
MP160 *April* (1995 Annual Doll, LE 2,500)	20in (51cm)
MP162 *Littlest Ballerina*	6in (15cm)
MP164 *Little Sister*	6in (15cm)
MP165 *Darren* (comes with soccer ball, LE 2,500)	

Christmas

MV122 *Currier & Ives Christmas*	9in (23cm)
MP166 *Blue Patsy Ornament**	3in (8cm)
MP167 *Pink Patsy Ornament**	3in (8cm)
MV242 *Victorian Angel Tree Topper*	12in (31cm)
MV243 *Renaissance Angel Tree Topper*	12in (31cm)
MV247 *Annual Christmas Doll*	9in (23cm)

First Christmas ornaments ever produced by Effanbee.

Illustration 408. The 9in (23cm) collector quality vinyl beauties of the Enchanted Garden Collection include: Violet and *Poppy.*

All The World Loves A Clown

MP141 *Patches*	12in (31cm)
MP142 *Bubbles*	12in (31cm)
MP163 *Littlest Clown*	6in (15cm)
MV236 *Dimples* (vinyl)	9in (23cm)
MV237 *Mickey*	9in (23cm)
MV238 *Pierrot*	9in (23cm)
MV239 *Harlequin*	9in (23cm)

Angels

MP140 *Pink Angel*	12in (31cm)
MP156 *Grandma's Little Angel*	
MP161 *Littlest Angel*	6in (15cm)
MV241 *Guardian Angel*	9in (23cm)

1996 CATALOG LISTING

The Patsy Family

P226 *Porcelain Patsy* (holding vinyl Wee Patsy, LE 7,500) 14in (36cm)
V500 *Candy Kid* (molded from 1946 original, add. coat, bonnet & muff set) 13in (33cm)
V521 *Patsy Trunk Set* (molded from 1928 original composition doll, 2 add. costumes & trunk made in the 1930's suitcase style) 13in (33cm)
V522 *Black Patsy Joan** 17in (43cm)
V523 *Skippy* (molded from the original doll) 13in (33cm)
V524 *Happy Birthday Patsy Joan* 17in (43cm)
V525 *Patsy Joan with wig** 17in (43cm)
V528 *Wee Patsy Travel Set* (w/paper doll book by John Axe, doll house travel case, Wee Patsy girl & boy dolls, 5 accessories — rocking chair, clothes tree, Jack-in-the-box, train & black cat) 5-1/4in (13.65cm)
V530 *Patsy* (molded from 1928 original) 13in (33cm)
V531 *Christmas Patsy Joan* (w/Wee Patsy) 17in (43cm)
V535 *Wee Patsy* 5-1/4in (13.65cm)
*Each of these Patsy Joan dolls has been molded from the original 1946 doll.

Storybook Collection

MV214 *Queen of Hearts*	9in (23cm)
MV215 *Mary Had A Little Lamb*	9in (23cm)
MV216 *Miss Muffet*	9in (23cm)
MV217 *Little Bo Peep*	9in (23cm)
V503 *Snow White*	9in (23cm)
V504 *Red Riding Hood*	9in (23cm)
V505 *Cinderella*	9in (23cm)
V506 *Rapunzel*	9in (23cm)
V515 *Sleeping Beauty*	9in (23cm)

Enchanted Garden

Same as 1995 listing.

Special Memories

Same as 1995 listing with the following addition:
MV241B *Guardian Angel* 9in (23cm)

Illustration 409. 9in (23cm) Indians of the Americas come with a certificate that gives a description of the American region from which each doll originates. The dolls include: *Southeast Indian, Woodlands Indian, Northwest Indian, Plains Indian,* and *Southwest Indian.*

Indians of the Americas

V516 *Plains Indian*	9in (23cm)
V517 *Southwest Indian*	9in (23cm)
V518 *Southeast Indian*	9in (23cm)
V519 *Woodlands Indian*	9in (23cm)
V520 *Northwest Indian*	9in (23cm)

Plains Indian V516
Southwest Indian V517

Best Friends Collection

Same as 1995 listing with the following additions:

MV265B *Blonde*	9in (23cm)
MV265 *Brown Hair*	9in (23cm)

Accessories:

MV264
V507
V508
V509
V510
V511
V512
V513
V514
V536 *Bed*
V537 *Armoire*

Vinyl Babies

Same as 1995 listing with the following additions:

MV259 *Bonnie*	14in (36cm)
MV262 *Amy*	14in (36cm)
V526 *Katy Travel Set* (w/trunk, pillow & 2 add. outfits)	9in (23cm)
V527 *Honey Bun Trunk Set* (w/trunk, 2 add. outfits, bib, & pacifier)	
V532 *Debbie*	14in (36cm)
V534 *Kira*	14in (36cm)
MV256 *Butterball Basket*	12in (31cm)
MV258 *Chrissy*	12in (31cm)
V538 *Honey*	12in (31cm)
V539 *Penny*	12in (31cm)

Porcelain Collection

Pride of the South (Each doll is 15-1/2in (39cm), numbered, comes with a Certificate of Authenticity, and is limited to an edition of 2,500 pieces.)

P201 *Mint Julep*
P202 *Peach Melba*
P203 *Rose Water*
P204 *Magnolia*

MP132 *Beth* (LE 2,500)	
MP150 *Cinderella* (LE 2,500)	22in (56cm)
MP151 *Alexandra's Wedding* (LE 5,000)	22in (56cm)
P207 *Miss Kitty* (LE 2,500)	22in (56cm)
P208 *Can Can* (LE 3,500)	22in (56cm)
P209 *Alexandra's Winter Fantasy* (LE 2,500)	22in (56cm)
P210 *Mardi Gras* (LE 2,500)	20in (51cm)
P211 *Guinevere* (LE 2,500)	22in (56cm)
P212 *Juliette* (LE 2,500)	20in (51cm)
P213 *Glinda* (LE 2,500)	22in (56cm)
P223 *Benjamin* (LE 2,500)	13-1/2in (34cm)
P224 *Fairy Princess* (LE 2,500)	17in (43cm)
P227 *Ashley* (LE 2,500)	16in (41cm)
P228 *Gabriel* (w/satin cloud pillow)	12in (31cm)

Illustration 410. 17in (43cm) *Happy Birthday Patsy Joan*. See pages iv, v, vii, ix, 2-3, 287-290 for more *Patsy* information.

Fairy Princess

Same as 1995 listing.

Our Littlest Collection

MP161 *Littlest Angel*	6in (15cm)
MP162 *Littlest Ballerina*	6in (15cm)
MP164 *Little Sister*	6in (15cm)
P215 *Littlest Snowflake*	6in (15cm)
P216 *Littlest Flower Girl*	6in (15cm)
P217 *Little Mary Sunshine*	6in (15cm)
P219 *Betsy Bows*	6in (15cm)
P220 *Billy Buttons*	6in (15cm)
P221 *Little Christening Baby*	6in (15cm)
MP156 *Grandma's Littlest Angel*	19in (48cm)
MV243 *White Tree Topper*	12in (31cm)
P218 *Littlest Elf* (all porcelain)	6in (41cm)
P225 *Holly Annual Christmas Doll*	19in (48cm)
V501 *Annual Christmas Doll*	
V502 *Red Tree Topper*	12in (31cm)

Legend Series

V529 *George Burns*	17in (43cm)

INDEX

293

294